# FRONTIER JUSTICE:

## The Rise and Fall
## of the Loomis Gang

*THE LOOMIS HOME*

# FRONTIER JUSTICE:

## The Rise and Fall of the Loomis Gang

## E. FULLER TORREY, M.D.

# FRONTIER JUSTICE
## The Rise and Fall of
## The Loomis Gang

Sixth paperback printing, 2017

ISBN 0-932052-91-6


**Library of Congress Cataloging-in-Publication Data**

Torrey, E. Fuller (Edwin Fuller), 1937-
  Frontier justice : the rise and fall of the Loomis gang /
E. Fuller Torrey.
    p.  cm
  Includes bibliographical references and index.
  ISBN 0-932052-92-4. — ISBN 0-932052-91-6 (pbk.)
  1. Gangs—New York (State)—History—19th century.
2. Loomis family.  3. Criminals—New York (State)—
Oneida County—Biography.  I. Title.
HV6452.N72L668     1992
364.1'06'609747—dc20                          91-40675
                                                    CIP


North Country Books, Inc.
220 Lafayette Street
Utica, New York 13502
www.northcountrybooks.com

# DEDICATION

*To John and Jeri Karin,
in appreciation for their
friendship over many years.*

Lewis C

Camden

Hastings
Center

Oswego County

Oneida Lake

Higginsville

176

Erie Canal

Syracuse

Chittenango

Oneida
Canastota

Oneida
Castle

Oneida
Reservation

Onondaga County

Stockbridge

Peterboro

On
Fa

Cazenovia

Morrisville

Madison

Madison County

Hamilton

Cortland County

DeRuyter

Chenango County

Smyrna

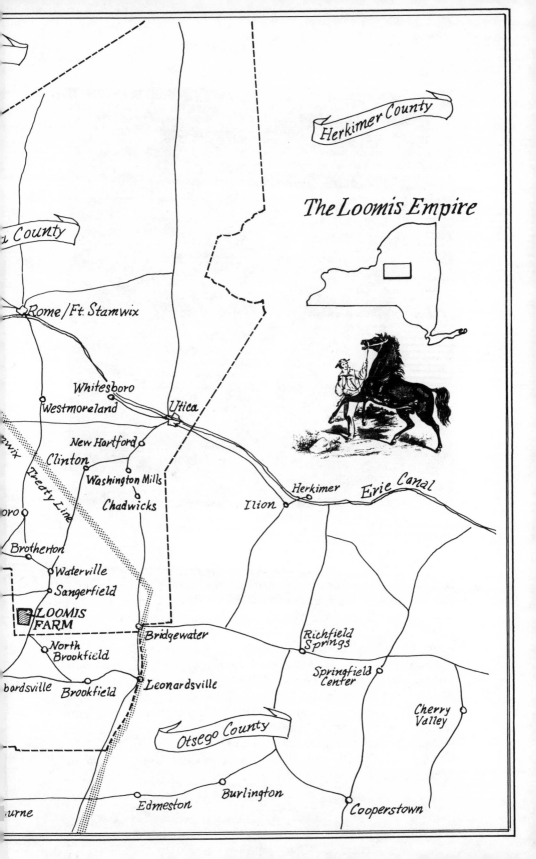

Herkimer County

The Loomis Empire

County

Rome / Ft. Stamwix

Whitesboro

Westmoreland

Utica

New Hartford

Clinton

Washington Mills

Chadwicks

Ilion

Herkimer

Erie Canal

oro

Brotherton

Waterville

Sangerfield

LOOMIS FARM

Bridgewater

Richfield Springs

North Brookfield

Springfield Center

bardsville

Brookfield

Leonardsville

Cherry Valley

Otsego County

Burlington

Edmeston

Cooperstown

urne

## *About the Author . . .*

Dr. Torrey grew up in Clinton, New York, just fourteen miles from the Loomis homestead, and for one summer worked on a job building a road adjacent to Nine Mile Swamp. He was educated at Princeton, McGill and Stanford Universities, and served in the Peace Corps in Ethiopia. He is the author of twelve books including *Surviving Schizophrenia, Nowhere To Go: The Tragic Odyssey of the Homeless Mentally Ill*, and *The Freudian Fraud. The Roots of Treason: Ezra Pound and the Secret of St. Elizabeths* was nominated by the National Book Critics Circle as one of the five best biographies of 1983. He is a clinical and research psychiatrist and advocate for individuals with serious mental illnesses and has appeared on Donohue, Oprah, Geraldo, 60 Minutes, 20/20, and other programs. His home is now in Washington, D.C.

# ACKNOWLEDGMENTS

I am deeply indebted to the work of George W. Walter who researched the Loomis gang from 1930 to 1953. When he died in 1972 he left behind an important collection of Loomis information. Many people assisted me in locating historical data including Russell Hubbard and the staff of the Madison County Historical Society; the staffs of the Oneida Historical Society and Utica Public Library; Ms. Linda Hazelden and Ms. Philippa S. Brown of the Waterville Historical Society and Ms. Wendy Sexton of the Waterville Public Library; E. Stevens Wright of the Onondaga Historical Association; Ms. Betty Smith of the Susquehanna County Historical Society; the staffs of the New York State Historical Association, Rome Historical Society, Cherry Valley Museum, Cornell University Library, and Syracuse University Library; Frank K. Lorenz and Prof. David Ellis of Hamilton College; Howard D. Williams of Hamilton; Judge John J. Walsh of Utica; and the staff of the Library of Congress in Washington. Ms. Lewis and Mr. Engel of the Mohawk Valley Psychiatric Center located the original psychiatric records of Gerrit Smith.

I am also grateful to the following:

The Cornell University Press for permission to quote from David M. Jordan's *Roscoe Conkling of New York: Voice of the Senate*; © 1971, Cornell University.

The Syracuse University Press for permission to quote from H. F. Jackson and T. R. O'Donnell's *Back Home in Oneida: Hermon Clarke and His Letters*.

The Colgate University Library for permission to quote from J. B. Hogan's unpublished manuscript "That Loomis Legend."

The Madison County Historical Society for permission to quote from unpublished material in the George W. Walter collection.

Ms. Ellen L. Peletz and the Madison County Historical Society for permission to use the line drawing of Gerrit Smith's Mansion House, originally published in B. J. Giambastiani, ed., *Country Roads Revisited*, Madison County Historical Society, 1984.

The Waterville Historical Society for permission to use photos of Waterville.

The National Gallery, Smithsonian Institution for permission to use Matthew Brady's photo of Gerrit Smith and John G. Jarvis' photo of Roscoe Conkling.

The Rome Historical Society for permission to use a photo of the Rome Courthouse.

Ms. Philippa S. Brown for permission to use her drawing of the Loomis home and the hanging of Plumb Loomis.

Ms. Kathleen Karin for permission to use her photo of Nine Mile Swamp.

Early drafts of the book were read by Russell Hubbard, Robert L. Taylor, and Nicholas R. Burke whose suggestions were very helpful. Ms. Judy Miller provided excellent typing and editing of the manuscript. Ms. Sheila Orlin and North Country Books kindly gave the book a home as a furtherance of upstate New York history. And my largest debt is to my wife, Barbara, my best reader and critic.

# CONTENTS

# EPIGRAPH

"By now it is evident that, historically, American life has been characterized by continuous and often intense violence. It is not merely that violence has accompanied such negative aspects of our history as criminal activity, political assassination, and racial conflict. On the contrary, violence has formed a seamless web with some of the most positive events of U.S. history: independence (revolutionary violence), the freeing of the slaves and the preservation of the Union (Civil War violence), the occupation of the land (Indian wars), the stabilization of frontier society (vigilante violence), the elevation of the farmer and the laborer (agrarian and labor violence), and the preservation of law and order (police violence). The patriot, the humanitarian, the nationalist, the pioneer, the landholder, the farmer, and the laborer (and the capitalist) have used violence as the means to a higher end."

Richard M. Brown
*Strain of Violence: Historical Studies of
American Violence and Vigilantism*, 1975

"They were conquerors, and for that you want only brute force —nothing to boast of, when you have it, since your strength is just an accident arising from the weakness of others. They grabbed what they could get for the sake of what was to be got. It was just robbery with violence, aggravated murder on a great scale, and men going at it blind—as is very proper for those who tackle a darkness. The conquest of the earth, which mostly means taking it away from those who have a different complexion or slightly flatter noses than ourselves, is not a pretty thing when you look into it too much. What redeems it is the idea only."

Joseph Conrad
*Heart of Darkness*

# PREFACE

I have known of the Loomis gang for as long as I can remember. The stories of their horse thieving and murdering, of the scalping of Wash and the hanging of Plumb, were part of the folklore of my town just fourteen miles from Nine Mile Swamp. And I remember believing that the swamp itself could instantaneously swallow a horse and rider in the quicksand of its dark recesses; small boys are impressionable.

The discovery that childhood stories are much more than that is one of life's unexpected pleasures. The Loomises traversed history, their lives intersecting our predecessor's efforts to shape a nation. My great-grandfather bought and resold Indian land in Pennsylvania at a handsome profit just as Jedediah Sanger bought and resold Indian land in central New York to George Loomis. My father bought hops from farms around the Loomises after they were gone and did business with Hermon Clarke and other men who had participated in the final raid. The story of the Loomis gang, then, is also the story of all who count themselves as genealogical and historical pastiches of nineteenth century America.

American history is a strange and wondrous tale. Although it is usually presented as having been a linear progression from wilderness to civilization, our history was in reality, like the world itself, a series of random collisions between revolving egos and meteoric ambitions. Such collisions are violent, and violence is therefore the heritage of our nation. As historian Richard Hofstadter noted in *American Violence*: "What is impressive to one who begins to learn about American violence is its extraordinary frequency, its sheer commonplaceness in our history, its persistence into very recent and contemporary times, and its rather abrupt contrast with our pretensions to singular national virtue." This, then, is the essence of my story.

All the facts of the story are true insofar as I can ascertain. My sources are indicated in the Notes section, and all direct quotations are taken from contemporary newspaper accounts, court records, or interviews used by George Walter in his book *The Loomis Gang*. I have taken the liberty of attributing thoughts to some characters but have tried to make such thoughts compatible with the historical circumstances and with the known facts.

# MAJOR CHARACTERS

George Washington Loomis (George) - the father

Rhoda Mallet Loomis - the mother

    Calista

    William (Bill)

    Cornelia

    George Washington, Jr. (Wash)

    Grove

    Lucia

    Wheeler

    Charlotte

    Plumb

    Denio

W. J. Bissell - Waterville shopkeeper

Hermon Clarke - clerk at Bissell's who joined the Union army

Roscoe Conkling - Utica lawyer, District Attorney, and later, United States Senator

James Filkins - constable

Gerrit Smith - Peterboro abolitionist and philanthropist

# CHAPTER I

# Prologue

News of the Cherry Valley massacre reached the Loomis home in Windsor, Connecticut, as it reached other American homes in November, 1778. The Loomises took a great interest, for they were among the staunchest supporters of American independence. They also were among the leading aristocratic families in New England, having lived there for five generations and boasted of prominent offspring who had become judges, educators, ministers and missionaries. Family members were highly educated and prided themselves on keeping abreast of important events on both sides of the ocean. In late 1778 a new Salieri opera had opened at La Scala in Milan, a child prodigy named Beethoven was being presented to German society, and Jean Jacques Rousseau had recently died leaving behind the idea that the primitive state of mankind is morally superior to the civilized state.

The news from Cherry Valley was of unprecedented violence. Prior to then the war had been fought between combatants with civilians not being intentionally injured. At Cherry Valley a force of Tories and Indians, marching quietly up Cherry Valley Creek from the Susquehanna River, had surprised the frontier settlement and randomly murdered thirty-two men, women and children.

Newspapers reported the scene in gory detail, as the *New Jersey Gazette* which informed readers that "Robert Henderson's head was cut off, his skull bone was cut out with the scalp. Mr. Wells' sister was ripped up, a child of Mr. Wells, two months

1

old, scalped and arm cut off, and many there as cruelly treated."
A farmer named Mitchell, working in the fields when he saw the
Tories and Indians running toward his house, hid and watched
his family being slaughtered. His smallest child was killed by a
Tory whom Mitchell recognized as being from a nearby village.
When the Tories and Indians finally left, Mitchell piled the
remains into a cart and took them to the Fort. A soldier's diary
described the "shocking sight my eyes never beheld before of
savage and brutal barbarity; to see the husband mourning over
his dead wife, with four dead children lying by her side, mangled,
scalpt, and some of the heads, some of the legs and arms cut off,
some of the flesh torn off their bones by their dogs . . ."

At their stately home in Connecticut, Daniel and Sarah Loomis
discussed the massacre. It presaged, they said, a long and bitter
war because violence would beget more violence. The Loomises
already had six children, but at the time of the Cherry Valley
massacre they conceived a seventh. He was born August 17,
1779, and named George Washington Loomis in honor of the
General whose increasingly effective troops promised victory.

Despite the death of his mother when he was five, George
Loomis grew up warmly indulged by his older sisters, Charlotte,
Anna and Clarissa. He had the confidence of a man insured by
his birthright and assured of his heritage. Loomis was a name
which people recognized, a name which another need not ask you
to repeat because it was obvious by the way you said it that yes,
you were from *that* Loomis family. George Loomis learned early
that proper pedigree conferred privilege in frontier America,
privilege which could be rationalized for improbity as easily as it
could for beneficience.

When George Loomis' father died in 1798 George, age 18,
went to live with his sister, Charlotte, in Vermont. He had
already begun exhibiting a fondness for horses and predilection
for collecting those which did not belong to him. He had a good
eye for them, and learned that stolen horses could be driven to
Connecticut and sold with no questions asked. The areas around
Brandon and Rutland were being rapidly depleted of fine horses
when George Loomis was warned by the sheriff. Unable to resist
the lure of easy gold, he persisted in his activities until 1802 when
a posse chased him over the border into New York State. It was
time, George decided, to visit his sister, Clarissa, who had settled
in Sangerfield with her physician-husband, Stephen Preston.

Riding up the Mohawk Valley, his saddlebags bulging with

three thousand dollars in gold, George Loomis reflected on the workings of the world. It was not, he thought, a question of whether a person could take things which did not belong to him, but rather who would be allowed to and what they would be allowed to take. As he was fond of telling his family in later years, when something is stolen by the finest of men, it is no longer considered stolen.

Sangerfield lay just thirty-seven miles of rolling hills west of Cherry Valley. As George rode he was aware he was traveling in the footsteps of his illustrious namesake who, while waiting in 1783 for peace negotiations in Paris to conclude, had ridden up the same trail through Cherry Valley and Sangerfield looking for land to buy. George Washington was an inveterate speculator in real estate, having watched his half-brothers acquire 200,000 acres as charter members of the Ohio Company and beginning his own investments as a teenager in the Shenandoah Valley where he was surveying. Throughout his career he had continued to buy and sell land, even paying attention to these business interests at the height of the Revolution.

Washington's companion on that trip had been George Clinton, former delegate to the Continental Congress, brigadier general in the War, and then first governor of New York State. Clinton also speculated heavily in land; according to a biographer, "during the later years of the Revolution he was salting away in land whatever funds he could obtain from the state on his salary." Clinton and Washington had already entered into joint investments, including an estate in Alexandria, Virginia, which Washington had purchased with a loan of £2,000 from Clinton. On the 1783 trip the two men tried to purchase the springs at Saratoga and land at Fort Stanwix, later known as Rome, which was an ancient Oneida Indian portage between the Mohawk River and Wood Creek; unsuccessful, they settled for 6,071 acres of prime farmland south of the Mohawk. Clinton loaned Washington another £2,500, a portion of which was used for his half of the purchase. According to a letter by a local settler, "they say that the General and Governor Clinton got it amazingly cheap from Colonel Willet who was in command at Fort Stanwix." Presumably the official positions of Washington and Clinton were directly related to their ability to buy land at such highly favorable rates.

The land in central New York coveted by General Washington and Governor Clinton was known to be among the most fertile in the newly independent United States. Over six million acres of it, however, were owned by the Oneida Indians, a small but powerful member of the six-tribe Iroquois nation. Widely respected for their oratory and statesmanship, the name "Oneida" meant "People of the Upright Stone" because of a sacred, two-ton granite boulder which, according to tribal mythology, "would follow them wherever they should go" as long as they kept the laws of the Great Spirit. It was the altar around which tribal councils and religious ceremonies took place, and it rested in a butternut grove on a ridge overlooking their farmland. The Iroquois were widely respected in the United States and Europe, and had in fact influenced the evolution of both the American and the Communist systems of government. Thomas Jefferson and Benjamin Franklin, helping plan the American Constitution, had studied the Iroquois system of voting by proportional representation at tribal councils. Later Karl Marx, writing *Das Kapital*, read Lewis Henry Morgan's 1851 book about Iroquois methods of communal sharing. If the Iroquois were the elite of eighteenth century American Indians, the Oneidas were the elite of the Iroquois.

In 1783 the Oneidas were also well known as one of only two Indian tribes in America which had sided with the colonists in the Revolutionary War (the Tuscaroras were the other). All others, including the other Iroquois tribes, had fought for the British, alarmed by land-grabbing propensities of the colonists and exhorted by crown officials to "feast on a Bostonian and drink his blood." The Oneidas had fought bravely in battles such as Oriskany, often in direct combat against their Iroquois brethren, and several Oneidas had achieved officer rank for their military endeavors. They had also supplied George Washington's troops with food and provided valuable intelligence to their American friends; in fact an Oneida had specifically warned the colonists of the impending raid against Cherry Valley but his warning had not been heeded.

As General Washington and Governor Clinton assessed the Oneida farmlands in 1783, they were aware of the devastation which had been wrought by the war on the tribe. Oneida villages had been destroyed by British raids, their crops burned, many of their young men killed, their social system disrupted, and their political affiliation with the other Iroquois tribes permanently broken. The majority of Oneidas and Tuscaroras were homeless and gathered behind American lines near Schenectady, living in squalid huts and suffering from famine and smallpox. Philip Schuyler, the aristocrat from the Hudson Valley who had served with George Clinton in the Continental Congress and in the war and who was one of George Washington's closest friends, was moved by their pathetic condition in 1780 and requested Congress to grant them immediate aid. America, Schulyer said, was "bound by every principal of honor" to assist their faithful Indian friends. Following the signing of the Treaty of Paris in 1783 Congress again addressed the fate of the Oneidas and Tuscaroras, passing a resolution stating that ". . . whereas the Oneida and Tuscarora tribes have adhered to the cause of America, and joined her armies in the course of the late war, and Congress has frequently assured them of peculiar marks of favor and friendship, the said Commissioners are therefore instructed to reassure the said tribes of the friendship of the United States, and that they may rely that their land which they claim as their inheritance will be reserved for their sole use and benefit, until they may think it for their advantage to dispose of the same." One year later at a new Treaty of Fort Stanwix, Philip Schuyler, Governor Clinton and James Madison again assured the Oneidas that they were "secured in the possession" of the six million acres which were their tribal farming and hunting grounds. Indian tribes other than the Oneidas and Tuscaroras, all of which fought against the colonists, were told bluntly that "you are a subdued people; you have been overcome in a war which you entered into with us, not only without provocation but in violation of your most sacred obligations." Predictably, most of the land of those other tribes was simply taken from them.

"Revolution," it would be said years later, "means to murder and create, but the American experience has been projected strangely in the realm of creation alone." In 1785, within two years of the Congressional resolution affirming rights to their land, and eight months after Governor Clinton and other officials signed the Treaty of Fort Stanwix, the leaders of the Oneidas were summoned to meet with Governor Clinton to discuss selling approximately one million acres, including some of their best hunting lands. Good Peter, a chief speaking for the Oneidas, told the Governor that they had no interest in selling because the lands in question "are very dear to us, as from whence we derive the rags which cover our bodies." Good Peter also noted that Indian tribes which had sold their lands had seen their game sources disappear and had been slowly reduced to poverty. The land requested by Governor Clinton all lay west of the Fort Stanwix Treaty Line, the boundary which had defined Oneida Indian land since 1768.

The Governor expressed annoyance at the Indians' refusal to sell but urged them to meet again the following day. He then put on display a wide assortment of food and gifts which the Indians were to receive if they agreed to sell; Governor Clinton had been told a month earlier that "because the Indians were then very hard pressed for provisions and other necessaries, the treaty (negotiations) was being held at a very opportune time for the state." The display of food and gifts, combined with the urging of state officials (and probably some bribery), brought about factionalism within the Indian camp. Four days after the discussions began the Oneidas compromised and agreed to sell half the tract the Governor had requested—one-half million acres at two cents an acre.

One of the greatest land rushes in history had begun and the Oneida Indians were in the way. Rights, agreements, obligations, treaties, and principles of honor all were trampled beneath the feet of speculating officials and land-hungry settlers rushing westward to claim the spoils of the American Revolution. From abroad the defeated British cynically watched the American treatment of their Indian allies. First the Americans fell on their knees and gave thanks to God, it was said; then they rose and fell on the Indians.

The pressure to obtain Oneida Indian land increased as settlers poured into the region. In 1788 Governor Clinton again approached the Oneidas, poverty-stricken and increasingly beseiged by settlers encroaching on their lands, and persuaded them to sell over five million acres for one-tenth of a cent per acre plus an annuity of six hundred dollars per year forever. "Clinton's Purchase," as it was called, included some of the most fertile land in central New York and reduced the Oneida Indian land to 300,000 acres compared to six million acres they had held four years previously. Governor Clinton presided over the negotiations and, following the signing, seated himself on a log. The Oneida chief "came and seated himself very close by him. Out of courtesy the governor moved along, when the Indian moved also, crowding still closer. The Governor then made another move; the Indian hitched along again close to him; and thus the moves were several times repeated, when at last Governor Clinton found himself off the log! Being considerably nonplussed he requested the meaning of this curious operation. The Chief sagaciously replied: 'Just so white man crowd poor Indian; keep crowding; keep crowding; by and by crowd him clear off! Where poor Indian then?'"

It was not only the Oneida Indians whose lands were rapidly shrinking, but those of the other Indian tribes as well. The State of New York was determined to seize all Indian land and turn it over to settlers. The federal government, still in Philadelphia, had become increasingly uneasy about the state's activity and in 1790 determined to stop it by passing a law known as the Indian Non-Intercourse Act. This law forbade the sale of any Indian land without the express consent of the federal government. Washington, who had become President a year earlier, met with a delegation of Indians and assured them: "Here, then, is the security for the remainder of your lands. No state, nor person, can purchase your lands, unless at some public treaty, held under the authority of the United States. The General Government will never consent to your being defrauded, but it will protect you in all your just rights." The Oneida Indians continued to be mistrustful of the word of the government, so the following year a delegation of their leaders went to Philadelphia where they met with Washington, Alexander Hamilton and Philip Schuyler. Do not worry about your remaining lands, they were told; the federal government will not allow them to be sold.

Four years later the State of New York purchased another 100,000 acres from the Oneidas, one-third of their remaining land. No federal authorization had been given nor was any federal representative present at the sale. The purchase was never ratified by Congress and thus was clearly in violation of the Indian Non-Intercourse Act. The United States Attorney General heard that such a sale was in progress, and asked the federal representative to the Iroquois to warn the Oneidas that such a sale was illegal. The Attorney General, in his instructions to the federal representative, added that "having done this much, the business might there be left." The negotiations were concluded in Albany and the document signed by several Oneidas, none of whom were chiefs and none of whom could read or write. Philip Schuyler and two other men signed for the State of New York. The sale price was three cents per acre per year to be paid indefinitely. Similar land surrounding the Oneidas was then being sold at between one dollar fifty and four dollars an acre. Two years after this purchase the Oneida land was sold to developers at three dollars fifty-three cents an acre.

The profits to be made from the buying and selling of Indian lands were enormous. On the land which Washington and Clinton bought along the Mohawk River on their 1783 trip, for example, "before his death Washington had almost doubled the money he had invested in the project, and he still had one thousand acres worth five or six dollars each." In 1799 Washington asessed his total land holdings at $488,137, a vast sum of money at the time.

George Clinton also profited handsomely from his land investments. In 1792, however, allegations of favoritism and irregularities in the sale of state lands were made against him. It was said that he had sold over three and one-half million acres to one friend at very favorable terms, and had sold fifty thousand acres to another friend who then turned nine thousand acres of it back to Clinton. These charges arose at the same time as Clinton was accused of rigging his own re-election as governor by having ballots from three counties invalidated on technicalities; "had the votes of these counties been tallied it is certain that [John] Jay would have been elected." At the time of the 1795 land purchase from the Oneida Indians Clinton had decided not to run for re-election and was temporarily leaving public office.

One of the largest landowners in the area of the Oneida holdings was Philip Schuyler, the chief negotiator of the 1795 purchase for New York. As state surveyor-general Schuyler had responsibility for land development, and as head of the Commissioners for Indian Affairs he had responsibility for the Indians. In 1795 he had already served one term as United States Senator and was one of the most influential men in the state. His wealth was intimately bound up with land development, as noted by a 1792 traveler through the region: "The increasing population, the rage of speculation in land by Americans, Dutch and Englishmen, double actually the value of the lands . . . The families of Livingston, Beeckman, van Renselaer, van Cortland, Schuyler, in one word all the powerful families in the state, merchants excepted, acquired their actual wealth and respectability by the purchase of new lands, and their judicious settlements on these."

Schuyler's son-in-law, Alexander Hamilton, invested much of his money in New York land, as did John Jay and Aaron Burr. Abraham and Samuel Ogden bought and resold large tracts of land in northern New York; Abraham had loaned George Washington his house for a headquarters in Morristown, New Jersey, during the Revolution and his son was Hamilton's law partner. Another New Jersey businessman, William Cooper, purchased vast tracts between Cherry Valley and Sangerfield and moved there in 1790 with his infant son, James Fenimore. Later Cooper hired Alexander Hamilton "to extricate him and his partner from the legal consequences" of acquiring additional land "by questionable methods."

The person who benefited most by the state's acquisition of Oneida Indian land was Peter Smith, son of an established Dutch family in the Hudson Valley. Early in his career he went into the fur trading business in partnership with a German immigrant, John Jacob Astor. Smith bought furs from the Iroquois in exchange for "Indian money"—beads, shells and pieces of glass —and in the process got to know the Indian leaders and their lands. In 1792 Smith married Elizabeth Livingston, daughter of one of the leading aristocratic families in the state and close friends with Philip Schuyler. The following year Smith began investing in land and bought 37,000 acres near Utica jointly with Astor (who had become close friends with Governor Clinton).

The land Peter Smith coveted most was a fertile area immediately south of Oneida Lake and part of the rapidly decreasing holdings still owned by the Oneidas. Because of the 1790 Indian Non-Intercourse Act it was illegal for Smith to purchase it, so in 1794 he negotiated a 999-year lease with the Oneidas for 60,000 acres. The federal government, concerned about Smith's quasi-legal land dealings, sent a federal official "to try to curtail Smith's activites but the canny Utican (Smith) was too much" for the official. In 1795, when New York State purchased 100,000 acres from the Oneidas for three cents per acre per year, most of Peter Smith's leased land was included; he was then able to buy it officially from the state for three dollars and fifty-three cents per acre and subsequently sold portions for fifteen dollars per acre. Continuing acquisition of Indian lands brought Smith's holdings to over one-half million acres and made him the largest landowner in the state. In the heart of the land purchased from the Oneidas Peter Smith founded the village of Peterboro and the township of Smithfield, and there built a large home which he named the Mansion House. From Utica he moved permanently to the Mansion House with his wife and newborn son, Gerrit.

Another settler who profited greatly from Oneida Indian land dealings was Jedediah Sanger, who migrated to central New York in 1788. He had been a successful merchant in New Hampshire, owning a tavern, store and farm, but a fire had destroyed his assets. Some claimed he had left New Hampshire in the middle of the night to escape his creditors but others denied this. Whatever the case he arrived with sufficient funds to purchase one thousand acres of land at fifty cents an acre from George Washington and George Clinton, settled on the land in the town of New Hartford, and immediately built a saw mill and grist mill. He continued buying land, some of it in partnership with Philip Schuyler, and in 1791 purchased with two other partners 67,130 acres of the Oneida land know as "Clinton's Purchase," also for fifty cents an acre.

Sanger was an ambitious and persuasive man. In 1793 he started the first newspaper west of Albany, and the following year became a founding trustee (along with Alexander Hamilton) of the new school for Indian education, the Hamilton Oneida Academy. At a meeting of settlers to select a Town Supervisor, Sanger lost by a vote of 50 to 34. According to records of the meeting "many people being deprived of the privilege of voting for Supervisor etc. moved to have the proceedings of the day made null and void, which passed in the affirmative." The following day another vote was taken and it was "found that Jedediah Sanger was unanimously elected Supervisor with the number of 119 votes, which choice was publicly declared in said meeting."

Sanger's persuasiveness was also shown by the naming of Sangerfield. The settlers to whom he resold the land he had purchased in 1791 quickly multiplied so that four years later they were ready to incorporate into a town. The majority wanted to name the town New Lisbon, but Sanger offered a cask of rum and fifty acres for a church if they would instead name it after him. The rum carried the day, and notes from the first Sangerfield town meeting recorded that "after the meeting was opened, they voted to adjourn to the barn" where Sanger's rum had been stored.

Clarissa Loomis Preston and her husband, Stephen, were among the original settlers in Sangerfield in 1795, attracted by the land Sanger was offering for less than four dollas an acre. Sangerfield was at the time the frontier, with bears and panthers still abundant, and wolves and lynx occasionally seen. By the time George Loomis rode into town in 1802 to join his sister, the surrounding woods had been cleared and many of the wild animals gone. Sangerfield boasted two hundred inhabitants, and a cluster of homes one mile away was growing into the village of Waterville. Stores and taverns lined the Sangerfield village green, avatars of civilization for the increasingly heavy traffic pushing westward. "Wagons, stagecoaches, herds of cattle and sheep, Yankee peddlers, itinerant artisans, and farm vehicles formed an ever-moving pageant on these roads. Teamsters, as proficient with their tongues as with the long whiplash, walked beside the wagons, which carried wheat, flour, cheese, potash, and whiskey." Men like Stephen Preston and George Loomis sipped rum as they watched the endless procession, wondering how much farther west the frontier could possibly go.

As the wild animals were killed or driven away, the number of Oneida Indians in the area also dwindled each year. The path from the main Oneida villages to their favorite hunting grounds passed directly through Sangerfield, but by 1802 it was unusual to see them hunting. The Oneidas who remained were sullen; once great orators mumbled drunkenly, and eyes which had been able to spot a deer a mile away gazed vacantly at the past. Disease, alcoholism and famine were endemic among them. This was, it was said, the plan of the Lord; as a Puritan leader in New England had previously explained: "By this means Christ, whose great and glorious works throughout the earth are all for the benefit of his churches and chosen, not only made room for this people to plant, but also tamed the hearts of these barbarous Indians."

George Loomis surveyed carefully the available land around Sangerfield. The price of land was rising rapidly but George wanted land with special features, including a place to hide stolen horses and high ground which could be used as a lookout. Finally he purchased fifteen acres for $14.78 per acre, still considered a good price. It was part of "Clinton's Purchase' for which Governor Clinton had paid the Oneidas one-tenth of a cent per acre and which Jedediah Sanger had then bought for fifty cents an acre. Situated four miles southwest of Sangerfield, the land included a high pinnacle and abutted the great swamp which the Indians called Skawanis.

Like many of the settlers, George Loomis wrote to Connecticut urging his brothers and sisters to join Clarissa and himself; Willard, Walter and Sarah agreed to come. Another local resident reported to his brother in New England that "the Yankees have taken care of the wolves, bears and Indians, Ephraim, and we'll build the Lord's Temple yet, build it out of these great trees."

George Washington Loomis laughed cynically. He understood the forces driving people westward and they had little to do with the Lord's Temple. The frontier meant gold for the strong and enterprising, while the weak and stupid would go the way of wolves, bears and Indians. Each time he saw an Oneida he was reminded that their reward for siding with the Americans in the Revolution had been the privilege of being swindled out of their land rather than having it stolen outright. That was, he knew, the spirit of the new land. Like himself it was a land conceived in violence, developed by men of correct pedigree and race, and dedicated to moral principles of free enterprise which reposed in the eyes of the beholders. As he liked to tell his family in later years, he also was a father of his country.

# CHAPTER II

# Meeting

The crime wave following the 1852 meeting of the Loomis gang bore testimony to the success of their own organization. Hidden clearings in the swamp overflowed with Morgans, Hunters, and an equine assortment collected from fields throughout the state. Strings of horses could be seen being led to the Loomis farm at night, and by morning identifying markings on many had been changed. Homes and stores were burglarized in surrounding villages, wayfarers robbed, stage coaches relieved of valued burdens. Clumps of men gathered on the streets of Sangerfield, Waterville and North Brookfield asking anxiously how things had come to such a state and what might be done. A definitive answer would not be found for almost fourteen years.

The meeting took place in October, 1852, fifty years after George Loomis had ridden into Sangerfield. The fifteen acres he had purchased had grown to over four hundred acres of meadows and wooded hillsides. On the pinnacle, five hundred feet above the Loomis homestead, seventy men and almost that number of wives and mistresses gathered in the autumn sunshine. Next to the Loomis home ran the Oxford Turnpike and a man passing that afternoon remembered "the wagons and rigs all headed in toward the house and the horses tied there. They were just as thick as they could be." Beyond the turnpike the Loomis land ran to the edge of Skawanis, prosaically renamed Nine Mile Swamp by the settlers because it stretched for nine miles from Sangerfield south to Hubbardsville. When George Loomis died

13

in 1851 a few oldtimers still referred to the land as "Clinton's Purchase." George Loomis bequeathed his land, genes, and sociopathic propensities to his large family.

The men had gathered on the pinnacle to coordinate the expanding activities of the Loomis gang, on the threshold of becoming the largest family crime syndicate in nineteenth century America. A report of the New York State Legislature in 1865 would describe them as "bands of associated depredators . . . the law has been powerless when exerted against this gang." By that time their reputation had become international as London's *Quarterly Review* featured them in an article about crime in America; the Loomis gang, it said, had achieved "freedom for thieves—and thralldom for honest men."

Wash Loomis emerged from the meeting as the undisputed leader of the gang. Although he had been the second of six sons born to George and Rhoda Loomis, it was he who had been given his father's name and baptized George Washington Loomis, Jr. It was as if George and Rhoda had presciently realized that Bill, nee William Walter Loomis four years earlier, would not be a leader. Bill was affable enough, but according to contemporary accounts he "had no mental activity" and was content to be controlled by his younger and brighter brother.

Wash, by contrast, was a natural leader. Just twenty-nine years old, he had dark curly hair, a full black beard and moustache, and dark blue eyes which were said to "read a man at a glance." In later years many compared Wash to John Wilkes Booth to whom, it was said, "he bore a remarkable resemblance." As he moved easily among the men and women who had been invited to the meeting Wash was infallibly polite, asking about other members' families, about the crops, and seeming to invariably remember which name went with which face. Once, when asked how he had acquired his skills of remembering names and putting people at ease, Wash laughed and allowed as how he was practicing to be a politician.

From the time he had been a small boy it was clear to George and Rhoda that Wash was the Loomis son to watch. His teachers noted his unusual "perceptive faculties" and the fact that "he was a keen observer of human nature and seemed endowed with magnetic power." Strong boys regarded Wash with respect, as something more than their equal, while weaker boys migrated to his side in hopes that his strength would become their talisman. As Wash grew older his peers described him as a man who was "generous to a fault, told a good story, and always kept his word . . . Few could resist the fascination of his manners and conversation . . . He was a born diplomatist, and never resorted to force when his ends could be obtained in any other way." Girls as well were attracted to Wash and it was said that "he dressed with exquisite neatness, sported the finest turnout in the county, attended all rural dances and festivals, and was a general favorite with the fair sex."

When Wash had finished the Tinker Hollow School just down the road from the Loomis farm it was agreed that his education needed to continue. Consideration was given to sending him to Hamilton College fourteen miles away in Clinton; the college had been founded to educate Indians but by the 1830s there were almost no Indians left to educate. The college, however, had acquired a reputation for students with unruly behavior and the Loomises, like many local families, were hesitant to entrust their son to such a milieu. Instead George and Rhoda Loomis decided to send Wash to study law with James B. Eldridge in the nearby village of Hamilton; a respected lawyer, Eldridge had just completed three years as Judge for Madison County. Wash Loomis' training proved to be extremely useful over the years in helping the Loomises avoid the legal consequences of their activities.

Wash Loomis had shown an aptitude for larceny from his earliest years and this was nurtured by his mother. As he later explained to a friend: "We sometimes traded little things like boys do, and learned quickly to deceive and cheat. Mother smiled approval when she learned of what we did and told us not to get caught nor to allow anyone to get the better of us. We were always supposed to seize the advantage. When we stole little things, Mother approved. As long as we were not caught she said it was all right. If we got caught we got licked."

Rhoda Loomis extended these lessons to many of the young people who visited. She was a firm believer that everyone had their price and could be corrupted if it was met. Young men who showed an attraction to liquor were plied with the finest whiskies which the Loomises stocked. As they grew older they might be encouraged to fraternize with "blooming girls who had been brought to the mansion as servants on the promise of good wages and started upon an infamous career." When the young men were leaving the house Rhoda "would place a hand on their arm and say: 'Now don't come back without stealing something, if it's nothing but a jackknife.' The first time they might return with the carcass of a sheep or lamb or a tub of butter. Their dexterity was praised and the fruits of the marauding were placed upon the table."

Wash excelled at these boyhood thefts and moved to more valuable items as he grew. The challenge to steal was virtually a compulsion, and he enjoyed the process almost as much as the booty. While disarming others' suspicions with charm and verbal skills he calmly went about his plunder, and was forever trying new schemes to relieve others of their property. He was caught only rarely, but when he was such stories circulated widely. On one occasion, while staying overnight at an inn, he came down in the morning complaining that his boots had been stolen. The innkeeper was trying to calm his agitated guest and offer payment for the boots when an employee of the inn announced that he had seen Wash hide boots beneath hay in the barn. The boots were retrieved, and Wash sent unceremoniously on his way.

Wash Loomis was especially fond of gold and devised various strategems to enlarge his collection. On one occasion he presented himself at the home of a farmer near Morrisville who was rumored to keep gold hidden in his house. Wash claimed to be a buyer of gold and offered to pay a high premium for any gold pieces the farmer might have. Wash watched as the man went upstairs and retrieved his hidden box, then offered the man a price so low he had to refuse. As recounted by the farmer's stepson:

"The next day being Sunday we went to the Baptist Church, stepfather ahead, mother following, and I lagging along behind. A man passed stepfather, bowed and smiled and met mother, who recognized him as the man who had called about the gold. She called to stepfather and told him that probably the man was going to our home, so we all turned back and found the man near the house, but he walked on to the bridge and then came back and went away, not stopping. One day next week, when I came home from school, mother said, 'Son, I have cleaned your bedroom today and you will have to sleep up in the spare room.' Later I went up to bed and sleep. Some time in the night I was partially aroused by cattle lowing, but rolled over and went to sleep again. Then something hit my head and I roused up and saw a man pulling up the curtain. He had already raised the window and was partly in the room. I tried to call mother, but there was such a big lump in my throat I could hardly make a sound. However, mother thought she heard me call and told stepfather to go up with the lamp and she would grab a towel and come as she thought I had a spell of nose bleeding. They came up and mother said, 'What is the matter, son, is your nose bleeding?' 'No, no!' I said, shaking. 'Look! Burglars!' pointing to the window. 'We're robbed, we're robbed!' cried stepfather, and ran to the chest, which he found locked. When mother had quieted me we all went downstairs. There was not much sleep for us that night."

On those few occasions when Wash was caught he used his legal training skillfully. In 1844, when Wash was twenty-one, he was arrested for stealing money from a store in the village of Waterville. He delayed the trial numerous times using a variety of legal tactics and, when finally convicted, carried appeals all the way to the New York State Supreme Court where the conviction was reversed on technical grounds. On other occasions Wash used his training to help family members or other Loomis associates. When Bill Loomis was arrested for passing counterfeit bills, for example, Wash talked to the complainant until the latter was completely confused, and when the case came to trial all charges were dropped. A reporter described his legal skills as follows: "Wash was a genius. He would train a witness in manufactured evidence until he actually made him believe that he was telling the truth."

Following his conviction in 1844 Wash increasingly moved toward employing others to steal for him and he would then dispose of the stolen goods. One of these was Riley Ramsdell who had been Wash's friend throughout childhood, and in 1845 Wash and Riley were indicted twice for larceny. Bail was set and paid in each instance, and the two simply forfeited it by failing to appear. Bill Loomis was also engaged in stealing, and in 1847, was indicted with Wash for taking "with force and arms" seven buffalo robes valued at five dollars each from a store in Camden. As usual bail was paid but the trial was never held and charges were eventually dropped. During these years, according to a newspaper account: "Burglaries were of nightly occurrence. Clothes lines were robbed, farmers lost their sheep and horses, and there was a multitude of petty thefts."

Everyone in Oneida County, in which the Loomis farm stood, and in adjacent Madison County knew where most of the stolen goods were going. Those who doubted soon became convinced by whispered stories of crawl spaces in the Loomis home and holes beneath the floorboards in their barns. One such story concerned a young woman working for the Loomises at hop-picking time:

> "A sudden shower appeared, and all the pickers ran into
> the Loomis woodshed out of the rain. The boards in the
> floor of the woodshed were apart about two inches, and
> looking through this crack she saw a whole milk pan full of
> watches and chains."

The increasing thefts, combined with the stories, led to talk
among local citizens of doing something about the lawlessness.
Without warning, on a snowy December afternoon in 1848,
several sleighloads of armed men arrived at the Loomis farm and
demanded to look around. Holding the family under guard the
men began what became known as "the big search." "An almost
inconceivable variety of articles" was found which were identified
as having been stolen, including clothing, buffalo robes, furs,
umbrellas, saddles, harnesses, and parts for wagons. Some were
found beneath trap doors, others in a hayloft behind "square
holes covered with boards." Stolen goods were identified as having been taken in both Oneida and Madison counties and some
of the merchandise was immediately taken to Waterville for
preparation of Loomis arrest warrants. The remainder was left at
the Loomises with a guard. That evening, however, the Loomises
overpowered the guard and spent the night burning and hiding
the remaining evidence against them. Despite these efforts Wash
and Bill Loomis were arrested and charged with multiple counts
of grand larceny.

The evidence against the Loomises was overwhelming, and
talk in the community was that this time there was going to be a
conviction and jailing. Wash, free on bail, heard the talk, and
also heard rumors coming from California about the gold John
Sutter had accidentally discovered while building a sawmill.
Wash decided it might be a propitious time to go west and see if
gold really was running in the streams. In early 1849, acccom-
panied by his friend, Riley Ramsdell, Wash quietly rode west out
of town. When he was gone the judge in Madison County oblig-
ingly dropped all charges against both Wash and Bill, while in
Oneida County the multiple charges of grand larceny were struck
from Wash's record with the notation: "Absconded."

For almost two years central New York was free of Wash
Loomis and thefts decreased dramatically. Old George Loomis
turned seventy shortly after Wash left and was not well. Once the
vigorous leader of the family, he had become gentle and forgetful

in his older years. His younger brother Willard and older brother Walter, both former partners in counterfeiting and other crimes, had died in the 1840s and George was increasingly content to live in the past. Residents of Sangerfield and Waterville remembered him as "a genial old man who was always joking with the young folks and twitting them on their love affairs . . . In the fall his pockets were filled with fruit which he distributed liberally." Those who knew the Loomises said that "the big search" of 1848 was a sign the Loomises were failing; a younger George Loomis would never have permitted such an occurrence. To further herald the demise of the Loomis family rumors circulated in 1850 that Wash had been caught stealing in California and had been hanged by a vigilante committee. It seemed to many at the time that the depredations of the Loomises were over.

Such talk turned out to be remarkably premature. This became apparent in late 1850 when Wash Loomis reappeared in Sangerfield, riding a golden California mare and tipping his hat to the ladies. He looked very much alive with a full beard, expensive attire, and a gold signet ring which he claimed to have had made from dust he had panned. He boasted of gold he had found and of having been a member of the Oregon Territorial Legislature, but said little about why he had returned. Later a story circulated that he had been in a dispute with a man named Burns over a mining claim. Both had been drinking in a saloon when their argument became heated and Burns challenged Wash to step outside and settle the dispute in the time-honored western manner. Wash agreed, but on the way out the door, he shot Burns from behind. According to a newspaper account "the wound was a slight one but Wash's treachery told upon the community. They gave chase with a rope. He escaped into a canyon and was followed by a friend on horseback. Wash rode the pony over two hundred miles pursued by Burns' comrades."

Word of Wash Loomis' return spread quickly down the valleys of central New York. People who only months before had talked of the Loomis gang in the past tense shifted uneasily to the present. Speculation increased following February 26, 1851, when George Washington Loomis, the patriarch of the Loomis family, died after a brief illness. Wash's return had been none too soon, and he presided at the graveside service at the Sangerfield cemetery where his father was buried. Neighbors asked each other what effect George Loomis' death would have on the family's illegal activities. Those who knew the Loomises from afar hoped their lawlessness was at an end; those who knew Wash Loomis knew better.

If Wash Loomis was the leader of the Loomis gang, then just as clearly Grove Loomis was second in command. Less than two years younger than Wash, the two complemented each other and had been inseparable as young boys. In 1852 Grove, then twenty-seven years old, was described as "nearly six feet high, well developed and almost perfect in manly beauty . . . a fine-looking man with black curly hair and black whiskers." He was more flamboyant in his dress and manners than Wash, wearing "patent leather boots or shoes, a black coat and pants, a white vest or fancy plaid ruffled shirt front, and a large ring with studs in his shirt." He was also more overtly aggressive, counselling action when Wash was content with patience. He lacked Wash's tact and diplomacy, and neighbors said that it was fortunate that Grove had an older brother to keep him in line.

Grove had two loves in life—women and horses. His record with the first was not passed down with history, but as a judge of horses he was excelled by none. It was said of Grove that "his love for horses was inherited from his father, and grew into a passion. He kept none but blooded stock, and when pressed sailed over the country on horseback without regard to roads or fences. The finest horses stood in the barnyard night and day saddled and bridled, ready for use at a moment's warning."

Grove was an adept pupil for his father's tutoring on horses. While still a young man he began breeding them, and in 1844 crossed one of his Kentucky-Hunters with a mare owned by a neighboring farmer. The resulting offspring was a short-tailed filly named Flora Temple, sold to a horse trainer and raised as a trotter. Flora Temple was spectacularly successful, winning eighty-six of one hundred and three races and setting a world's record for the mile. "Babies were named after her, as were steamboats and cigars . . . she was a favorite subject of the famous lithographers Currier and Ives" and when she ran in the Camptown Races she was immortalized as "I'll bet my money on the bob-tailed nag, somebody bet on the bay." Grove Loomis never tired of retelling his role in Flora Temple's genesis. In later years one of Grove's horses, a Black Hawk stallion, was valued at over six thousand dollars.

Grove could have become wealthy as a legitimate breeder of horses but he craved excitement. While Grove was still a boy his father taught him how to pick the finest horses to steal and how to change their markings. To create a white marking on a horse a hot baked potato was bound tightly to the spot, repeating the process several times until the hair color had been bleached out. To darken a light marking silver nitrate was used. Other dyes and chemicals were used as needed, including paint on occasion, so that a horse stolen at midnight would be unrecognizable by sunrise the following morning.

So effective were the Loomises in changing a horse's appearance that many farmers in the area unknowingly bought back their stolen animals. On one occasion a farmer's roan horse was stolen; a few days later he replaced it with a black one which was being offered for sale. When the farmer brought the new horse home and led it to its stall "the animal whinnied joyfully—back home in a changed costume." On another occasion a pair of black horses was stolen from Thomas Jones, a farmer near Utica. Several weeks later Jones heard that a pair of horses was being sold at a farm near Camden. Riding there, he found two chestnut horses with white stockings, one with a white star on its forehead, and he purchased them. Abe Lovett, a Negro working for George Loomis at the time, recalled the incident: "Yessir, dat sure am funny. Mister Jones done bought his own team back. I stole 'em myself an' had their markin's changed. Mister Jones bought his own team an' never know'd it."

Old George Loomis and Grove had spent days riding the farm roads and lanes of Oneida and Madison counties. They had a good eye for horses, and when they saw a particularly fine one they would stop and talk pleasantly with its owner. Usually within a few days the horse had been stolen. To deaden the sound of a departing horse in the night burlap was tied around the horse's hoofs. As recalled by one local resident: "There was Mr. Wadsworth living in Washington Mills who had a fine team of horses that the Loomises were determined to get. When they saw some team they wanted they usually got it in time. One morning Mr. Wadsworth went to his barn and discovered that his team was gone. A search was held but he never found his team. A neighbor and his wife had got up about four that morning the team was stolen so they could catch the train in Utica. On the road the Loomises passed them driving the Wadsworth team. The neighbor thought it strange that the team moved along without making any noise. 'That's funny,' he said to his wife. 'Those horses' feet don't make any noise.'"

Horses were valuable assets to farmers in the nineteenth

century; it was commonly said that in the event of fire one should save his horse first and his wife second. The price for a good horse ranged from one hundred to one thousand dollars, occasionally even more. The Loomises stole some of the horses themselves, but far more were stolen by confederates with whom they developed business relationships. Some of these colleagues, like Abe Lovett, lived on the farm in cabins near the pinnacle; many others lived in the surrounding towns and used the Loomises as a stolen horse fencing operation. The Loomises paid approximately twenty-five dollars for an average horse, and if the horse was sold without difficulty the thief was given an additional bonus of fifteen dollars. George Loomis and his sons would change the horse's markings and sell it to buyers in another county for eighty to one hundred dollars.

As Grove Loomis grew into his twenties he increasingly took over the horse thieving business from his aging father. He had learned his lessons well and, in addition, had an audacity not possessed by his father. This trait was illustrated one September at the Brookfield County Fair when Grove, still a young man, admired the winner of the horse show, a magnificent animal with "white markings on its forehead and four white stockings. Arrayed in a glistening new harness, it was hitched to the finest carriage its owner could afford. After the exhibition the horses were tethered around the inside of the fairground fence. In the afternoon, while other events were taking place, the section where the horses were tethered was deserted except for a nine year old boy. The youngster stopped his play when he saw Grove Loomis approaching. As he had heard fearsome stories of the Loomises from his parents, he quickly hid. The boy saw Grove carefully glance around to see if anyone was watching. Grove then took a bottle from his pocket and began swabbing the horse with its contents. When he completed his work there were no markings on the horse. Grove removed the prize ribbon from its bridle, unhitched the animal from its post, backed the carriage from its place in line and slowly drove out of the entrance gate of the fairground. The few people who were standing near the gate paid no attention to either the horse or its driver as Grove drove away."

On occasion Grove's audacity led him into difficulty. Such was the case with young Herbert Throop of Sangerfield who had trained his horse to do tricks such as dance, kneel, roll over, and play dead. "One night the horse was stolen. Herbert and his father drove to the Loomis farm and demanded that Grove return the animal. While Grove registered indignation a horse whickered loudly from the nearby pasture. In stride and build the animal resembled Herbert's horse, but its markings and coloring were different. Grove insisted he had recently purchased it from outside the state. Walking to the fence Herbert voiced a command. To Grove's consternation the horse obeyed. At the boy's insistence the animal went through its entire repertoire of tricks. When the elder Throop led the horse from the pasture and started homeward, Grove did not interfere."

In his social relations Grove Loomis lacked Wash's charm and more often resorted to aggressiveness. An example of this occurred at the hop-dig in the Abbey barn in September of 1848. Grove, then twenty-five, was accompanied to the event by Wheeler, the next youngest Loomis son who was seventeen at the time and described as "the most unprincipled of the six brothers . . . his character shows not a redeeming ability."

Hop-growing was the most profitable agricultural activity in Oneida and Madison counties throughout the middle years of the nineteenth century. A farmer in the village of Madison began growing them in 1808, and within ten years was selling his product to brewers in New York at one thousand dollars a ton. By the 1830s almost every farm in the area including the Loomises "grew at least a few acres of hops, and the larger farms had their own hop kilns—wooden barnlike structures distinguished by squat twin towers—in which the hop blossoms were dried and bleached." New York State contributed ninety percent of the hops to the nation's breweries, and the Sangerfield-Waterville area was its hop-growing center. In September "the hop fields swarmed with men, women and children . . . Entire families descended on the fields, as if for a two weeks' holiday, to strip hops from dawn to dusk into large boxes—one chattering group often pitted against another, racing to fill more containers and accumulate more tickets entitling them to cash payments at the end of the day or week."

A hop-dig was a dance used to celebrate completion of the hop harvest, and that given by the Abbeys took place in a barn two miles south of the Loomis farm; "dried vines festooned the walls, fiddlers stamped time to their own shrill music, and hop-pickers danced on the same rough floors that recently had been covered with a foot or more of hop vines." Grove and Wheeler Loomis arrived with some friends to take part in the festivities. Allen

Abbey met the Loomises at the door and told them they were not welcome. Grove pushed Abbey aside, entered, and went directly to Abbey's girl friend asking her to dance. Pandemonium broke out as Abbey and his friends attacked the Loomises; chairs, shovels, and hop-poles were swung indiscriminately as women screamed and rushed for the doors. Abbey was felled by Wheeler Loomis' blow from behind and then stomped into unconsciousness by Grove's boots. Warrants were issued the next day charging Grove and Wheeler Loomis with assault with intent to kill; the trial, however, was delayed by repeated failures of witnesses to appear and the charges were eventually dropped.

Grove's equine acumen and innate aggressiveness won him respect if not affection from other members of the Loomis gang. When Wash was absent Grove's word was accepted as law. Grove was always trying to persuade the others to extend their horizons both geographically and in terms of new criminal activities. He had a vision of the Loomis gang which was not confined to central New York, not even to New York State, but rather encompassed the entire northeastern portion of the expanding United States. And it was this vision which he persuasively conveyed to the guests as he circulated that autumn afternoon in 1852.

The pinnacle on which the meeting was held was the highest point for miles around, affording uninterrupted views in all directions except west where its hegemony was challenged by woods sloping gently away. To the north and south the Oxford Turnpike could be seen for miles, circumambulating the swamp as it ran toward Sangerfield and snaking around hop fields and into gullies as it wound south. East of the turnpike the Loomis land continued to the edge of Nine Mile Swamp. Well ensconced in Indian lore for its wild animals and bogs, the swamp was choked with white pine and cedar. Through its center flowed Chenango Creek which formed part of the headwaters of the Susquehanna River to the south. In 1852 the swamp was still more than a mile wide in most places, a forbidding and mostly impassable morass which, from atop the pinnacle, appeared monadic. There were rumors, though, which were said to come from the Indians, rumors of hidden trails and small clearings in the midst of the swamp, but nobody except the Loomises were certain whether such rumors were true. Even in 1879, seven decades after George Loomis had purchased his land and after his family had made the swamp famous, the *New York Sun* would still describe it as "so thick and impenetrable that not more than ten men in the county can traverse it with confidence."

The main business of the meeting was the division of territory among gang members and coordination of efforts of the various factions. The world had changed, argued Wash and Grove, and it was time to modernize their operations. It was no longer George Loomis' world of the 1830s when thefts could be carried out in a leisurely fashion and there was little to fear of stolen goods being traced from one county to the next. Life had sped up in the 1840s, as if rushing somewhere. The coming of trains seemed to symbolize the change, great iron horses plying steel rails between Albany and Syracuse by 1839 and each year going farther west. The railroad between Utica and Rome had to pass through marshland so a system was devised to elevate the railbed on wooden piles; so exotic did this seem that "excursionists were able to fancy they were sailing through the air" and President Martin Van Buren came himself to try it out. Turnpikes also proliferated and improved in quality so that stagecoaches could travel faster each trip. In the late 1840s the practice of covering roads with wooden slats was introduced to further speed travel; these plank roads became very popular and provided passengers with a corrugated ride.

There were also the canals. The Erie Canal, opened in 1825, had brought profound changes to central New York. Linking the Great Lakes with the Atlantic Ocean had been the fulfillment of dreams of George Washington, George Clinton and Philip Schuyler and it was Clinton's nephew, Governor DeWitt Clinton, who accomplished the task. Freight costs between Utica and New York City were slashed by ninety percent opening vast markets for the products of the farms around the Loomises. Hop growing increased, commercial dairying took hold, and in the towns along the Canal, textile mills sprang up. So successful was the Erie Canal that the State immediately began building extensions of it, feeder canals linking it to more distant areas. One of these was the Chenango Canal, stretching ninety-seven miles from Utica to the Susquehanna River in Binghamton; through its one hundred and sixteen locks ran barges with Pennsylvania coal bound for the textile factories of Utica. Opened in 1837 its course was through the village of Madison just six miles west of the Loomis farm. The Loomises and their neighbors used it to send hops and other farm products to market; it could also be used to dispose of stolen horses and other goods.

Words also began traveling faster. Samuel F. B. Morse, a

successful portrait painter and sculptor in New York, became interested in electricity and moved to his cousin's home in Cherry Valley for several months in 1837. During this time he built the first telegraph machine and, with the help of a local melodeon manufacturer, invented the Morse Code. In 1842 Morse went into partnership with Ezra Cornell, who had grown up in Madison county and then moved to Ithaca; together they built a telegraph line between Washington and Baltimore. On May 24, Morse sent the first message: "What hath God wrought!" Cornell then built intercity telegraph lines across New York State and reorgainzed his company as the Western Union.

Trains, plank roads, canals and telegraph lines all meant faster movement and faster communication. Gang members could coordinate thefts and dispose of stolen goods with a speed that had been inconceivable a few years earlier. When George Loomis had extended horse thieving operations to his brother Willard's farm at Hastings Center, north of Syracuse, in the 1830s it had seemed like an extraordinary distance of forty miles. Now the Loomis family and their friends sat around drinking rum and casually discussing expanding further into Ontario and Pennsylvania, distances of one hundred and twenty miles or more.

Bill Loomis was given primary responsibility for Loomis business to the north. Bill was short and stocky and, although not as bright as his brothers, had an enterprising spirit. He was, as Wash and Grove knew, reliable and would not question their decisions. Bill was also on good terms with his cousins at Hastings Center—the two sons and daughter of his father's brother, Willard. In recent years, in fact, Bill had spent almost as much time at Hastings Center as he had spent at home. It was Bill who had convinced his father shortly before his death to buy one hundred and thirty acres of land in Hastings Center and it was widely assumed that Bill would eventually settle on the land. Bill did not get along well with his mother, it was said.

In the spring of 1852, while Bill was looking for horses to steal from farms to the east of Oneida Lake, he stayed overnight at the Burdick farm in Higginsville. Noticing his host's twenty-one year old daughter, Martha Ann, reciprocating his glances, Bill found reasons to return to the area increasingly often. By the time of the big Loomis meeting in October Martha Ann Burdick was pregnant and Bill, thirty-three years old, announced that he was going to marry her. Rhoda Loomis was bitterly opposed and did everything she could to stop it.

On February 11, 1853, Bill married Martha Ann Burdick, the first and only Loomis son to ever marry. They purchased a farm in Higginsville near that of her family; she accompanied Bill on visits to Sangerfield only rarely. Their farm sat beside the Sidecut Canal, a feeder connecting the Erie Canal with Oneida Lake, and it became the center for the Loomis gang's northern activities. Bill and Martha Ann had six children over the years; they were named for Bill's father (George), brothers (Wash and Grove), and sisters (Calista and Lucia), but no child was named for Rhoda.

Counterfeiting had always intrigued Bill Loomis, and at the farm in Higginsville he began turning out both counterfeit bills and coins. As his father had taught him he recruited accomplices to do the actual distribution thereby keeping himself at arm's length from the law. Two of his accomplices were Jesse and Bill Hitchings who owned a general store in Higginsville and gave counterfeit money to their customers as change. The local sheriff became aware of this, and obtained a sworn affidavit from a man that Bill Loomis was the person supplying the counterfeit currency. The sheriff then went to the store, made a purchase and when he received counterfeit change arrested both Bill Hitchings and Bill Loomis. Both men were jailed in Utica and bail was denied. When the date of trial arrived the man who had given the sworn affidavit had disappeared; Bill Loomis was therefore released and all charges dropped for lack of evidence.

Bill Loomis also proved to be adept at stealing, and a rash of burglaries occurred in area homes and business establishments. On one occasion Bill was said to pick a fight with a man in front of a butcher shop. The shop owner went out front to see what was taking place, and as he did a Loomis accomplice slipped in through the side door and made off with a side of beef.

Bill Loomis' principal energies, however, went to the stealing of horses which were then driven through the night to the Loomis homestead by Nine Mile Swamp. Bill posed as a buyer of horses and cattle, traveling from farm to farm assessing the stock and making occasional purchases to maintain the facade. When a particularly fine horse was spotted Bill Loomis would inform his accomplices who would then do the actual stealing. He operated over a broad geographical area of northern Oneida, Oswego and Lewis counties making it difficult to link the thefts to him. To one friend he boasted: "I never take things, but I can hide them where God himself couldn't find them."

Occasionally he was charged with horse theft but evidence for conviction was wanting. Once a particularly valuable horse was stolen from a farm in Camden by two Loomis accomplices. Unknown to the thieves the horse was followed, first to Bill Loomis' farm and then south to the farm of a Loomis gang member near Sangerfield. The thieves were convicted and sent to prison but the evidence was not sufficient to indict Bill or his brothers.

The most celebrated case involving Bill Loomis during the 1850s was the Wygart mare. In early 1855 a brown mare named Doll was stolen from the farm of Reuben Wygart south of Higginsville. A horse appearing to be identical was found on the Loomis farm in Sangerfield and both Bill and Grove Loomis were indicted. The Loomises insisted that the horse found on their farm had been purchased by them and was not the Wygart mare; Wygart and his friends were just as certain that it was his horse. On the day of the trial another brown mare was brought to the Wygart farm by Wash Loomis. "With a whinney at recognizing its old home, it trotted down the lane to the barn, and as it stood there one of the women in the house called out: 'Why there's our Doll.'" Wash then took the horse to the courthouse where a confrontation took place as to which was the real Wygart mare. Eventually it was decided that the horse Wash had brought (which he claimed he had "found" in Pennsylvania) was the real one, not the one found on the Loomis farm, so all charges were dropped. The Loomises then sued Wygart for damages, and eventually received a settlement. It was said that Wygart became so discouraged with the legal chain of events that he packed his belongings and took his family west. The Loomis reputation continued to spread.

As the center of the Loomis' northern operations Bill Loomis also had responsibility for maintaining their network for disposing of stolen horses in Canada. Horses were driven north from Higginsville or Hastings Center to Pulaski, then along the eastern shore of Lake Ontario through Sackets Harbor to Cape Vincent. There they were ferried across the St. Lawrence River into Canada and sold locally or taken downriver to Montreal for sale.

Loomis operations to the south were the responsibility of Grove. This included Otsego, Delaware, Sullivan, Chenango, Broome, and Cortland counties as well as a large area of Pennsylvania north of Scranton. The Loomises had cousins who lived near Scranton and they valued such family ties. The Loomises maintained an extensive network of accomplices throughout northeastern Pennsylvania and it appears to have been the most important outlet for their stolen horses and other goods. They also used this area to hide gang members who were being sought for arrest, such as a Loomis accomplice who was hidden in the town of Susquehanna, Pennsylvania, until charges against him were dropped by the court.

On one occasion a member of the Loomis gang was arrested and jailed in Montrose, Pennsylvania, for horse theft. Grove Loomis testified as to his innocence at the trial but the jury could not decide and the man was held in jail pending another trial. The man in fact was innocent in this particular case and when the real thief was found Grove Loomis vowed to make Montrose "pay well for every day" his friend had been in jail. A short time later, in November, 1854, a fire of unknown origin destroyed much of the business district of the town "and crossing the street the residence of Judge Post and all the buildings south on both sides of the street to the house of Mrs. Turnell and the storehouse of S.F. Keeler." The Loomises took credit for it.

Loomis operations to the east were the most delicate for they included Albany, the state capital; Wash Loomis kept this responsibility for himself. Horse thieving by Loomis accomplices took place in Herkimer, Fulton, Montgomery, Schoharie and Albany counties. In addition, the Loomises maintained an alternate network for disposing of stolen horses in Vermont where George Loomis had lived as a young man and where they had many cousins, the offspring of George's sister Charlotte. The most important business in this direction, however, was the cultivation of well-placed friends in Albany. Wash had learned from his father and mother that every man has a price, and the challenge was to learn what that price might be. Loomis friends in Albany included, it was rumored, several members of the state legislature; such friends were invaluable when it came time to appoint local officials such as county judges who would be hearing cases involving the Loomises.

It was only to the west that leadership of Loomis activities was put into the hands of a nonfamily member. The honor belonged to Big Bill Rockwell, "well over six feet and built in proportion," a handsome man with a full beard and "kindly face with ever a smile." His father had been an alcoholic but his mother instilled in her son a desire for material success. Rockwell was pursuing a variety of stratagems for achieving this goal when Wash Loomis encountered him selling patent medicine off a wagon in the village of Madison. Wash, having previously purchased a bottle of the tonic from Rockwell, walked up to the wagon and said loudly in front of the gathered assemblage:

"Here is your dope, you faker. It ain't worth a damn."

"I know it," returned Rockwell in a flash, "it don't work on wood."

Wash looked at Rockwell, the crowd quiet and expecting a fight.

"Men have died for saying less than that," Wash said in a tone suggesting he was not speaking metaphorically.

"Yes, but not by your hands," snapped back Big Bill. Standing on the wagon he seemed to tower over Wash and the rest of the crowd. Before Wash could act Rockwell added: "Say, big boy, come and see me at my hotel tonight. I'm staying at the Madison Hotel; we'll talk this over and have it out."

"I'll be there," answered Wash as he walked away, his ego and reputation comparatively intact.

It was a meeting of kindred spirits from the beginning, and after a couple of drinks Rockwell agreed to supply the Loomises with stolen horses. The friendship was cemented when Rockwell visited Wash's home and met his sister Cornelia who "showed a deep interest" in Rockwell from the start. Big Bill was, according to local talk, very much a woman's man and known in his hometown of Moravia for having seduced the most sought after young lady in the village. He owned a boat "and on many an evening Viola and him would be seen out rowing." Unfortunately Viola was later found drowned. Cornelia apparently disregarded such talk and it was said that Rockwell "had a comparatively easy conquest."

Over the next few years Big Bill Rockwell became "the terror of the Finger Lakes region," with thefts incurred by virtually "every household for miles around." The stolen goods were brought directly to the Loomis farm. Horses continued to be the main contraband, and many of the finest specimens from the fertile fields around Cayuga, Owasco, and Skaneateles lakes were led through the night to hiding places in Nine Mile Swamp. Wash Loomis eventually showed Rockwell how their system worked:

> "The horses were led into the swamp, each one by a different path, so as to make their tracks confusing. Following an

irregular, twisting course, they all converged to one point about two miles from where they entered the swamp. At that point the swamp was almost impassable. There was a sort of an island, comprising about one acre of land, almost entirely surrounded by water, forming a moat. The boys had constructed a temporary bridge, by which the island, as it was known to them, could be reached. The bridge was constructed in such a way that it could be put in place or taken down in an incredibly short time. It was composed of planks which would be hidden in different parts of the swamp when the bridge was not in use. The island itself was fringed in with scrubby trees and underbrush, hiding the interior, which had been cleared off by the boys, completely."

The meeting in 1852 not only formalized a reticulum of accomplices extending over one hundred miles in all directions, but also effectively organized their resources closer to home. Each of the surrounding towns had designated Loomis confederates who stole for them and acted as part of a network for disposing of stolen goods. A saddle stolen by Rockwell in the Finger Lakes region might turn up for sale in Oriskany Falls by Julius Glazier. Or some clothing taken from a store in Bridgewater might be disposed of in Syracuse by John Maxwell and William Bennett who lived nearby. The Loomis gang increased in size throughout the 1850s to well over one hundred members, and names like George and Sidney Peckham, DeWitt Dennison, William Ellis, Thomas Mott, Ezra and Laverne Beebe, Eli Tilly, Byron Tubbs, John Simms, Frank Jones, William Flemming, Jack Van Dee, John Stoner, Lorenzo Bixby, John Smith, Archie McGregor, Jack Keenan, Silas Clark, and Henry Carter turned up increasingly often on indictments throughout central New York. As their operations increased the Loomises dropped the facade of a family farm and were increasingly brazen. There were almost always men staying with them in the house and the shacks on the hill, "as many as fifty or sixty men around the farm at one time." Strangers were challenged and it was not a place that neighbors dropped by for a casual visit.

Without question the most notorious Loomis associate was Bill Alvord from the village of Madison, a tall powerful man with a trim beard and mean countenance. He had first been arrested in 1838, and by the early 1850s had already served three terms in prison and was "held in perfect terror by all honest citizens in Madison County." In 1853 he was arrested again for counterfeiting and, according to a contemporary newspaper account, he pleaded "strenuously for his freedom insinuating that if money would buy his escape it was ready in any amount." On this occasion Alvord's "liberal offers were respectfully declined." Between prison terms Alvord spent much time at the Loomises and his sister also lived with them.

By late afternoon at the 1852 meeting the business of dividing territory and allocating responsibility for gang activities had been concluded. The tables which had been brought to the pinnacle were filled with food, rum flowed freely, and a band which had been hired began playing traditional dance tunes of nineteenth century rural America. It was a festive occasion for the Loomises and their friends, eating, drinking and dancing amidst the splendor of an autumn sun accentuating red and yellow maples on surrounding hillsides. Glasses were raised in toasts to their successes, to the new Loomis gang, to the spirit of George Loomis, and to the spirit of America. The celebration continued, it was said, far into the night.

Early the next morning a neighbor boy, "about sixteen or seventeen at the time, took his gun and went up on the plateau" next to the pinnacle to hunt. "Nothing had been cleaned up. There was the remains of food on the tables, and the trampled earth marked the site of the dancing." Standing on the hill the power of the Loomises must have seemed awesome. As far as one could see in all directions was under their control, and their influence extended north into Ontario, east into Vermont, south into Pennsylvania, and west almost to Lake Erie. One had to look carefully on the horizon to perceive the problems which would eventually lead to their destruction.

# CHAPTER III

# Discord

To outsiders in the 1850s the Loomis gang appeared to grow more powerful with each passing day. The number of associates climbed toward two hundred as their activities spread in ripples from its cynosure in Sangerfield. Burglaries, petit larceny, grand larceny, armed robberies, and horsethefts were endemic. Crawl spaces in their home and barns overflowed with stolen goods just as Nine Mile Swamp could not contain the multitude of stolen horses. Profits were reinvested in gold, land, legitimate businesses, and above all in bribes for public officials.

Insiders, however, were aware that discord had settled permanently into the Loomis home and her name was Rhoda Loomis. Although sixty years old Rhoda was still a feisty and vigorous woman. All her life she had controlled the men around her with a subtlety imperceptible to the uninitiated, and as long as George Loomis had been alive she had continued to work her will through him. After George died, however, Wash and Grove had taken over control of the family and the gang. Rhoda was treated with respect but she was no longer in control. Rhoda Loomis was not a woman who suffered losses gracefully, even if the losses were to her own sons.

Those meeting Rhoda for the first time invariably underestimated her tenacity. She was a cultured and charming woman, and men were especially susceptible to her influence. Even entering her seventh decade one could see shadows of the beauty which had been the talk of Sangerfield in the early years of the century. She was slender with "glossy black hair, brushed back from her forehead, parted in the middle and caught in a loose knot at the nape of her neck." Her skin was said to be "like pale ivory and her only beauty secret was to wash her face every day with a fine linen handkerchief soaked in dew."

George Loomis had seen Rhoda's tenacity when he had first encountered her and it was that trait which had so intrigued him. It was 1811; Rhoda was eighteen and George thirteen years her senior. Zachariah Mallet, Rhoda's father had a propensity for forgery which brought him intermittently to the notice of the law. George Loomis had accompanied Sheriff James Kip to the Mallet home to serve a warrant for Zachariah's arrest. When their business became known and Kip tried to enter the Mallet home, Rhoda barred the door and attacked Kip with a shovel. When George came to Kip's assistance he too received a battering.

George Loomis found excuses to return to the Mallet home often. Although her mother had died when she was a young girl, Zachariah had indulged his only child and had seen to Rhoda's education. She had learned to read and write, unusual for a woman on the frontier, and had even taught school briefly. She was thus among the best educated and most widely read women in the area, which did nothing to detract from her beauty.

Rhoda Mallet also claimed a noble lineage which rivaled George Loomis' English roots washed over by five generations of New England aristocracy. The Mallets had been a Scandinavian family which had migrated to France. They were said to be "distinguished by a terrible weapon which did great execution, a long hammer with a point at the other end - a mallet with one side pointed." As Huguenots the family had been forced to flee religious persecution in seventeenth century France, and they settled in Stratford, Connecticut. Zachariah Mallet, a fourth generation American, had been one of the earliest settlers in central New York and among the first buyers of the Oneida Indian lands Jedediah Sanger had put up for sale in 1795. Rhoda never tired of telling people of her family's importance and was known by neighbors for a pride which often blended into haughtiness. "I want you to understand that I am French," she would say, "and high French too."

Rhoda's superior attitude, her love of fine things, and her lack of concern about how the fine things were obtained all resonated with George Loomis' view of life. He signed up with the New York Militia to fight in the War of 1812 and when he returned

persuaded Rhoda to marry him. It was a propitious time for
Rhoda to change households, for Zachariah Mallet had been
sentenced to a long prison term for forgery and perjury.

Rhoda moved into the cabin which George and his brother had
built on the hill overlooking the swamp. The Loomises immediately began a family which would take twenty-three years to complete; such large families were desirable because the labor was
needed to maintain a farm and because the infant mortality rate
was approximately fifty percent. Epidemics of cholera, typhoid,
typhus, smallpox, and malaria (known locally as "Genesee
fever") occasionally visited the villages of central New York
bringing death to children who had been perfectly well just days
earlier. Effective remedies were few, though most mothers kept a
copy of William Buchan's *Domestic Medicine* of home treat-
ments or tried special diets such as that advocated by Sylvester
Graham whose supposedly therapeutic crackers became very
popular and eventually bore his name. There were also medicines
such as the Indian tobacco plant (a strong emetic), Smith's Triple
Cure Tablets ("for catarrah, dispepsia and blood"), and Kicka-
poo Cough Syrup (with a picture of an Indian on the bottle and
an alcohol content of eighteen and one-quarter percent). Such
medicine rarely cured but children swore that it made them feel
better.

For young couples in the early years of the nineteenth century
there was realistically only one alternative to having a large
family - sexual abstinance. Local newspapers discreetly advertised "Golden Female Pills" as purported abortifacients but
these were as unreliable as were the homemade remedies for
douches and vaginal sponges. It was not until 1832 that Charles
Knowlton published *Fruits of Philosophy or The Private Companion of Young Married People*, the first popular birth control
manual, but even then inexpensive rubber condoms were still
several decades away.

The first Loomis child, Harriet, was born in 1815, the same
year that George learned of the death of his elder sister,
Charlotte, in Vermont. Another daughter, Calista, was born in
1817 but baby Harriet died shortly afterwards. Finally a male
heir, William, was born in 1819 and was followed by Cornelia in
1821, George Washington Loomis, Jr. (forever to be known as
Wash) in 1823, Grove in 1825, Lucia in 1828, Wheeler in 1831,
Charlotte in 1832, Amos Plumb in 1834, Hiram Denio in 1836,
and another Harriet in 1838. All lived except the second Harriet

who, like the first, died at two years of age.

Rhoda quickly demonstrated that George Loomis had been correct in assessing her strengths. She took over management of the farm, purchased more land in 1815, and by 1823 had tripled its size to 325 acres. She also took over management of the family and of George Loomis himself, although for many years he was not fully aware of this. The frontier family was theoretically a strict patriarchy with all household members expected to give unquestioned obedience to the male head. He was the conduit through which any member of the household attained legal standing or recognition in the community, even to the degree that prizes for needlework at the Oneida County agricultural fair were awarded to the male head of the household in which the work was done. Wives and children were a man's property and if they ran away the man said they had been "stolen" just as pigs or horses might be. As early as 1803 the local *Whitestown Gazette* carried notices such as: "Eloped from my bed and board my wife Peggy without any just reason. All persons are forbid [sic] harboring or trusting her on my account, on penalty of the law." On the other hand when the man wanted to terminate a marriage he simply announced in the newspaper that his wife "has conducted herself in an unbecoming manner which renders it unfit that I should live with her any more."

Despite these theoretical and legal constraints on the role of women, Rhoda Loomis and many others on the frontier learned how to bring about their desired ends. By wiles, charms, and subterfuge a man like George Loomis could be controlled. An 1823 pamphlet of a Presbyterian society in Utica entitled "Female Influence" circulated widely through the region giving instructions to women like Rhoda:

> "And who can so successfully wield the instrument of influence than women. By force of persuasion, how often has woman prevailed, especially when accompanied by submission and entreaty, where strength and courage and boldness would have accomplished nothing . . . A sensible woman who keeps her proper place, and knows how to avail herself of her own powers, may exert, in her own sphere, almost any degree of influence that she pleases."

Rhoda probably did not need such advice, for evidence suggests she opted for "strength and courage and boldness" more frequently then most. When George came home intoxicated one night, as was the local custom, she filled his bed-warming pan (which usually contained live coals) with snow. As she hit him repeatedly with it he cried out "you're burning me, you're burning me." Wash Loomis later told a friend that his father had been dominated by his mother: "We soon learned obedience to him was a matter of choice. If he wanted us to work on the farm, but we wanted to go fishing instead, we went to Mother. She made him let us have our way."

From the beginning Rhoda Loomis taught her children that they were special. According to one account Rhoda "did not want them to associate with other children in the neighborhood. She dressed them well, and this to some extent incurred the jealousy of their playmates." They all attended the local school at Tinker Hollow but Rhoda supplemented their learning, reading them exciting stories like *The Spy* (1821), *The Pioneers* (1823), and *The Last of the Mohicans* (1826) written by James Fenimore Cooper over the hills in Cooperstown. George Loomis was less enthusiastic about Cooper, characterizing him as an arrogant aristocrat living off land which his father had stolen from the Indians. Cooper's view of anyone striving after wealth did not endear him to his Central New York neighbors: "Of all the sources of human pride," he wrote, "mere wealth is the basest and most vulgar minded. Real gentlemen are almost invariably above this low feeling."

Following primary education Rhoda Loomis insisted that their daughters, as well as their sons, be given educational opportunities to fit their abilities. At the time, such education was restricted to families with money and provided by boarding schools, seminaries, and academies under private auspices. The nearby villages of Whitestown and Clinton offered several such schools, and all four Loomis girls were sent to them. The brochure advertising the Whitestown Seminary, which at least two of the girls attended, encouraged parents to "state very frankly and fully your wishes in reference to the studies, the intellectual and moral training of children, so that teachers may feel at liberty to give you all that information which an intelligent and considerate parent desires when entrusting a son or daughter to the authority of strangers." Calista, Charlotte and Lucia all displayed considerable musical talent, the latter two becoming accomplished pianists. Cornelia, the brightest of the girls, even taught school in Utica briefly following the completion of her education.

The expanding Loomis family rapidly outgrew the house on

the hill. The various activities of the Loomises were making them wealthy by community standards and Rhoda decided that it was time to build a house to reflect their standing. Accordingly in 1825 they constructed a large, three-story house, forty by fifty feet, with a hallway running the length of the house, two stairways going to the second floor, two parlors, two kitchens, and seven bedrooms. A front door faced the roadway to the east, a side door exited from a kitchen, while the back door led out through the woodshed. Most noteworthy were the variety of unusual architectural features including double-panelled walls, false floors, and concealed spaces beneath the stairs.

Whereas the original home had been built high on the hill near the pinnacle, the new house stood on a knoll near the edge of Nine Mile Swamp. The Oxford Turnpike had been relocated to the lower elevation and the Loomis home went with it. The large white Loomis house was set off by well-tended flower gardens and shaded by maple trees. Across the turnpike from the house the Loomises built two large barns for cattle and horses, a hophouse, and several sheds. The distance from the Loomis front door to the edge of the swamp was approximately two hundred yards. Behind the house a path ran uphill through the maple and butternut trees to large meadows, additional barns, and cabins for the Loomis servants and hired farmhands. Beyond the cabins lay the original homestead and the pinnacle.

Rhoda Loomis was a woman who both enjoyed her wealth and wished others to know that she had it. According to those who visited the Loomises, "the family lived in fine style. The table was covered with silver and while all were industrious there was no lack of servants. The girls dressed fashionably and the service of dressmakers was frequently required. The table was well supplied with meat, fowls and vegetables." One visitor, a young friend of Wash Loomis, recalled that the "homestead literally overflowed with guests. It was not unusual for twelve or more young people to arrive early and stay for both dinner and supper. Rhoda served good, hearty meals. Noonday dinner usually consisted of a plentiful variety. There were potatoes, turnips, baked squash, corned beef, boiled ham, sweet apples, white pot (custard), black applesauce, maple sugar for sweetin', a porringer of maple syrup, eight or nine mince pies piled on top the other, hasty pudding, nutcakes, and cheese - all washed down with steaming cups of tea, barley coffee, or milk." Books were valued and abundant in the house, and local newspapers as well as those from Albany and New York bespoke the educational achievements of the family.

When the Loomis children were young, with servants and farmhands few, they all helped with daily chores. Rhoda and the girls fed the chickens while the boys led the cows to pasture in the morning and returned them to the barn for milking and feeding in the evening. Water had to be carried to the house, and wood split and stacked for the winter. Women did the cooking, including baking in the tempermental Dutch oven that was buried in the burning coals in the fireplace, and in bad weather Rhoda taught the girls to spin, weave, and knit. The boys learned from their father how to plant corn, pumpkins, potatoes, beans, cabbages and turnips, and in the fall how to store the beans in the attic and the potatoes, cabbages and turnips in a hole in the ground protected from freezing by leaves and earth. Wild berries were collected, and occasionally squirrel, rabbits, partridge or pheasants were caught as a special treat.

The changes of seasons were marked by family activities that required participation of all members, but always managing and directing the activities was Rhoda. In spring the maple trees were tapped, in early years using alder stalks and birch bark containers and later with commercially made spouts and buckets. Even the young Loomis children helped collect the dripping sap and carry it to the huge kettles in which it was boiled down. The maple syrup was used as the main sweetner for cakes and pies, and dark maple sugar kept as candy for special occasions. Each fall found the family harvesting the hops and stacking them in the hop-house until they could be transported to Utica for sale, although as the children grew older the Loomises increasingly hired others to do such harvesting for them.

By the standards of other families in the area Rhoda Loomis spoiled her children. By her own standards, however, she was merely training them for the privileged positions which she believed they deserved. She availed herself of every opportunity to enrich their education and broaden their horizon. When they were young she took them to Utica, a half day's drive in the carriage, to see a circus advertising an equestrian rider who would perform "a number of new and surprising feats of agility on the horse . . . will toss the oranges and will ride with his toe in his mouth while the horse is in full speed." By the 1830s small circuses and traveling dramatic groups stopped regularly at villages such as Waterville and Sangerfield as well as in the larger towns.

Ambitious productions such as the "Grand Romantic Drama of
the Forty Thieves" and "The Grand Melo-Dramatic Equestrian
Spectacle of the Secret Mine" competed with itinerant theatrical
families who lived in their wagons and carried on top the scenery
for productions of "Macbeth" and "Love's Sacrifice." Among
other attractions were Siamese Twins, Tom Thumb, "giants,
magicians, ventriloquists, albinos, fire-eaters, jugglers, and once
a 'real mermaid.'"

In all educational undertakings Rhoda included her daughters
on terms of equality with her sons. When she undertook the
informal training of her sons in the art of stealing, therefore, her
daughters were enrolled in the same course. All four girls were
taught how to shop in stores in nearby villages, trying on clothes
to see what fit; invariably some of the clothes would be missing
when they left the store. Cornelia proved most adept at shoplifing
and became the subject of widespread gossip. According to a
local historian, on one occasion she "walked into a Waterville dry
goods emporium one afternoon and asked the clerk if she might
see his latest in muffs and fur scarves. Unaware of the identity of
his customer, the clerk displayed several fur pieces. 'They are the
latest we have,' he said. 'We got them from New York this week.'
'They are nice,' Cornelia admitted, 'but they are not exactly what
I have been looking for. I guess I will have to think it over.' Noticing some bolts of cloth on the shelves at the rear of the store she
said, 'My mother asked me to bring home some samples of gingham. Would you give me a few snatches of your latest?' While
the clerk obliged, Cornelia picked up the best-looking muff, bent
over, and pulled it up her leg. When the clerk returned she
smiled at him and said, 'I'm sorry I caused you so much trouble.'
After Cornelia departed with the samples of gingham, the clerk
discovered that a muff was missing, so he rushed to see Constable
Aurelius (Bill) Benedict. 'That was Cornelia Loomis up to her old
tricks,' the constable said with a laugh. 'If she hasn't left town,
I'll try to get your muff back.' Cornelia, indignant when Benedict
took her into custody, loudly protested her innocence. 'Where
are you taking me?' she asked. 'To the lock-up.' 'I won't go,'
'Yes, you will, even if I have to drag you.' 'My brothers will kill
you when they hear of this,' Cornelia cried. Ignoring the threats
the constable took her to the lock-up, where two women searched
her and found the muff. The clerk failed to press charges, so she
was released."

Cornelia and her sisters also learned that fur muffs, which

were quite expensive, could be stolen from places other than stores. One of their favorite ruses was to attend dances in surrounding towns; at the close of the dances several young women were usually unable to locate their muffs. After this pattern had been repeated at several dances, the mystery of the missing muffs was solved. As told by the son of a woman who attended the denouement:

"Before my mother was married she, with eighteen or twenty girls and as many fellows, were out to a country party one night. The lady of the house gave the girls a large bedroom upstairs in which to take off their things and pile them on the bed, dresser and chairs. In those days every girl or woman carried a muff. If you didn't have a muff you weren't in style. When the party broke up around two in the morning, a number of the girls couldn't find their muffs. They hunted high and low. Finally one girl, a little older and bolder than the rest, went around and pulled up the dress and petticoat of one of the Loomis girls and beheld that she had four or five muffs on each leg. She shoved her over backwards on the bed and called two girls to hold her hands and other girls held her feet so she couldn't kick. They disrobed her of the muffs and then led her to the door and shoved her out. That ended the Loomis girls going to any more parties."

Teaching her children to steal seemed perfectly natural to Rhoda Loomis. Everybody steals, she told her family, but only those who are stupid get caught. Stealing was a means not only for acquiring the fine things which she wished to have, but also for demonstrating the superiority of her family. It was, to the growing Loomis children, a survival skill which they were encouraged to master in order to be full participants in family activities. Rhoda emphasized this point by recounting her own participation in the "family businesses" over the years, detailing the profits which had been made and implying that the Loomis family future promised even greater glories.

When Rhoda and George had been married in 1814 George's illicit activities had been confined to horse thieving and occasional counterfeiting. Forms of currency other than whiskey or goods-in-kind were not well established on the frontier in the early years of the nineteenth century. There was no federal banking system, and bank charters were available from state legislatures to friends of those in power or under the table to the highest bidder. Ebenezer Purdy, a state senator, openly bribed fellow legislators to grant bank charters to corporations in which he was a stockholder. A public scandal erupted in 1805 when Purdy was knocked down in the senate chamber, the assailant being the president of a competing bank, and officials retrospectively agreed that there had been a "semblance of corrupt influence." Each bank was allowed to issue its own bank notes to be used as currency, and according to one historian, "never before or since in our history was counterfeiting easier."

In this atmostphere George Loomis and many others dealt in counterfeit currency. He and his brother, Willard, had a partnership with two friends. Business was apparently good until 1810 when George pushed his luck too far and attempted to pass a counterfeit hundred dollar bill onto Samuel Leonard, an officer of the law in Sangerfield. All four men were initially charged, but only two were indicted, convicted, and sent to prison. The Loomis brothers were not indicted because, according to later newspaper accounts, "a grand juryman was bribed by the worthy couple to use his influence and vote for them in the jury room, which arrangement was duly and successfully carried out." George Loomis had learned that the stern eye of the law metes out justice impartially except to those who have the financial resources to divert its attention; it was a lesson he was to impress upon his family.

Following their marriage Rhoda Loomis assumed control of counterfeiting operations and expanded them considerably. One new Loomis business became the lending of money, often counterfeit, and then foreclosure on collateral if the lender could not repay the loan. The Loomises were helped considerably in these efforts by having a respected and skilled lawyer, Othniel S. Williams, who settled in Waterville in 1814. Williams continued to give the Loomises legal advice even after he moved to Clinton in 1820, and taught them the importance of having the best counsel that money could buy.

Throughout the 1820s and 1830s George and Rhoda Loomis continued to buy and sell counterfeit notes, stopping only when centralized banking procedures were introduced with a standardization of the currency. The Loomises, in partnership with Willard, were also involved in selling liquor without a license and Willard was indicted for this in 1838. As the Loomis children were growing up their home increasingly became known as a place in which all manner of stolen goods could be found, including merchandise, sheep, chickens, hogs, cattle, or horses. As early as 1829 the Oneida County sheriff identified the Loomises as being behind much of the larceny in surrounding towns, and in 1836 a constable obtained a search warrant and visited the Loomises. He was courteously received by Rhoda, allowed to search the premises, but found nothing.

In June, 1837, the barn of Stephen Leonard of Sangerfield burned to the ground. It was Leonard who had brought counterfeiting charges against George and Willard Loomis twenty-seven years earlier. George Loomis was indicted for arson, arrested, and released on one thousand dollars bail. He obtained several delays in the trial, then failed to appear. He forfeited the bail but the charges against him were eventually dropped. The sheriff of Oneida County at the time was Erastus Willard who had appointed his son as under-sheriff; according to one historian "the old members of the bar say they both made themselves comfortably rich" while in office. David Moulton followed Willard; elected in 1840, he was removed by the Governor two years later "for want of moral honesty." Moulton was accused of various indiscretions including revealing the outcome of secret grand jury proceedings, taking bribes, and allowing prisoners to escape. Moulton was followed by Palmer V. Kellogg in 1844, a businessman known for "his shrewd and ingenious scheming to foil and outwit a competitor . . . His ambition was to succeed in life and make money and he succeeded. He entered the political arena with the same motto and the same methods." With such men as the guardians of public safety George Loomis learned that for the right price virtually any indictment could be dropped. Justice is an imperfect lady, he told his family, and like any lady, she can be compromised by patience and influenced by gifts.

About this time another story with a more ominous tone circulated in the area. A tin peddler, his wagon full of shiny pots, pans and various tools, set out from Hubbardsville for Sangerfield along the road passing directly in front of the Loomises. Somewhere along the road he and his wagon disappeared, never arriving in Sangerfield. According to an 1879 account in the *New York Sun*: "It was known that he had stopped at the Loomis mansion. It is said that an unauthorized posse searched the place for his body. They found a well on the farm filled with stones, and began to clean it out. Half way down they came to an immense boulder, which had evidently been drawn to the well by a yoke of oxen and rolled in. It choked off all further search, and the peddler was never found."

That Rhoda Loomis liked fine things was well known in the villages around Nine Mile Swamp. What was not as well known was the fact that Rhoda was prepared to do whatever was necessary to acquire these things. Controlling the men around her had always been her main means of acquisition. Therefore, when she saw control of her family and the gang slipping away from her following George's death in 1851, Rhoda reacted with the same fury as when she had attacked Sheriff Kip with a shovel many years earlier. The uxorial and matronly facade was set aside as Rhoda Loomis prepared to do battle. It made little difference that the enemies this time were her own sons.

Wash and Grove Loomis were supported by Bill, and often by Wheeler, in their increasingly frequent disputes with their mother in the 1850s. Bill remained at Higginsville most of the time, however, for Rhoda continued to berate him for marrying and she treated Martha Ann as a servant on the rare occasions when he brought her home. Wheeler, just twenty at the time of his father's death, shifted sides periodically with the fortunes of war, the consummate opportunist who is used by all but counted on by none.

Siding with Rhoda were the youngest sons, Plumb and Denio and the four girls. Plumb was described by outsiders as an unpleasant young man—"the worst of the lot" according to some observers. He was only eighteen years old but had "a cold, steely and expressionless eye and a poker face." He looked up to Grove, envious of his horsemanship and audacity, yet took orders unquestioningly from his mother. Audacity without character is merely indiscretion, and it was to be another fourteen years before Plumb would finally mature—with a noose encircling his neck.

Denio, the youngest and smallest Loomis, was thought to be "not quite right." He had been named after Hiram Denio, a well known judge in Utica who at the time of Denio's birth had been waging a fight for improved public education. Rhoda Loomis had honored the judge's commitment to education it was said, but not to justice. Because of his namesake and his owlish looks Denio was often referred to as "the judge." Aged sixteen at the time of the Loomis meeting in 1852, he was completely under the influence of his mother and remained so his entire life.

The support of Rhoda by her daughters became less important with each passing year. Calista, married to a lawyer in Whitesboro, died in 1854 giving birth to a son. Lucia married a farmer in Waterville and continued to actively participate in family activities until she died in 1858 from an epidemic fever passing through the village. Young Charlotte married a businessman shortly after her father's death and moved to New York City.

That left only Cornelia at home, and she sided strongly with her mother. The most intelligent and aggressive of the Loomis girls, Cornelia rode horses astride and emulated her brothers' criminal activities. She also, it was rumored, had shocked her family by openly propositioning Big Bill Rockwell. On one occasion Cornelia and Charlotte approached a farmer in Brookfield about two fine oxen he was offering for sale. The asking price was high—three hundred and sixty dollars—but Cornelia finally agreed. When they asked for a yoke to drive the oxen home, however, the farmer insisted on another two dollars to cover the cost of the yoke. Cornelia paid it all, but when the farmer deposited the money at the bank the following day he was told that it was counterfeit except the final two dollars. Enraged, he swore out a warrant against the Loomis girls and succeeded in getting the oxen returned. There are other accounts of Cornelia traveling the countryside passing counterfeit bills, sometimes dressed in male attire, and she became widely referred to in neighboring towns as "the outlaw queen."

The issues dividing the Loomises were many. The one most openly discussed involved the organization and activities of the gang. Rhoda wanted things to remain as they had been when George was alive—as a family unit involving a few friends. It was safer, she agreed, and meant dividing the fruits of their labors the least number of ways. Wash and Grove, on the other hand, envisioned a gang which would control criminal activities throughout New York State and across its borders. No scheme was too dangerous, no activity too brazen to command their attention. They had been raised to believe that everything was potential plunder and everyone an incipient felon; the only difference between aristocrats and outlaws, they argued, was that the latter got caught.

Although the size and activities of the Loomis gang were the issues which got argued far into the night in the Loomis home, they were in fact not the most important causes of the increasing family discord. As the gang enlarged it included more and more individuals who were merely illiterate thugs, the social and genetic jetsam who comprise the criminal classes in all societies. These were men Rhoda Loomis had always disdained, and as long as George had been alive they had never eaten at the Loomis dinner table. If it had been necessary to employ them, as it sometimes was, they had been relegated to the shacks on the hill and always kept in their place as Loomis laborers. With the growth of the gang, however, the social barriers broke down and the Bill Alvords of the world increasingly shared the same dinner as Rhoda, Wash, Grove, Cornelia, and the other Loomis family members.

Much more threatening, from Rhoda's point of view, were the women who frequently accompanied these gang members. Mistresses, wives, and sisters turned up increasingly often, initially to just stay overnight while stolen horses were being delivered but later to stay for increasingly longer periods. The fact that the Loomises possessed five unmarried males who had, it was rumored, more then their share of the world's gold encouraged women associated with the gang members to come and see for themselves.

The outcome was inevitable. Not only did these women, most of whom could neither read nor write, fail to accord Rhoda Loomis the respect she believed was her due, but some of the women became romantically and sexually involved with her sons. Rhoda had bitterly opposed Bill Loomis' marriage to Martha Ann Burdick and she was determined to insure that there would be no more such mistakes.

In September, 1854, the conflict at the Loomises became public knowledge when a young woman, holding an infant son and pleading for help, stumbled into a home in the village of North Brookfield. She was Jane Alvord, the sister of Bill Alvord, and had been living with the Loomises for several months. Early in 1854 she had given birth to the child whose paternity was said to be one of the Loomis sons. Precisely which Loomis was the father was uncertain for it was rumored that more than one claimed eligibility.

From the time the child was born, Jane said, Rhoda Loomis had harassed her and tried to drive her away. In recent weeks Rhoda had threatened to kill her and Jane had been warned by one of the sons that his mother was serious. Jane had taken her child ostensibly to go berry picking down by the swamp, but instead had fled by a path through the swamp to North Brookfield, She was given shelter and never again returned to the Loomises. Many village residents discounted the alleged threat on her life by Rhoda Loomis. Others, who had known Rhoda over the years, disagreed and reminded listeners of the disappearance of the old tin peddler. Rhoda Loomis, they said, was a woman quite capable of murder. Eventually they would be proven correct.

# CHAPTER IV

# Opposition

As the Loomis gang dramatically increased its activities in the 1850s the surrounding villages stirred uneasily but impotently. The gang was becoming so large and powerful that most folks simply glanced off distractedly when the subject of their misdeeds came up. In North Brookfield, a hamlet of less than two hundred people three miles across the swamp from the Loomis farm, a substantial number of men were said to be on the gang's payroll. Sangerfield, four miles northeast, remained a village of two hundred inhabitants virtually unchanged from the day George Loomis had arrived in 1802; Loomis cousins, gang members, and sympathizers were abundant.

Courage for most persons requires company and it was only in Waterville, one mile north of Sangerfield, that opposition to the Loomises was developing. The town had grown to over one thousand residents and was the commercial center for the area. By the early 1850s it boasted six stores, two taverns and hotels, two grist mills, two machine shops, a tannery, woolen factory, and a bank. Its dirt streets were set off by raised wooden sidewalks and punctuated by hitching posts, and in the summer the circus came and the Waterville Brass Band gave concerts on the village green.

The most important store in town was that opened in 1852 by W.J. Bissell. A slight, plain-talking man who seemed unable to grasp the niceties of subtle discourse, Bissell stood behind the counter and told anyone who would listen exactly what he thought. He sold seeds, tools, food, patent medicines, cigars, and candy - everything a family might need except clothes. The store "was a natural gathering place in all seasons: no farmer . . . could stay away from Bissell's for long and many, no doubt, visited as much as to talk as to trade."

Bissell's antipathy to the Loomises was not grounded in personal animosity, but rather arose from a naive worldview of right and wrong. While other townspeople discussed the Loomises quietly in the privacy of their homes, aware that many were on their payroll and repeating conversations to them, Bissell would publicly catalogue their crimes and offer blunt assessments regarding their moral character. The leading citizens of Waterville gathered daily to hear Bissell hold forth—the Palmers, Eastmans, Clevelands, Towers, Montgomerys, Greens, Terrys and Goodwins—nodding quietly and shifting uneasily on their feet. They agreed privately, but when Bissell's attention shifted elsewhere the conversation turned to safer subjects such as the Eastman's new baby, George, who was born in 1854 (and destined to patent the Kodak camera and roll film), or the visit of Dan Rice's circus, featuring an elephant that could walk a tightrope. Or the public lecture in January, 1855, by P.T.Barnum, a Connecticut state legislator and exhibitor of midgets and Siamese twins. Barnum gave a talk entitled "The Philosophy of Humbug" which was widely discussed and reprinted in the town's new weekly newspaper, the *Waterville Times*:

> "Faith now rules the hearts of men. Of this faith is born the giant of America, the most Noble Don Humbug. Many imagine this to be a mysterious word, but it is merely the conventional name of the philosophy of the last century . . . Our Declaration of Independence is sheer humbug, declaring all men to be created equal and meaning to except all but white men."

Nobody could remember who had first proposed "the California solution" for the Loomis problem. Many thought it must have been Bissell for he was the one who kept raising it. By the mid-1850s "the California solution" was being widely discussed throughout the United States, a euphemism for the activities of the San Francisco Vigilance Committee which had been formed in 1851. Corruption and lawlessness had reached such proportions in that city that when a newspaper editor crusading against corruption was murdered, "within a matter of days the vigilantes tried and hanged [the two murderers] . . . Two months later they hanged two more men and altogether they expelled [from the city] twenty-eight men" believed to be involved in the corruption. Six thousand of San Francisco's leading citizens signed statements of support for the vigilance committee.

Support of the vigilante action was widespread; the *Boston Journal* noted that "in California . . . the officials, and particularly the juries, are corrupt and venal, and it is the consequent uncertainty of the administration of justice which had impelled the people to take the matter out of the hands of the courts, and in their sovereign capacity to mete out justice to notorious offenders." The *New York Times* asked: "What can a community do but fall back on its natural rights, and personally maintain that standard of peremptory justice which the exigency demands and the authorities are too corrupt to enforce?" And the *New York Tribune* editorialized that the Vigilance Committee had earned "a certain meed of respect . . . As necessity knows no law, we do not propose to prescribe laws for necessity." As Bissell liked to remind the listeners in his store, even President Andrew Jackson had once advised farmers in Iowa to take justice into their own hands and lynch a murderer.

Bissell himself claimed that the proposal to use "the California solution" for the Loomis problem had originally been made by Roscoe Conkling. An outspoken and implacable opponent of the Loomises, young Conkling had been the only elected official to campaign against them. As District Attorney in 1850 Conkling had even put one of the Loomises in jail, an unprecedented event. Bissell strongly admired Conkling and held him up as an example for his listeners of responsible civic behavior.

The Loomises, by contrast, loathed Conkling. Their problems with him had begun in 1848 when Bill and Wash had been indicted for grand larceny following "the big search." Wash's departure for California resulted in the dropping of charges against him but those against Bill in Oneida County continued to stand. Employing a variety or legal tactics the Loomises managed to delay Bill's trial for over a year. There seemed reason to believe that, as public interest waned and cash gifts found their way to the proper pockets, the remaining charges against him would be quietly dropped as had happened so often in the past to Loomis family members. That had been the way it had always been; never once in his more than fifty years of criminal activities had George Loomis been convicted of a crime or gone to jail. The Loomises assumed that judicial immunity was part of their family heritage, and incarceration created for persons other than themselves.

The Loomis' plans for getting Bill's charges dropped were abruptly interrupted in April, 1850, when the District Attorney of Oneida County, Calvert Comstock, unexpectedly resigned. To the astonishment of everyone Governor Hamilton Fish appointed Roscoe Conkling to fill the remaining term. Conkling, only twenty years old, had just completed studying for his profession with Utica lawyer Francis Kernan and had passed the New York State bar only two months previously; he was not even old enough to vote. However his father, a former congressman and federal judge, was good friends with Governor Fish. The Loomises, along with most people in central New York, marveled at such brazen patronage and ridiculed the appointment of young Conkling.

Roscoe Conkling, however, was no ordinary young lawyer. He had a six generation American pedigree that exceeded even that of the Loomis family, and a belief in his own abilities that blended into arrogance. Nor was he easily overlooked. A broad-shouldered six feet three inches, he had a full, "exquisitely-curled" beard and reddish-blond curly hair. "In the center of his broad forehead hung a Hyperion curl" which was to become his trademark for political cartoonists in later years. When Conkling arrived at the Rome courthouse to begin his duties as District Attorney he was remembered by one observer as looking "like a tall blonde young lady [with] a tall silk hat, a frock coat with a velvet collar; his cheek was as fresh as a rose and he had long red ringlets clustered about his neck."

A young lady Conkling was not, although he was notably fond of them. In addition to a daughter by marriage, Conkling was later rumored to have fathered by other women a man "whom old-timers point out . . . bears a striking resemblance" to him and "a lady, a school teacher . . . who sometimes is designated as the product of another Conkling liason." "And his reputation as a rake, albeit a highly circumspect rake, harmonized with his appearance as a beau, his always immaculate turnout, his dazzling personal beauty."

Conkling combined physical presence with a rare blend of self-righteousness and invective to become a formidable opponent in a courtroom. He drank little and despised tobacco, and if he entered a room where someone was smoking he "would throw open the nearest window to allow the noxious fumes to escape." According to a colleague, "method, order, arrangement were his triune synonyms, and these qualities governed his mental nature as well as the use of the materials with which he worked. He would not read the newspaper till he had smoothly folded it the size of an even quarto or octavo; nor would he put a bank-bill into his wallet until it was folded midway the length, and then exactly over the middle width."

It was eloquence, however, for which Conkling was best known. Widely read, he could invoke Pitt or Burke as fluently as Shakespeare or Milton; a biographer noted that "he could quote whole pages of the Bible and was very fond of doing so." In the courtroom he stood erect with his head back, "the left thumb hooked into the side trousers pocket, the right foot slightly advanced" and never shouted. He prepared his courtroom speeches and summations meticulously, rehearsed them in the privacy of his room, then delivered them with precision, "very slowly always, his anger cold, rich, musical, his invective a trifle elephantine but crushing . . . During his set speeches, his greatest, he would refer occasionally to notes on the backs of envelopes, reminder notes resembling newspaper headlines; but usually this was no more than a trick to give the impression of extemporaneous speaking when in fact the speech had been perfectly memorized."

The Loomises attempted to influence the newly appointed District Attorney but to no avail. Conkling had an aversion to corruption among public officials which was extraordinary for his day. The only effect of the attempted bribe, in fact, was to bring the Loomis case to his attention. Although it had been languishing for over a year, Conkling ordered two potential witnesses against Bill Loomis to court on May 9 and 11, and when they failed to appear he ordered their arrest. Within three days the Loomis trial took place, and Conkling obtained a quick conviction. Bill Loomis was sentenced "to be confined in the county jail two months and to pay a fine of seventy-five dollars and to stand committed to the county jail until paid not exceeding six months after the expiration of the first two months." A member of the Loomis family had actually been convicted and gone to jail. Of the first fourteen indictments brought by Roscoe Conkling to jury trial, convictions were obtained on Bill Loomis and eleven others.

The populace of North Brookfield, Sangerfield and Waterville were as incredulous as were the Loomises at the outcome of the trial. It was widely assumed that the Loomises could buy their way out of any legal difficulty, for that was the way it had always been. Local observers speculated that if George Loomis had not grown old and forgetful it would never have happened. The fact that Wash, with his legal acumen, had gone to California, had also weakened the family's ability to meet such challenges.

From the Loomises point of view Roscoe Conkling represented a serious threat to their way of life and they vowed to get him out of office. As a political appointee Conkling was merely filling a term of office due to expire in eight months in November, 1850. Conkling saw the position as an initial step in an illustrious public career and, as expected, declared his intent to run for re-election. The Loomises, through bribery, threats, and their criminal network, were said to control at least five hundred votes in Oneida County and they went to work to insure that every one of these voted against Roscoe Conkling.

When the votes were counted in November, Conkling, running on the Whig ticket, had lost the election to the Democratic candidate by 8,070 to 7,454. The Loomises took full credit for the margin of defeat and widely boasted of having forced Conkling out of office. Conkling, returning to the private practice of law at age twenty-one, heard the boasts. He was a man who neither forgot nor forgave.

Despite his election defeat in 1850 Conkling continued rising in Whig and then Republican circles, speaking frequently in Sangerfield, Waterville, and other villages in Oneida County. In 1852 he campaigned for Whig Presidential nominee General Winfield Scott, and in 1856 stumped the villages on behalf of Republican nominee John C. Fremont. At every opportunity Conkling decried public corruption and crime, often singling out the Loomises as examples of unprosecuted crime and reminding his listeners that he had put one of them in jail.

Conkling's influence increased with each passing year. In 1853 he narrowly missed being nominated as New York State Attorney General, a possibility which caused much concern to the Loomises. Two years later Conkling broadened his power by marrying Julia Seymour, younger sister of New York's Democratic Governor Horatio Seymour. Meanwhile he continued practicing law, becoming widely known for his ability to win cases thought to be hopeless and for his oratorical skills. In a closing summation in the case of a man accused of murder, for example, Conkling urged the jury to find him not guilt with the following plea:

"The day is too bright and too beautiful for such a deed. Nature and man should shudder! Heaven and earth should give note of horror; the skies should be weeping; the winds should be sighing; the bells should be tolling; the court-house should be hung in mourning; the jury-box should be covered with crepe - the day when a father, a husband and a citizen is sent to a prison or a gallows upon such testimony as this."

One of Roscoe Conkling's listeners and admirers in the 1850s was a blacksmith in North Brookfield who shared Conkling's dislike of the Loomises. Jim Filkins was a short but heavy-set man with sandy hair and a goatee framing a badly pockmarked face. He had been born in Richfield Springs and moved with his father, a blacksmith, to a succession of villages in the area. He learned his father's trade and moved to North Brookfiled at age twenty-two to work in his uncle Isaac's store. Shortly thereafter he went to work for Joe Avery who ran the local blacksmith shop, married a local girl, and settled down to a blacksmith's life of anonymous respectability.

That Jim Filkins disliked the Loomises was known to local people though the source of his antipathy was obscure. The Loomises used Avery's blacksmith shop so Filkins surely knew them well. He was a year younger than Wash and year older than Grove. In later years rumors circulated that Filkins had been involved with the Loomis gang and even "served a year or two in Albany prison" for stealing money before having a falling out with them. Other rumors involved a young woman who was said to have rejected Filkins in favor of Wash. What is certain is that Filkins himself was not well liked in the community; local residents interviewed after he had become well known characterized him as an unpleasant man with a quick temper.

Public criticism by W.J. Bissell and Roscoe Conkling and personal dislike by Jim Filkins were certainly known by the Loomises in the mid-1850s. Such opposition must have seemed like minor irritations, however—gnats flying around a creature growing larger and more powerful with each passing day. Business for the Loomis gang had never been better.

Under Wash's direction larceny in central New York had become endemic. Nothing was too large nor too small to be stolen, and the Loomis farm swallowed the contraband which flowed into it from all directions. According to one newspaper account detailing recent thefts in the village of Madison:

"Horses, harnesses, leather boots, shoes, buffalo and wolf
robes, cloth, clothing, etc. were taken. Not long ago ladies'
underclothes were taken from the yard of Allen Curtis, the
same night a small quantity was missed from the yard of
John Dye. The next night an attempt was made to enter Mr.
Dye's home. A few nights later an attempt was made to pick
the lock of Curtis and Dye's carriage house. It failed. On
Tuesday night of the fifth, two valuable robes and thirty
chickens were taken from Henry Taylor and a piece of cot-
ton cloth from D.Z. Brockett. On Sunday evening of the
tenth, a robe was stolen from Rev. C. Swift's carriage while
he conducted religious services at the Durfee School
House."

Serious thefts, once unusual, became commonplace. Stagecoaches were periodically stopped and robbed by masked men
who were widely presumed to be Loomis gang members. On one
occasion a stagecoach on the Peterboro road was stopped but,
unknown to the thieves, one of the horses pulling it was known as
a "kicker." As the leader of the masked men passed the horse it
"lashed out in true fashion and knocked the would-be holdup
man into a ditch, whereupon [the driver] whipped the horses up
and ran all the way into Peterboro thus saving the day."

To those who had watched the Loomises over the years it was
clear that the gang was becoming increasingly ambitious in their
burglarious goals and sophisticated in their techniques. In
Deansboro, for example, they broke into a store, "knocked off
the knob on the safe with a sledge hammer, drilled through the
outer wall of the safe door and then blew it open with a charge of
gunpowder." On the road between Waterville and Utica a factory manufacturing pistols was entered by forcing a window with
a crowbar and axe; fifty-two pistols were taken, many of which
were later found hidden in the Loomis home. Samuel Colt had
patented his revolver (six chambers revolving around a single
barrel) in 1836 but it was not until the 1850s when bullets replaced the ball and powder that pistols became popular for use by
criminals.

That the theft of the pistols was an ominous occurrence
became apparent a few weeks later when a farmer near Waterville, trying to stop the burglary of his barn, was shot and seriously wounded with a pistol. Pistols could be used on either side,
however, and when a thief broke into a store in Oriskany Falls on
February 23, 1855, the store owner, who had been sleeping
upstairs, shot and wounded the intruder exiting a window; the

*Waterville Times* speculated that the wounded man had been a Loomis. As the 1850s progressed, violence became an increasingly frequent companion of local crime. On March 14, 1856, a sixty-year-old farmer living west of Morrisville was found axed to death, apparently for resisting a burglary. A neighbor was charged with the murder, brought to trial and acquitted. Many claimed the crime was the work of the Loomis gang.

It was a time of general prosperity in central New York and the Loomises were determined to take their share. The rich soil yielded more corn, wheat and oats each year as farming methods improved. The price of hops continued to rise and in the autumn, following the harvest, farmers' mattresses were stuffed with cash and gold. Each year the stores in North Brookfield, Sangerfield, and Waterville displayed more goods for sale—or for theft.

Prosperity also meant better horses in the pastures to be stolen. Grove's task was to decide how much each was worth, which ones needed their markings changed and where to send them for sale. When a particularly fine specimen arrived Grove would occasionally keep it for breeding and reward the finder with extra money. Late at night Grove and his visitors often could be seen sitting around the lantern, sipping rum and discussing equine attributes.

Disposing of so many stolen horses presented logistical challenges for the Loomises. The well-worn routes down the Oxford Turnpike to northeastern Pennsylvania, and north through Hastings Center to Ontario continued to be used but these could only absorb so many horses for marketing. It was during these years, therefore, that the Loomises began using the canal system of New York State to dispose of horses and other stolen goods. Small barges were purchased and kept at Bill Loomis' farm on the Sidecut Canal at Higginsville. Horses were driven from Sangerfield to Higginsville, loaded aboard, and taken down the Erie Canal to Albany where buyers were always available, no questions asked. At Albany the horses could be put on large boats and sent to New York City or farther south for resale. Bill Alvord was given the responsibility of operating the barges when he was not in prison, and wherever Alvord's barges stopped more horses and other goods were noted to disappear. His boats became known as "thief boats" and their appearance evoked fear in villages along the canal.

At the same time as most inhabitants of central New York were increasingly fearful of a visit from the expanding Loomises, those who lived immediately around the farm were noting a curious friendliness from them. This was all the more noteworthy because George Loomis had never gotten along well with his neighbors, treating them with contempt and implying that they were beneath his social station. On one occasion, for example, when the Loomis' dogs had attacked the son of neighbor Horace Terry, Terry came to the Loomises and suggested that they get rid of the offending dogs. George Loomis confronted Terry in the yard and shouted at him: "I wish my dogs had eaten him up!" Terry then sued the Loomises and obtained a judgment of fifteen dollars.

Following the 1852 Loomis meeting this all changed abruptly. Wash Loomis realized that neighbors could provide a buffer against those who would interfere with their operations, and he instructed gang members accordingly. The Loomises had been especially damaged by the 1848 "big search" in which several sleighloads of law officers had appeared at their door without warning. Wash conceived the idea of a perimeter of friendly neighbors surrounding their farm and he set out to make this a reality.

The sudden benevolence of the Loomises toward their neighbors became widely discussed on the farms around Nine Mile Swamp. It was seen in small acts, such as when Plumb Loomis gave a neighbor turkey eggs without charging. As the neighbor recalled, Plumb said: "'You'll need about eleven if you're going to set a hen on them'; so he went out and found me five more. I tried to pay him for them, but he wouldn't take the money. My wife and I figured maybe there was something tricky about the eggs since he gave them away so freely; but do you know ten of them hatched out just fine! Funny how we never trust a man with a reputation like theirs, isn't it?"

The Loomises help for their neighbors also was seen in larger acts, such as when Ed Abbey's wife became insane; he tried to get her admitted to the New York State Lunatic Asylum in Utica but they refused to take her because all the beds were full. Mr. Abbey "told Grove about it, so Grove went to the hospital and fixed things up, and took Ed and his wife down. This time Ed got his wife in without any trouble."

On several occasions the Loomises intervened on behalf of neighbors who were being taken advantage of, such as the farm hand "who was employed by all the different farmers in that area whenever they needed a little extra work done" and who had also been employed on the Loomis farm. The man had worked several days for one farmer for the price of a cow, and when he had completed his requisite service the farm hand took the cow home as agreed. The cow began yielding great quantities of milk under its new owner, and when the farmer learned this he decided to claim the cow back, which he did. Hearing this, the Loomises told the farm hand "not to be surprised to see a cow tied to his fence one morning, which is exactly what happened, only it was a different colored cow. However, it gave the same amount of milk and appeared to be the same as the other cow except in color. The former owner came over, saying that he had lost his cow but that she was of a different color than the one in the farm hand's barn." Such incidents gave the Loomises a Robin Hood reputation among some of their neighbors.

Given the magnitude of the Loomis' operations it was inevitable that friends of the family would be victimized by mistake. On one such occasion a new horse and buggy were stolen in Waterville from a friend of Grove Loomis. Hearing of the theft Grove recovered the horse and buggy, tied them to a tree near town, then picked up his friend and drove around until the horse and buggy were "found." Another time "Perry Risley, who lived up the road from the Loomises, missed his yoke of oxen from his barn one morning. He went to the Loomis home. 'I think my oxen have strayed from my barn,' he said to Wash. 'If you should see them wandering around I wish you'd let me know.' 'I'll have my men see if they can find them,' Loomis said. The next morning the oxen were in Risley's yard." .

Neighbors rapidly learned that being on good terms with the Loomises was important, and that direct appeals to their friendship were often effective. Such was the case with Tim O'Connell who had two oxen which the Loomises wished to buy. "Realizing that they might be stolen if he refused, Tim agreed to sell. The Loomises paid him $100 and drove the oxen away. When the Irishman went to the bank to deposit the money he discovered that forty dollars was good money and the rest counterfeit. Tim went to the Loomises and handed Wash the counterfeit money. 'I ain't the complainin' kind,' remarked Tim, 'but by jashus I don't want this kind of paper.' Wash took the bills and grinned. 'I'm sorry, Tim,' he said. 'I didn't know my brothers gave you this.' He reached into his pocket and extracted a large roll of bills. He counted out sixty dollars and handed them to his neighbor. 'Here's your money,' he stated, 'and take my word, it is good.'"

There was, it was said, no limit to the effort the Loomises would go to to earn the friendship of neighbors. This was perhaps best illustrated by the experience of Robert Roberts, a farmer who had a fine team of horses stolen. Roberts knew the Loomises, and as he recounted to a friend:

"I promptly hitched up another horse and drove to the Loomises. Wash was at home and acted as if he had been expecting me. I knew he wondered why I had come alone instead of bringing a deputy sheriff. 'I've lost my team, Wash,' I said, 'Will you help me find them?' He seemed surprised at my request, for I neither demanded or threatened him as his other victims had done. 'Certainly I will, Mr. Roberts,' he replied, 'but you will have to accompany me.' I agreed and later that day we started out together in one of Wash's carriages. We journeyed southward for four days, far into Pennsylvania. Whenever we were hungry or needed a place to spend the night, Wash would stop at some farm or wayside tavern. There was always a table set for us or beds ready for us to sleep in. No one asked either of us any questions and we did not pay a cent out for the hospitality shown us. I sensed it was all a part of the vast Loomis organization. When we inquired about my horses we were always told that they were a short distance beyond. Eventually we located them and brought them back with us to my farm. I was grateful to Wash for aiding me in getting the team back. 'How much do I owe you, Wash?' I asked after our return. 'Why, Mr. Roberts,' Wash answered, 'I wouldn't think of charging a neighbor anything.'"

The assiduous cultivation of their neighbors' friendship paid regular dividends for the Loomises. When deputy sheriffs or other officers of the law headed toward the farm they usually found that their arrival had been expected. When evidence against the Loomises was sought, neighbors were remarkable in having heard or seen nothing which would implicate the Loomises in any wrongdoing. If the fidelity of a neighbor was in doubt tests were even devised by the Loomises to ascertain it, such as the incident recalled by a man who lived down the road from the Loomis farm:

"I always kept a great fierce shepherd dog when I lived there as a young man; this dog used to growl when a stranger was around - he barked right out for a friend. One night, he woke me with his growling at my elbow, and, in spite of my wife's protests, I went to the front door. There, standing at the foot of the steps, was a man with a gun in each hand. He said he was going over to shoot up the Loomis gang and wanted me to come along. He offered to pay me twenty-five dollars before we went and to give me one of the pistols. I said, no, they always treated me fine - why should I want to shoot them? Well, he said they had done so-and-so; I said I knew that, but they had never harmed me. He finally went away - I really think if it hadn't been for my wife who begged me not to go, I would have gone just to see what he'd do - and I found out later that he was one of the gang himself, sent to test me out."

As the Loomis gang expanded in the 1850s Wash and Grove became increasingly concerned about betrayal from within as well as from without. In earlier days, when operations had consisted of George Loomis, his brothers, and a few friends, there were few such worries. With over one hundred confederates involved, and more being added every year, one could no longer be certain of a gang member's fidelity and various stratagems were therefore devised to test and maintain it. On one occasion, for example, when a Loomis associate threatened to expose them and left for Utica to do so, he found himself arrested as soon as he arrived in the city. He was charged with stealing a watch which the Loomises had planted on him. On another occasion a disaffected gang member claimed he had been shortchanged sixty dollars by the Loomises and was going to Clinton on business. The Loomises encouraged him to borrow one of their better horses and, on his arrival in Clinton, had him arrested for stealing it. "At the trial he swore that the horse had been a loan but he couldn't prove it . . . Finally Plumb [Loomis] suggested to his hired man that if *he* would forget about the alleged debt of sixty dollars, *they* would drop the matter of the horse."

The ultimate method of keeping order in the Loomis gang was to kill those who threatened to break ranks. In the middle 1850s a Negro member of the gang who was living on the farm complained that he had been cheated out of his proper share of proceeds and he threatened to go to the sheriff. Wash assured the man that an equitable solution would be found, and assigned him to do farm chores with other gang members living there. The group was going to cut hay with hand scythes in the upper meadow; as they walked up the path behind the Loomis home toward the meadow a scythe suddenly flashed through the air and into the abdomen of the Negro who fell, partially disemboweled. Later that afternoon Perry Risley, who lived on the farm adjacent to the Loomises, was asked to come and see the man's body who, the Loomises said, had fallen on his scythe in a terrible accident. A coroner's inquest was held but all witnesses agreed that it had been an accident and no charges were ever brought. Twenty years later a newspaper reported the rumor that the man who had wielded the scythe had been "an Irishman employed by the Loomises."

In Bissell's general store in Waterville there was no doubt in anyone's mind about what had taken place at the Loomis farm. It had been murder, Bissell assured listeners. Talk drifted to rumors of other Loomis gang members who had disappeared, and to the old tin peddler who had vanished many years earlier. Bissell's listeners nodded vigorously when he said that something should be done; Bissell's proposal, as usual, was "the California solution." In North Brookfield Jim Filkins heard the stories and agreed - something should be done. And in Utica Roscoe Conkling heard the stories and also agreed - something should be done. The question was what, and by whom?

# CHAPTER V

# Milieu

The 1850s were extraordinary years in young America. The nation had broken free of Mother Britain yet had not matured enough to govern itself wisely. Like an adolescent caught between its past and future, the country was undergoing cataclysmic social upheavals. Corruption and crime were rife, and the rules of the new economic order—who could take what from whom— not yet established. Inequality of individuals was assumed; the Indians were being destroyed, but the status of Negroes and women was yet to be determined. Above all a question hung in the air above the New Jerusalem: could social justice be achieved without violence? By a curious coincidence the answer would be provided by events within a few miles of the Loomis farm, and the Loomises themselves swept along in the consequences.

Corruption and crime were commonly found at all levels of government. Among local officials it was not a question of *whether* a sheriff, judge or district attorney had his price but rather how high his price might be. When Wash and Grove Loomis offered bribes, the firm expectation was that the bribes would be accepted. A large number of officials in both Oneida and Madison counties accepted "gifts" from the Loomises over the years, and some of them were on their regular payroll. One example whose favors to the Loomis family recur repeatedly in the family annals was Charles Mason, a District Attorney for Madison County and later appointed as Judge. His friendship with the Loomises began one evening when his wife went to a wedding in the village of Hamilton during which her watch, a precious family heirloom, disappeared. "The next day word was carried to the Loomises that she was overcome with grief at the loss of her grandmother's keepsake, and in two day's time the watch appeared mysteriously in Mrs. Mason's home." Judge Mason availed himself of abundant opportunities to repay the Loomis favor by dismissing charges, reducing bail, delaying trials, and setting minimum fines.

The Loomises did more than simply corrupt the system of justice to insure their own immunity, however. Under Wash's tutelege they learned how to use the system to punish their enemies. An example of this came to public notice in 1866 when the New York State Legislature conducted an investigation of the Loomis gang. In Oswego County a husband and wife were found to have been held in jail because the Loomises wanted them there. The couple had been connected with the gang until their daughter ran away with one of the gang members, enraging the mother who publicly began discussing the gang's activities. According to the official report:

> "She was repeatedly warned to desist, and menaced with punishment if she continued to operate against them; but she paid no attention to their threats, and continued her hostile action. One evening, just at dusk, a Jew peddler came in with his pack and requested her to let him stay all night. She assented, proposing to him to leave his pack in the front room, while they went into a rear apartment to get supper. They sat in the room until bedtime, and the peddler, in his affidavit, distinctly declares that she was never once out of his sight. When he was ready to retire, she lighted a candle for him, but before going to bed, he went into the front room to look at his pack, when, to his consternation, he found that it was gone.
>
> The next morning he entered a complaint before a justice, who was himself generally believed to be connected with the gang, against the couple at whose house he had lodged; and, although the complainant swore that the woman was never out of his sight from the time he left the pack in the front room until he discovered that it was lost, and the husband proved, or offered to prove that he was at a Methodist meeting during the whole time that the peddler was in his house, yet the justice committed them for trial. A respectable farmer now came forward and offered to be their bail, and was accepted by the magistrate. He told the

woman, at the same time, that if she would say no more about the gang and their affairs, she would hear no more about the larceny charge. But she was smarting so severly about the loss of her daughter that she could not restrain her propensity to talk, and frequently gave information which was adverse to the interest of the parties who she believed were keeping her daughter in concealment. When the bondsman found that she would not keep quiet, he surrendered both her and her husband, and they were then committed to jail, where they had remained up to the time of our visit. Their cases had been put over from court to court on account, it was alleged, of the absence of material witnesses for the prosecution. It was generally believed in the neighborhood that they would be kept there, on one pretense or another, just as long as it suited the interests of their prosecutors."

At the time of the investigation the couple had been held in jail for eighteen months.

The Loomises influenced local officials by one of three mechanisms. The most common was outright bribery. Equally effective, however, was the influence on elected officials by controlling a deciding block of votes. The Loomises had learned the importance of this in 1850 when they helped bring about Roscoe Conkling's defeat for District Attorney of Oneida County. Throughout the 1850s they worked assiduously to broaden their influence, utilizing the extensive network of the gang and sometimes buying votes outright. During these years they could often determine the outcome of elections in Oneida and Madison counties by throwing their support behind one candidate or the other. Party affiliation was not allowed to interfere with expediency, and the Loomises were recorded as having supported candidates "sometimes in one party and sometimes in another." Politically ambitious officials, including district attorneys, sheriffs and judges, thought carefully before alienating the Loomises.

The third means of influencing local officials was by way of Albany. Many officials, including judges, were appointed from Albany as part of the political spoils system; well-placed friends in the state capitol, therefore, could insure that appointed officials would understand the special needs of the Loomises. Many state appointments were virtually open to the highest bidder, and the Loomises were never shy about making their wishes known. Money was the usual item of barter, although history records one man being recommended for a state appointment because of his

"large family of interesting females." In another instance a well-
known young woman in Albany recommended a male friend as
state Commissioner of Deeds claiming that she had an "active"
command of six to ten votes in the state legislature and an ability
to "neutralize" double that number.

The most influential Loomis friend in Albany was undoubtedly
Thurlow Weed. As a young man Weed had worked in Sangerfield on its weekly newspaper and so he was known by George
and Rhoda Loomis. It was also well known in Central New York
that in 1815, still a young man, Weed had been indicted in
Cooperstown for assault and battery when a young lady accused
him of "some rudeness to her person." He was found not guilty,
but left Cooperstown for Albany where he rose rapidly in political
circles. In 1824 he became prominent when his fellow Whigs
challenged the power of the Albany Regency and engineered the
victory of presidential candidate John Quincy Adams. "My Lord
Thurlow" was the way detractors referred to him.

When the Whig party finally ousted the Regency Democrats,
Thurlow Weed and William Seward became the most powerful
men in the state capital. Weed had regularly denounced the
Regency for nepotism and corruption, especially Democrat William Marcy who popularized the phrase "that to the victor belong
the spoils." Yet when the Whigs took power the first thing Weed
did was to have himself appointed State Printer, the most lucra-
tive patronage job available. Weed acknowledged that the job
gave him "at least one man's fair proportion of this world's
goods" and rapidly amassed a large portfolio of real estate and
stocks. In subsequent elections "bribery by the Whigs was open
and flagrant, and a profusion of hired bullies appeared in Albany
polling places to the vast discomfort of Democratic voters . . .
Whigs were arrested for bribing voters at the polls." When confronted by this mockery of the democratic process Weed replied
that the practice had been used equally effectively by the
Democrats while in office.

By the late 1850s the New York State Legislature had become,
according to historians, "outrageously corrupt." Weed was the
leader of a group accused of accepting one million dollars in
bribes as "campaign contributions," and the New York *Evening
Post* editorialized against "the daring and corrupt schemes con-
templated in Albany." When Weed was approached by another
politician about a proposed candidate for office and asked if he
knew him personally, Weed is alleged to have replied: "Do I

know him personally? I should rather think I do. I invented him!"

In such a milieu the Loomises found willing recipients for "campaign contributions" in exchange for the appointment of local officials who would be mindful of Loomis family interests. Thurlow Weed was the kind of man Wash Loomis understood and felt comfortable with. According to one historian:

> "Manipulation was an instinct with Mr. Weed; an object to
> be pursued for its own sake, as one plays cards; but he
> appeared to play with men as though they were only cards;
> he seemed incapable of feeling himself one of them. He took
> them and played them at their face value."

Wash Loomis moved easily among the Thurlow Weeds of Albany, his charm and cultured manners belying his family's true business. He was a gentleman from Sangerfield and he purchased judicial protection for the Loomises with the utmost discretion.

The corruption in Albany, however, was nothing compared with that in New York City. One of the most predictable pleasures for the Loomis family was reading about the latest outrage in the New York newspapers and then discussing it over dinner. During the 1840s roving gangs of muggers and murderers known by names such as the Plug Uglies, Roach Guards and Dead Rabbits, controlled the city from their headquarters at Five Points, that cesspool of crime which Charles Dickens had visited and described as "reeking everywhere with filth and dirt . . . men and woman and boys slink off to sleep, forcing the dislodged rats to move away in quest of better lodgings . . . all that is loathsome, drooping and decayed is here." When the gangs fought each other the leader of the Dead Rabbits "carried a real dead rabbit atop a spear into every battle."

By the early 1850s such gangs had become highly organized. Names such as the Swamp Angels, Slaughter Housers, and Daybreak Boys regularly were in the news, the last especially feared for their activities in the hours just before dawn; between 1850 and 1852 they were credited with "twenty murders and the theft of $100,000 in property." Like the Loomises, these gangs were no longer "loosely organized, self-trained hoodlums" but rather "a tighter network of professional craftsmen . . . who required special knowledge and skills to succeed at their work" and "who invented their own internal power structure." The Loomises noted the professionalization of crime in New York City approvingly, as an older brother watching a younger one grow up.

As the 1850s evolved the gangs in New York yielded headlines to outrages of public trust which exceeded anything seen to date. For these were the days of William Tweed, "a craggy hulk of a man," six feet tall and three hundred pounds, who "looked like something that God hacked out with a dull axe." He had begun modestly as a bookkeeper in the family business, then became a fireman and in 1852 was elected Alderman for the city of New York. His group of Aldermen became publicly known as the "Forty Thieves" because of their blatant sale of ferry and street car franchises and government land to the person offering the largest bribe. Within a year two of his associates had been indicted but Tweed had moved on to Washington as a congressman. When he returned to New York in 1855 he was estimated to have accumulated one hundred thousand dollars and was living "in elegant style." Known as "Boss Tweed," he was "immensely likeable," suave in the private clubs and vulgar when necessary on the streets, a corpulant presence building a foundation of improbity which would immortalize his name in the "Tweed Ring." One venture which came to public attention was his purchase of three hundred benches from one city agency for five dollars each; he then sold them to another city agency for six hundred dollars each.

In addition to Tweed's activities, New York City increasingly symbolized to upstate observers the ascendancy of institutionalized immorality. Prostitution was so rampant that in 1858 it was estimated that if all the women of ill-repute marched up Broadway single-file the line "would reach from City Hall to Fortieth Street." Treatment with patent medicines such as "Unfortunate's Friend" did little to stem the tide of venereal disease. And in 1855 brothel owners "became so incensed by the extortionate payoff demands of the police that they finally complained to the new mayor, Fernando Wood." Wood himself had been elected with a reputation "as New York's most underhanded and unethical merchant."

Both in Albany and New York white collar crime was as pervasive as that of the gangs although it less often came to public attention. The 1840s had seen Wall Street rocked by a "series of bankruptcies, defalcations, and other scandalous business events which undermined the confidence of the business community." The prestigious Merchant's Exchange, "built by a corporation of businessmen to crown the glories of Wall Street" defaulted in 1842. Bank officers of the Manhattan Bank were found by investigators to have been manipulating stock; "after the report of the investigators was made public the Cashier of the bank, Robert White, attempted a rebuttal by attacking one of them with a club on Wall Street." The Secretary of the New York Life and Trust Company was convicted of embezzling a quarter of a million dollars for use in "lottery, gambling, women, and real estate speculation."

Corruption appeared to have reached all levels of the social strata. In 1854 Robert Schuyler of the aristocratic Schuylers "was discovered to have issued 20,000 shares of spurious stocks in the New Haven Railroad of which he was president," and almost simultaneously embezzlements were discovered in two of the city's largest banks. The *New York Times* decried "the gross betrayal of official trust" in business, while the *Evening Post* took note of the "extraordinary increase of defalcations, embezzlements, frauds, and robberies committed by men in places of trust."

The police in New York City, as elsewhere in the state, were assumed to be corrupt. Since they were directly appointed by aldermen in each city ward their jobs depended on the re-election of the alderman and the policemen acted accordingly. Among the most dishonest policeman in New York City was the Chief, George Matsell, "a blubberous man of some three hundred pounds . . . a master of rhetoric and bombast" who systematically collected kickbacks from "gamblers, brothels, abortionists and thieves." In 1856, when Matsell was finally exposed, it was found that he had built "a twenty-room mansion on a three-thousand-acre estate" from the proceeds of his position.

The Loomises regularly read newspapers from Albany and New York and so were keenly aware of the moral milieu. Indeed it would have been difficult not to be. The most important cattle buyer in the Sangerfield-Waterville area, for example, was Daniel Drew who was accused of feeding the cattle salt prior to taking them to market thus causing them to drink large amounts of water and weigh more. When Drew moved on to Wall Street as a major investor, the term "watered stock" followed him there. So widespread was corruption in financial circles that one businessman said he would "hardly trust John Jacob Astor with twenty dollars unless secured with real estate worth a hundred." One can imagine the delight of the Loomises as they read editorials such as one by the *New York Times*: "Hundreds escape punishment after having been brought before our Courts; and thousands of those whose hands and hearts are stained with many crimes, have not been brought even within the presence of a judge."

At the same time as corruption and crime appeared to be engulfing American society in the 1850s, the question of individual inequality came prominently to the fore. This was the era of the Know-Nothings, the political party founded on suppression of immigrants and Catholics. At its height of power in 1854 and 1855, it captured the governorships of Massachusetts and Delaware and was especially strong in New York. Bigotry was institutionalized and encouraged, and probably never before nor since in America has the belief been as pervasive that some individuals, because of genetic and geneological attributes, are superior to others. For families like the Loomises who counted themselves among the elite it provided another self-serving rationalization to justify their behavior.

At the close of the Revolutionary War there had been a widespread belief in the newly independent colonies that all men were created equally. It was an enlightenment view, imported from Europe by Jefferson and his peers, "that environment, not innate racial differences, accounted for the marked gaps in achievement between different people and nations." Almost immediately the belief in equality was challenged. American Indians owned land coveted by the settlers pouring westward; the most effective rationalization for seizing this land was to claim that Indians were inferior beings in the human hierarchy. By the end of the eighteenth century the Indians were being referred to as "the animals vulgarly called Indians" and the belief in a social elite in America had been permanently established.

In the early years of the nineteenth century the belief in an elite was given scientific credence by Charles Caldwell, a physician who popularized phrenology in the United States. Some races were genetically inferior, he argued, and a scientific study of skulls had proven it. These studies became increasingly widely known so that by 1839, when Dr. Samuel Morton published his *Crania Americana*, phrenology was among the most fashionable subjects of the day. The skulls and brains of Indians were much smaller than Caucasians, it was said, with Negroes falling in between. Morton and other leading phrenologists lectured in cities like Utica and Syracuse, introducing their subject by announcing to the audience that their "eyes never rested on such a collection of excellent brains . . . big-headed, moral, intellectual and energetic Pilgrims, enlightened and civilized." In Rome in 1841 Thomas Cole was painting "The Voyage of Life" depicting Caucasian man being given the virgin wilderness by God, and in 1845 a journalist in New York coined the ethos of the elite in a single phrase when he boasted of "our manifest destiny to overspread and to possess the whole of the continent which Providence has given us for the . . . great experiment in liberty."

For the Loomises and other educated Americans who read Morton's book and listened to the phrenologists, it must have seemed that history had proven them correct. The Oneidas had all but disappeared from the six million acres they had once owned. From time to time they came to public awareness but they were increasingly mere atavisms of a distant past. In 1818 two Oneidas were scheduled to be hanged in Rome for murder; when a reprieve was issued at the last minute the disappointed crowd vented its anger by erecting a gallows and hanging them in effigy. Five years later an old Oneida, who had fought with the Americans in the Revolution, was convicted of murder and hanged before a huge crowd estimated at forty thousand people in Morrisville. According to a contemporary account of the proceedings "the intensity of feeling which this trial produced between the two races, white and red, showed that it involved principles reaching beyond the fact of his having indulged a barbarous nature in destroying a fellow creature. It was the culminating strife between the elements of barbarism and civilization, and became the death struggle of barbarism in this region."

Most Indians in Central New York died more prosaic deaths, especially during the cholera epidemic of 1832. The Oneidas remained near starvation and were susceptible to all passing diseases. An English tourist passing through Oneida County noted Indian children "nearly in a state of nudity" as they ran beside the stagecoach begging for coins. Official concern about the Indians was minimal, especially after Andrew Jackson became President in 1829. He was called Sharp Knife by the Indians for having slain thousands of Cherokees, Chickasaws, Choctaws, Creeks, and Seminoles, and his first message to Congress was a proposal that all Indians east of the Mississippi River be moved west. This finally was effected in 1838 when soldiers herded the remaining Cherokees to Oklahoma over the "trail of tears"; one out of every four Indians died from cold, hunger, or disease on the march. The same year, in Albany, a bill was signed which "provided for the removal of all Iroquois in New York State, including the Oneidas, to Kansas territory." Some of the Oneidas simply refused to go.

What appeard to be the final chapter in Oneida Indian history took place in 1849 when a strange procession passed through Sangerfield and Waterville en route to Utica. Reduced to less than two hundred people, the "People of the Upright Stone" had finally sold the land on which their sacred stone rested. Officials of the newly-opening Forest Hills Cemetery in Utica heard about it and decided the two-ton stone would make an impressive entrance for their cemetery. They offered to transport the stone to Utica for safekeeping and the Oneidas accepted the offer. According to historical accounts "the huge boulder was carefully loaded upon a wagon drawn by four horses, and in the autumn of 1849, accompanied by a delegation of Oneida Indians and two of the trustees of the cemetery association, it was conveyed with considerable difficulty to its present site. It is said by some who remember the occasion, that before the Indians departed from the cemetery, they assembled around the stone and betrayed in their leave-taking pitiful manifestations of grief, several of them kneeling beside the boulder and kissing it."

The stone was initially placed upon a grassy knoll at the cemetery entrance. Later a marble base was made for it and a bronze tablet affixed with the following inscription:

SACRED STONE OF THE
ONEIDA INDIANS

---

THIS STONE WAS THE NATIONAL ALTAR OF THE
ONEIDA INDIANS, AROUND WHICH THEY GATHERED
FROM YEAR TO YEAR TO CELEBRATE SOLEMN
RELIGIOUS RITES AND TO WORSHIP THE GREAT
SPIRIT. THEY WERE KNOWN AS THE TRIBE OF
THE UPRIGHT STONE. THIS VALUABLE HISTORICAL
RELIC WAS BROUGHT HERE FROM STOCKBRIDGE,
MADISON COUNTY, N.Y., IN 1849.

As prophesied, the stone had indeed followed them "wherever they should go."

At the time of the Loomis meeting in 1852 the Indians had virtually disappeared, and the issue of individual inequality had

shifted to Negroes. Harriet Beecher Stowe's *Uncle Tom's Cabin*
had been published earlier in the year and had already sold
almost 300,000 copies, an extraordinary number for that time.
Much of the gossip at the Loomis meeting, however, centered on
Gerrit Smith of Peterboro, a candidate for the Madison County
congressional seat and who was running on a Free Soil Party
ticket advocating the abolition of slavery.

Gerrit Smith was well known to the Loomises, as indeed he was
to everyone in Central New York. He had inherited one-half
million acres of former Oneida Indian land from his father, Peter
Smith, and was the largest landowner and one of the wealthiest
men in the state. Smith's twenty-eight room Mansion House
dominated the village of Peterboro just fifteen miles northwest of
the Loomis farm; travelers from the Loomises to Hastings Center
passed directly by the Mansion House so news of Gerrit Smith's
activities was regularly available for Loomis gossip.

Smith had become, in the 1840s, a leading advocate for the
abolition of slavery. His Mansion House was a major stop on the
underground railway guiding slaves from southern states to
freedom in Canada and was also a meeting place for politicians
and reformers interested in the issue. Among his regular guests
at Peterboro were Horace Greeley, William Lloyd Garrison,
Frederick Douglass, Henry Stanton, Henry Ward Beecher
(whose sister was writing *Uncle Tom's Cabin*), Thurlow Weed,
and Alfred Conkling with his son, Roscoe.

Encourage by Smith, Roscoe Conkling became a staunch abolitionist in the early 1850s as he rose in local and state political
circles. Just prior to the 1852 meeting at the Loomises, Conkling
had been in the news when he was hired by Smith to legally
defend some abolitionists in Syracuse. During a speech at a
Republican rally in which Conkling was condemning slavery, a
man in the crowd called out loudly: "Do you want me to marry a
black wench?" Conkling "pretended not to hear the remark
distinctly, and said, with great politeness of manner: 'Will the
gentleman who asked me a question have the kindness to come
forward and repeat it?' The Republicans who were present cried
out! 'Turn him out! turn him out!' 'Oh no, don't turn him out,'
said Mr. Conkling; 'I'm sure the gentleman asked some question
which deserved a reply; let him come forward.' So they pushed
the fellow forward to the middle of the hall, where he puffed out
his chest and said defiantly: 'Do you want me to marry a black
woman?' Mr. Conkling looked the man all over carefully for

about two minutes. It was so silent that one could have heard a pin drop. Then he said, with a drawl: 'Do I want you to marry a black woman? No, I can't say that I do—I have too much compassion for the black woman.'"

Gerrit Smith had also become prominent in nearby villages because of his sponsorship of local abolitionist rallies. Many of Smith's guests participated in these rallies in towns such as Madison, Morrisville, Sangerfield and Waterville. Elizabeth Cady, the niece of Gerrit Smith, described such outings in her memoirs:

> "Two carriage-loads of ladies and gentlemen drove off every morning, sometimes ten miles, to one of these conventions, returning late at night. I shall never forget those charming drives over the hills in Madison County, the bright autumnal days, and the bewitching moonlight nights. The enthusiasm of the people in these great meetings, the thrilling oratory, and lucid arguments of the speakers, all conspired to make these days memorable as among the most charming in my life."

The days were also memorable for Elizabeth Cady because she was falling in love with Henry Stanton, and became engaged to him at Peterboro after knowing him less than a month.

In 1848 a new visitor had arrived at Gerrit Smith's door in Peterboro, a man destined to profoundly alter American history. His name was John Brown and he was a wool merchant living in Springfield, Massachusetts. An enigmatic, Job-like figure, Brown's personal life had been a series of failed businesses and personal tragedies (four children had died of dysentery within eleven days). He was, however, a zealous abolitionist who already, in 1848, had confided to Frederick Douglass a plan "to establish five bands of armed men in the Allegheny Mountains who would run off slaves in large numbers." Gerrit Smith had recently given away 120,000 acres of land in the Adirondack Mountains to landless Negroes so that they could qualify to vote (land ownership was a requirement for eligibility at the time), and John Brown offered to help teach the Negroes how to farm the land. Gerrit Smith accepted his offer and gave him some land in the Adirondacks, in the town of North Elba, to which he moved his family.

The Loomises delighted in ridiculing Gerrit Smith and his friends. The abolition of slavery was a foolish idea, they said, for it was well known that Negroes were genetically inferior. This had been conclusively proven by scientists such as Dr. Caldwell who wrote that in genital organs the Negro "resembles the ape fully as much as he does the Caucasian." The Negroes, said the Loomises, would always be ruled by men such as themselves for that was the way it was intended to be. The Loomises in fact employed several Negroes to steal for them, including Abe Lovett and Salem Loucks who lived in shacks on the hill and were almost like members of the family. Salem Loucks had developed a profitable venture in partnership with the Loomises who, according to the *Utica Morning Herald*, took "the Negro south several times and sold him . . . he invariably came back to Sangerfield and divided the spoils with his sellers."

Gerrit Smith was also ridiculed by the Loomises and their neighbors because of his extraordinary self-righteousness. His ego, it was said, was as large as his land holdings. In an autobiographical note Smith described himself as "a man so noble and commanding in appearance . . . the most affable and agreeable of men" and compared himself to Jupiter as the "guardian of community morals." The Loomises were in complete agreement with one of Smith's critics who had said of him: "A fool's tongue is long enough to cut his own throat." The Loomises had no way of knowing in 1852 that Gerrit Smith's self-righteousness, wealth and friendship with John Brown would ultimately, if indirectly, affect the fortunes of their own family.

In 1852 Rhoda Loomis and the other women in the Loomis household were interested in Gerrit Smith for another reason as well. He had been one of the main supporters of the first Women's Rights Convention which had been held in Seneca Falls, seventy miles west of the Loomis farm, in 1848. Among the organizers of the convention had been Smith's daughter, Elizabeth; Smith's niece, Elizabeth Cady, who had married Henry Stanton; and Susan B. Anthony. The issue was the same as it was for the Negroes—individual equality. Elizabeth Cady Stanton summarized it as follows: "It struck me as very remarkable that abolitionists, who felt so keenly the wrongs of the slave, should be so oblivious to the equal wrongs of their own mothers, wives and sisters when, according to the common law, both classes occupied a similar legal status." If slaves could be freed, why couldn't women be freed as well?

The main question in 1852, however, was not equality for women but simply women's dress. Mrs. Stanton and her friends had been publicly observed wearing a short skirt with long undertrousers gathered at the ankles in place of the traditional long skirt. This shocking apparition had even been pictured in Amelia Bloomer's periodical on women's rights, much to the amusement of the popular press, and Mrs. Bloomer's name was becoming synonymous with the attire. With the encouragement of fathers and older brothers, boys on the street of Seneca Falls ran behind the women chanting:

> "Heigh! ho! in rain and snow,
> The bloomer now is all the go,
> Twenty tailors take the stitches,
> Twenty women wear the breeches.
> Heigh! ho! in rain or snow,
> The bloomer now is all the go."

The women at the Loomises knew the idea for short skirts with undertrousers had not originated in Seneca Falls, but rather just a few miles from Sangerfield in the village of Oneida. There, in 1848, John Humphrey Noyes had settled with a commune of free-thinking men and women and begun the Oneida Community. These were truly liberated women, encouraged to get an education equal to men and allowed to work at men's chores. They also had a system of "complex marriage" which was said to be scandalous—sexual exclusiveness had been abolished and both men and women were encouraged to use sexual love for "amative" ("a medium of magnetic and spiritual interchange") as well as "propagative" purposes.

Perhaps most shocking to the inhabitants of surrounding villages, however, were not the rumors of sexual dalliance but rather the dress of the women in the Oneida Community. Noyes believed that if women were truly going to be equal they would need to discard their long dresses and in 1848 he wrote: "Woman's dress is a standing lie. It proclaims that she is not a two-legged animal, but something like a churn standing on castors!" Accordingly that summer Noyes' wife and two other women cut their skirts to knee-length and used the excess material to make ankle-length pantalets. To make matters even worse they cut their hair almost as short as men's hair.

The practices of the Oneida Community provoked lively discussion throughout Oneida and Madison counties. Complaints were filed against Noyes and his followers in the courts but these were dismissed; some said the two hundred members of the Community were just industrious farmers with odd personal habits, other claimed they were agents of the devil. When a prominent weekly newspaper in New York City lauched a vitriolic attack, Henry James called that attack "an unmanly sight to see a great prosperous newspaper . . . gather together the two wings of its hebdomadal flatulence . . . for a doughty descent upon this starveling and harmless fieldmouse."

The women's dress in the Oneida Coumunity caused almost as much local discussion as did their advocacy of "amative" love. Mrs. Stanton, a regular visitor to Gerrit Smith's home just seven miles from the Oneida Community, became intrigued with it. Together with her cousin Elizabeth Smith she designed a modified version of it and the two women began wearing it on the streets of Peterboro. It elicited little more than raised eyebrows until they took the dress to Seneca Falls and shared it with Amelia Bloomer.

Although the Loomis women were interested in the idea of women's rights, they talked of it only among themselves. Wash, Grove, and the other Loomis men found the idea of equality for women as least as absurd as the idea of equality for Negroes. Women were necessary, of course, and could be very helpful as long as they stayed in their place. Loomis men, like virtually all men in Central New York, agreed enthusiastically with an editorial printed in the *Waterville Times* in response to the stirrings for women's rights:

> "Woman has done much to ameliorate the condition of our race, but in a sphere widely different from the one she now seeks. Civilized man has fully appreciated this last of heaven's divine favors, and has never knowingly consented that she should occupy a degraded position . . . True, there are a few who feel that they have been overlooked in this matter of awarding praise, but whenever we read or hear the fitful ravings of such a female . . . Lunacy in such cases is to be expected."

Corruption and crime and the inequality of individuals were, then, dominant issues in the 1850s. They recurred repeatedly in the newspapers and dominated conversations in Bissell's general store when the Loomises were not being discussed. For most people in central New York the name Loomis had become virtually synonymous with corruption and crime, and Bissell's advocacy of "the California solution" was increasingly persuasive as a resolution for the Loomis problem. A few miles to the west Gerrit Smith was coming to a similar conclusion regarding the use of violence as a resolution for the problem of slavery.

Smith had won a Congressional seat in 1852 in a major upset, but his career in Washington was brief. Early in 1854 the Kansas-Nebraska Act was introduced giving the inhabitants of the territories of Kansas and Nebraska the right to decide on slavery themselves. Smith and other abolitionists vigorously opposed it with the motto: "No slavery in Nebraska, no slavery in the nation; slavery an outlaw." When the bill passed Smith was bitterly disappointed and resigned his seat halfway through his term. The reason he gave for his resignation was "pressure of my far too extensive business," but in fact he had decided that the abolition of slavery was not going to take place in Congress.

Back in Peterboro Gerrit Smith became increasingly persuaded by the arguments of John Brown and others that force would be necessary to achieve abolition. In 1855, both men attended an abolitionist meeting during which John Brown "made a very fiery speech" and said he was prepared to take four of his sons and three other men to Kansas to help fight against slavery if he had arms and financial support; "funds were contributed on the spot, principally by Gerrit Smith." Brown also proposed to go to Louisiana to liberate slaves and retreat into Texas, and was still planning liberation projects in the Allegheny Mountains as well.

With pro-slavery settlers pouring into Kansas from the south and abolitionists like John Brown coming from the north it was inevitable that bloodshed would occur. When the pro-slavery forces sacked and burned Lawrence, Kansas, early in 1856 Brown and his followers murdered five pro-slavery adherents at Pottawatomi Creek in retaliation. Two months later a force of two hundred and fifty southerners attacked Brown's forces at Osawatomie; despite losing one of his sons in the battle Brown fought courageously. Also fighting with Brown in their battle was the brother of Susan B. Anthony, demonstrating the continuing ties of the abolitionists and feminists through Gerrit Smith's extended family. Watching Osawatomie burn, Brown vowed: "I have only a short time to live—only one death to die, and I will die fighting for this cause. There will be no more peace in this land until slavery is done for." A reporter for the *New York Tribune* was on the scene and called Brown's men "not earnest, but earnestness incarnate." John Brown became a national figure, a symbol of irreconcilable opposition to slavery and of a willingness to use violent means to achieve that end.

Gerrit Smith was fully supportive of Brown's efforts and wrote friends about "our sacred work in Kansas." One week after Brown had killed the five settlers at Pottawatomi Creek, Gerrit Smith published a letter in a Syracuse newspaper proclaiming that "I am ready to go with it in putting slavery to a violent death" and called for the raising of one thousand men and one million dollars in support of the Kansas efforts; Smith himself pledged ten thousand dollars. John Brown may have been a murderer to some, but to Smith his violent means were justified by a sacred end.

By late 1856 John Brown returned east, visiting Frederick Douglass in Rochester and then going to Peterboro. Brown's visits to the Mansion House were subjects for discussion and speculation in the surrounding villages for he had become a nationally known figure. From Peterboro, Brown went to Boston where he met Ralph Waldo Emerson, William Lloyd Garrison, Samuel and Julia Ward Howe, and Henry Thoreau; Thoreau was particularly impressed calling Brown "a volcano with an ordinary chimney-flue."

With Gerrit Smith's help, John Brown was prepared to try and free the slaves. In conversations with others Brown claimed that "a few men in the right, and knowing they are, can overturn a king. Twenty men in the Alleghenies could break slavery to pieces in two years." He was committed to armed conflict if necessary: "Any resistance, however bloody, is better than the system which makes every seventh [Negro] woman a concubine." In February, 1857, Brown set in motion the next phase of his plan by ordering one thousand pikes—a bowie knife with an eight-inch blade affixed to a pole six feet long. Such a weapon, he said, would be much more effective than a rifle because few men knew how to use rifles. "Give a slave a pike," Brown said, "and you make him a man."

John Brown anticipated violence in his new endeavors. He made arrangements with Amos Lawrence, another wealthy abolitionist and friend of Gerrit Smith's, to look after his family in the event that he was killed. In June, 1857, Brown again met with Gerrit Smith. That Smith was familiar with the outline of John Brown's plans is apparent from a letter which Smith wrote to a friend following this meeting: "We must not shrink from fighting for Liberty—and if Federal troops fight against her, we must fight against them."

John Brown returned to Kansas to recruit men for his intended raid. He took them to a remote town in Iowa and "spent the next several months training and drilling." In January, 1858, he returned to Rochester and stayed three weeks with Frederick Douglass; during this stay he wrote a provisional constitution for the slave communities which he hoped to liberate and which would be living in mountain strongholds in Virginia and Pennsylvania.

On February 18, 1858, John Brown traveled to Peterboro once again, igniting rumors in the surrounding villages. Accounts of abolitionist activity were featured prominently in newspapers; the local *Oneida Sachem* of February 20, 1858, had "President's Message on Kansas Affairs" on page one. Brown remained at Peterboro for one week during which time the details for a raid on Harpers Ferry were finalized. He was adamant in insisting on the feasibility of his plans—his raid would ignite the spark and precipitate a conflict setting the slaves free. "If God be for us," he argued, "who can be against us?" F.B. Sanborn, another prominent abolitionist, was also in attendance at Peterboro and described Gerrit Smith's final decision to proceed with the plan:

> "As the sun was setting over the snowy hills of the region where we met, I walked for an hour with Gerrit Smith among woods and fields (then included in his broad manor) which his father purchased of the Indians and bequeathed to him. Brown was left at home by the fire, discussing points of theology with Charles Stuart. Mr. Smith restated in his eloquent way the daring propositions of Brown, whose import he understod fully, and then said in substance: 'You see how it is; our dear old friend has made up his mind to this course, and cannot be turned from it. We cannot give him up to die alone; we must support him. I will raise so many hundred dollars for him; you must lay the case before your friends in Massachusetts, and ask them to do as much. I see no other way.' I had come to the same conclusion, and by the same process of reasoning. It was done far more from our regard for the man than from hopes of immediate success."

The date for the raid was set for July 4, 1858, to symbolize the new freedom. John Brown, exhultant, wrote to his wife and son that Gerrit Smith and his friends "are ready to go in for a share in the whole trade . . . Mr. Smith and family go *all* lengths with me." To another abolitionist Brown wrote: "I expect to effect a mighty conquest . . . God has honored but comparatively a very small part of mankind with any possible chance for such mighty and soul-satisfying rewards."

John Brown had decided that violence was a necessary means to achieve social justice, and had convinced Gerrit Smith and his friends as well. Rumors of Brown's intended raid circulated in the villages and towns of Central New York. The Loomises, and men like W.J. Bissell, Jim Filkins and Roscoe Conkling heard the rumors and wondered what would happen next.

# CHAPTER VI

# Raids

In February, 1858, at the same time as Gerrit Smith and John Brown in Peterboro were finalizing plans for the raid on Harpers Ferry, Jim Filkins in North Brookfield made a decision to fight the Loomises. He did so by filing for the job of constable. Since the village lay just three miles from the Loomis farm across Nine Mile Swamp, volunteering for the job of constable was distinctly unwise unless a man had unusual abilities to see no evil, hear no evil, and speak no evil; Jim Filkins had none of the three.

Filkins was not well liked by others in the town but they gladly voted him into office. Nobody else wanted the job, and Filkins' dislike of the Loomises was well known. W.J. Bissell and a few others in Waterville continued to publicly speak out against the gang, and Roscoe Conkling, just elected mayor of Utica, availed himself of every opportunity to urge justice to descend upon their heads. But in fact the power of the Loomises had never been stronger and they appeared to be virtually immune from prosecution. Indictments and arrests took place but then charges were inexplicably dropped or the cases languished. During the term of Calvin Hall as Sheriff of Oneida County from 1855 to 1858 it was noted the "indictments against the Loomis' for minor offenses cover pages of the record"; yet not one of them spent a day in jail. In Madison County the miscarriage of justice was even more blatant. When DeWitt Dennison was arrested for passing counterfeit bills in Hamilton, for example, Judge Mason allowed Dennison to post bail and then simply dropped charges.

Filkins' election as constable occurred at a time when the Loomises were inciting a flurry of law enforcement activity in surrounding towns. On February 25, 1858, a woman named Jane Barber had been arrested in Utica for passing counterfeit money. On questioning by the police she named Grove Loomis as her friend and accomplice, and a warrant was issued for his arrest. A search of the Loomis farm failed to disclose his whereabouts, and almost a month passed before he was found hiding at a house in Oriskany Falls. Benjamin H. Peebles, the local constable, approached Grove and handcuffed him after a brief struggle at which point "an excited crowd gathered and some of Grove's friends threatened to attempt a rescue"; Peebles pulled out his revolver and promised to shoot anyone who interfered as Grove was taken to the local jail. A few hours later Wash appeared, having been apprised of the situation by Grove's friends. Entering Grove's jail cell Wash cried out angrily: "What are you doing with my best boots on? Take them right off and put on these old ones." Grove complied, and Wash walked out of the jail smiling and wearing two boots packed full of Grove's remaining counterfeit bills.

Sufficient evidence had already been collected from Jane Barber, however, to earn Grove a cell in the Utica jail with bail set at eight thousand five hundred dollars. On April 9, Grove was discovered tunneling out of the jail. Roscoe Conkling, who had assumed the duties of Mayor the previous month, instructed the Sheriff to take whatever measures necessary to insure Grove's continued presence in jail whereupon Grove was fitted with "fetters and chain." Wash, William, and Wheeler Loomis thereupon put up the bail money and secured his release. They could have had Grove simply disappear for a few months until arrangements could be made to have the charges dropped, but the amount of bail to be forfeited was imposing. Obstructionist and delaying tactics might delay the trial but the case had generated much publicity and the evidence held by the District Attorney, Jairus H. Munger of Camden, was strongly incriminating. Clearly a new tactic would have to be devised to keep Grove Loomis from going to prison.

In times of need Wash Loomis usually adopted a strategy his father had taught him and so he hired the best lawyer that money would buy. On this occasion it was an Englishman, J. Thomas Spriggs who had settled in Utica as a young man and whose ambitions outstripped his ethics. He had been appointed District

Attorney of Oneida County in 1853 to fill an expiring term, just as Roscoe Conkling had been three years previously; unlike Conkling, however, Spriggs had shown himself responsive to the needs of the Loomises. The following year Spriggs had been elected Oneida County Treasurer; thus when Wash Loomis hired him to assist Grove in 1858 the Loomises could be certain that Spriggs was on close terms with Oneida County officials, including District Attorney Munger.

Late one night a week after Grove had been released from jail, Munger was walking home through the village of Camden after playing cards with friends. The streets of the village were virtually deserted as cold wind from the Tug Hill plateau belied the spring season. As Munger passed the Methodist Church a short distance from his house, two masked men emerged from the shadows, threw him to the ground, and placed a blanket over his head. His pockets were searched and wallet taken; it contained eleven dollars of his own money and all the counterfeit bills to be used as evidence against Grove Loomis.

Many, including Utica Mayor Roscoe Conkling, were outraged. Robbing a District Attorney exceeded all bounds of criminal propriety. Munger said that he had not seen his attackers so he could not recognize them. The indictment against Grove Loomis would, unfortunately, have to be dropped for lack of evidence. Nobody doubted the identity of the perpetrators; even the *New York Tribune* in covering the story added that "it is supposed that [the counterfeit bills] were taken from him to prevent their being used against Loomis at the trial." In Bissell's general store there was indignation and much speculation about why the District Attorney had been carrying the evidence against Grove on his person; some said it showed bad judgment, but the older men just looked at each other and nodded their heads knowingly.

At the same time as the Loomises were extricating Grove from the counterfeiting charges, they came to public notice for sheep stealing. The Loomises had always kept sheep on their farm both for wool and mutton. In June, 1858, "so many sheep were stolen from the [local] farmers that they organized a party and began to follow the clues that led to the Loomis farm" where the Loomis herd of sheep appeared to be increasing miraculously each night. Wash heard the talk of a posse being organized by the farmers and decided that it was time to direct attention elsewhere.

Jeremiah Clark owned a farm near Hamilton and was a well-known sheep thief. In fact "he was arrested and sentenced so many times for sheep-stealing that he would often jokingly give Auburn Prison as his home address." Wash therefore sold Clark a large herd of sheep, then announced loudly to surrounding farmers that the Loomises, too, had had sheep stolen and the sheep had been traced to Jeremiah Clark's farm. Wash, Grove, Plumb and Denio went to Clark's farm to retrieve the sheep Wash had sold him but succeeded in doing so only after a fight in which Jeremiah Clark was viciously beaten. Clark swore out warrants against all four Loomises charging them with robbery.

When Wash heard of the charges he became angry and decided to teach Clark a lesson. As recounted in the *Waterville Times* Plumb and Grove Loomis "met him in a piece of woods near his house and threatened to blow his _____ brains out if he opposed their tying him hand and foot. Not being desirous of losing his brains he kept quiet and was bound by the Loomises and taken by them to their house." There he remained until the following day when Deputy Sheriff Fitch Hewitt appeared with a warrant for Clark's arrest, on complaint of the Loomises, for sheep stealing. The entire party moved down the road to the farm of Judge Livermore, and lawyers were summoned to represent both the complainant and the defendant. Clark's lawyer immediately pointed out that "the warrant for his client's arrest was not worth a snap—that it was improperly made out and his client therefore was at liberty to return to the scenes of his youth at any moment. On hearing this Jeremiah Clark slid out of court and, while the Justice was preparing a new warrant, took to his heels and fled pursued by the accusers who could no more gain on him than a balky horse could gain on a streak of lightning. The last seen of Mr. Clark, he was putting for the swamp." The newspaper account then ends on an editorial note: "Thus ended the trial—which really was not trial at all—of an innocent appearing man on the charge of stealing 50 sheep from the Loomises *in broad daylight*. The case is a singular one."

The original warrants for the arrest of the Loomises for robbery were still outstanding; Jeremiah Clark added charges of kidnapping against Plumb and Grove. Jim Filkins was given the assignment of serving the warrants and arresting Plumb as his initial task as constable. Community outrage against the Loomises following the robbing of District Attorney Munger had reached a new peak, but no law enforceement official had had the courage to confront the gang directly. Most people doubted that Jim Filkins would be any different from the rest.

At 3 A.M. on July 8, 1858, Jim Filkins approached the Loomis farm with seven men who had agreed to accompany him. Surrounding the house, Filkins called for Plumb to come out. According to a newspaper account Plumb, seeing the house surrounded, jumped out a side window and headed for the swamp. Filkins, not to be denied in his new role, "outran him, jumped on his back and handcuffed him. This unusual treatment alarmed Plumb and he shouted murder. The constable threatened to brain him if he didn't shut up . . . Filkins said he counted fourteen different men in and around the house, all spruce young fellows. Plumb only was captured."

Plumb Loomis was taken to the hotel in Brookfield for safekeeping until he could be arraigned before a judge later in the day. Wash and Grove were outraged by the arrest of a Loomis by the little blacksmith from North Brookfield and vowed to free Plumb. A few hours later Grove Loomis, conspicuously armed with two revolvers, rode up to the hotel in Brookfield and demanded that Plumb be immediately set free "or suffer the consequences." Filkins and Deputy Sheriff Henry Keith met Grove at the door and, with hands on their own revolvers, steadfastly refused to consider the request. Grove backed down and left, and Plumb was taken to a second floor bedroom where he was handcuffed to another officer to prevent escape. Two hours later Plumb had disappeared, apparently having jumped from the window onto the back of a waiting horse. The story was told that the officer had fallen asleep allowing Plumb to slip out of his handcuffs, but most persons believed the officer had simply been bribed.

Jim Filkins had been initiated and the battle joined. A few nights later he raided the Loomis homestead again in an attempt to capture Plumb and Grove. He was accompanied by several deputies including Fred Hall and Ephraim Conger. Hall was stationed up the hill behind the house to cut off escape in that direction. While Filkins and Conger were searching the yard "Grove's hounds in the woodshed started howling. As the din grew louder lights appeared in the windows of the house. Filkins and Conger approached the woodshed door, which opened suddenly to disgorge several hounds. Baying and panting, they started up towards the spot where Hall was stationed. Seeing the dogs, he scattered them with a volley of stones, but they immediately reassembled and started towards him. Panic-stricken, he pried a big boulder loose and rolled it down the hill. The rock missed the dogs completely and bounded against the woodshed as Filkins and Conger were entering the kitchen. The impact caused a few dogs in the kitchen to rush for the doorway. They missed Filkins but tripped up Conger, who sprawled on his face in front of Wash Loomis. 'What's the mater with you, Eph?' Wash laughed heartily. 'What have you and Jim been drinking?'" Thoroughly humiliated, Filkins searched the house and then retreated with his men to plan a different strategy.

A few days later Plumb and Grove were located in Oriskany Falls hiding at the home of Plumb's girlfriend. Constable Peebles of that village took two deputies, Tilley and Thompson, to arrest them. As described in the *Utica Morning Herald*:

> "As Peebles and Thompson neared the premises they met Grove and Plumb making for their team. Peebles made a grab for Grove and as he did so Plumb struck at him with a cudgel which the officer took on his arm and thus saved his head. Grove then turned to run but was met by Tilley who presented a revolver and told him to stand. Grove's only answer was a shot from his own revolver which just grazed Tilley's cheek, who then took aim and fired at Grove. Two or three shots were exchanged when Peebles got rid of Plumb and came up. Grove started to run up the road with Peebles and his assistant after him. Grove turned around and fired a shot which was returned by Peebles. Grove then threw off his overcoat which impeded his flight and the race kept on for forty or fifty rods and eight or ten shots were exchanged. Grove finally leapt a fence and in the darkness succeeded in effecting his escape though it is believed he was hit and slightly wounded."

The Loomis attorney, J. Thomas Spriggs, thereupon filed a brazen motion in Oneida County to have all indictments against Plumb and Grove dropped for the stated reason "that they had thus far resisted arrest." The court simply ignored it.

The Loomises by this time had become truly public figures throughout Central New York. The *Waterville Times* noted that "the Utica papers are almost daily freighted with the movements of the Loomis family. The people in this section must be pleased with the distinction thus conferred upon their neighbors. The Loomises will yet figure in a sensational story, and acquire a Captain Kyd [sic] notoriety." When Wash Loomis was arrested in Higginsville on one of his indictments and brought to the Rome courthouse "quite a crowd gathered around to take a look at one

of the notorious family. Their character was fully discussed."
The editor of *The Roman Citizen*, watching the proceedings,
publicly offered the opinion that "should a bolt of lightning extir-
pate the whole family at once it should be a blessing." J. Thomas
Spriggs, the Loomis' lawyer, challenged the formidable editor to
a fight but then thought better of it.

Warrants for the arrest of Wash, Grove and Plumb Loomis for
stealing Jeremiah Clark's sheep were still outstanding, and
Filkins utilized the warrants to raid the Loomis homestead once
again the following week. Accompanied by deputies Fred Hall
and James Humphrey, Filkins reached the farm at daybreak and
came upon Wash, Grove and Plumb in the barnyard feeding
horses. Spotting the law officers, Wash and Plumb broke for the
house while Grove, the consummate horseman, leaped astride
the one he was feeding, headed toward the fence at full gallop,
cleared it, and disappeared into the woods with benefit of neither
saddle nor bridle. Humphrey, meanwhile, pursued and caught
Plumb at the back of the house, threw him to the ground and
called to Filkins and Hall to help him.

Suddenly from the back door of the Loomis home burst Cornelia Loomis and Adeline Glazier, Plumb's portly girlfriend who
was said to weigh one hundred and eighty pounds. Knocking
Humphrey off of Plumb, Adeline proceeded to bash Humphrey's
head on the ground and then sit on it while Plumb scurried for
the swamp. Hearing Humphrey's cries, Fred Hall came to his aid
but Adeline, refusing to budge, scratched Hall's face with her
long fingernails. Although normally a mild-mannered Quaker
this was too much for Hall who grabbed Adeline's ample breasts
and squeezed until she screamed and vacated her perch on Humphrey's head. Filkins, meanwhile, had subdued Wash, and when
Humphrey and Hall had fully recovered, the three headed for the
Morrisville jail with their prisoner in tow. As happened so often,
Wash was released on bail the same day.

The activity of Cornelia Loomis and Adeline Glazier in helping
Plumb Loomis escape was not unusual. As raids on the Loomises
became more common, Rhoda Loomis and the other Loomis
women found imaginative ways to help their men. On one occasion Deputy Sheriff Henry Keith arrived at the Loomises with
some men and a warrant for the arrest of Salem Loucks, wanted
for horse theft. Rhoda Loomis and Cornelia, dressed only in
nightclothes, met the men on the front porch and refused to let
them search the house. Certain that Loucks was hiding within,

Keith ordered his men to surround the house and watch all exits. Suddenly two Loomis girls ran out the side door with a man between them and headed for the swamp. The deputies pursued and stopped the trio, only to discover that the man with the girls was not the one being sought. Loucks, taking advantage of the diversionary activity, had exited out the opposite side of the house and had disappeared over the hill.

Filkins' raids on the Loomises were widely discussed in the surrounding villages, for no one had previously shown such bravery (according to some) or stupidity (according to others) in pursuing the family. Law officers in almost every local jurisdiction held warrants for the arrest of one Loomis or another but enthusiasm for serving the warrants was wanting.

Hearing of Filkins' raids, Deputy Sheriff George Klinck in Utica decided to arrest Wash on an outstanding warrant for robbery. Three days following Filkins' successful arrest of Wash, Klinck and three deputies (Wood, Latham and Ives) surrounded the Loomis home at three in the morning. Klinck rapped sharply on the front door.

"Who is it?" a woman's voice asked.

"Deputy Sheriff Klinck. Open the door or I will break it down!"

A man's voice responded from within: "If you do so, you will be killed."

Klinck continued to pound on the door.

"Who do you want?" asked the woman.

"Wash Loomis," shouted Klinck.

For a few moments everything was silent in the Loomis house. Then there was the sound of movement, followed by a cacophony of shouts, screams and barking from behind the house where Wood had been stationed to prevent anyone slipping out that way. Seven men, four women, and six vicious dogs had erupted from the back door and as the dogs tore at Wood's clothes the men and women pelted him with stones. Wash and Grove bolted for the swamp as the other officers ran to assist Wood but Wash's way was blocked by Latham. Wash flashed a pistol:

"I'll blow your brains out if you don't get out of here," he threatened.

Ives came up behind Wash and grabbed him. Wash broke free, but was collared by Klinck. At that moment Silas "Si" Clark, a member of the gang, rounded the corner of the house and Wash tossed him the pistol.

"Shoot them, Si," he urged, "Shoot!"

Silas Clark raised the pistol, cocked the trigger, and aimed it at Klinck. Undaunted, the Deputy Sheriff cooly drew his own revolver from its holster:

"Shoot, damn you," he shouted at Clark, "but I'll blast a hole through you first."

Silas Clark hesitated, then lowered his pistol. The Loomis women gathering around told Clark what they thought of his cowardice in no uncertain terms. The officers handcuffed Wash and put him in a carriage to return to Utica.

Wash was in jail but there was not a judge in Utica who was willing to bring him to trial. Two judges flatly declined to take the case, a third absented himself because his daughter had died. The Mayor, Roscoe Conkling, called for justice and the *Utica Morning Herald* complained of the inefficiency of the courts. Finally Judge Wilcox of Whitesboro agreed to hear the case but it was a very brief affair. As Wilcox explained to reporters after the hearing: "After waiting about two hours for the witnesses on the part of the people to arrive or at least some of them and none of them appearing and no bail being offered in view of all circumstances, affidavits and statements in the case, I became satisfied that it was my duty to discharge the defendant and I did discharge him."

Deputy Sheriff Klinck, like Filkins, was discouraged by such blatant miscarriages of justice but was not ready to give up. He still had a warrant for Grove's arrest for passing counterfeit bills so he returned to the farm several times in July and August attempting an arrest. The Loomises were getting tired of confrontations at three in the morning and had begun posting sentries around the property twenty-four hours a day. Each time Klinck and his men approached, the alarm was given and Grove headed for the swamp. Grove, turning the raids into a game of hide-and-seek, wrote a letter to the *Waterville Times* ridiculing Klinck as an "August fool."

As Jim Filkins continued raiding the Loomises, increasing numbers of other law enforcement officials emulated him. Fitch Hewitt, a Deputy Sheriff in Madison County, had collected several warrants for Grove's arrest for stealing horses and counterfeiting. In August, 1858, Hewitt and his deputies surrounded the farm and searched the house for Grove but to no avail. It was a game Grove was apparently enjoying, for after the raid he wrote to the *Waterville Times*: "I laughed quite heartily at the temerity of our amiable sheriff, Fitch Hewitt, Esquire, who looked cautiously into our stove oven the other day, expecting to find me there. I sent word to Fitch that I was baked some years ago, and that if my gun had been loaded I would have peppered him on the spot." The newspaper, reflecting growing frustration among the citizens of Waterville, editorialized: "The time is coming when Grove will discover that the swamp is no place of refuge . . . he will find himself surrounded by determined lawmen who will pounce on him 'like a hawk on a June bug,' and will carry him with exultant shouts to the county jail."

As efforts to arrest the Loomises led increasingly to violence, public sentiment against them further solidified. In an October, 1858 edition, the *Waterville Times* sarcastically reported: "The Loomises amused themselves the other evening by firing at officers attempting to arrest them. The fire was returned. The Loomises are getting to be rather pleasant fellows for neighbors." One month later, when the Utica newspaper likened Grove Loomis to Robin Hood, the Waterville paper bristled at the comparison calling it "ridiculous": "Grove Loomis is neither a Robin Hood, a Wallace, nor a Marion. He is simply a successful rogue, and destitute of those qualities which make the hero . . . The *Herald* has slandered immortal heroes."

At this time suggestions were being made in Sangerfield and Waterville for the formation of a local Anti-Larceny Society to combat the Loomises. The notoriety of the family had spilled over on their neighbors, and the *Waterville Times* complained that "the community is really being made to believe that every man in Sangerfield, except the editors of this sheet, is a knave, a villain and an outlaw . . . many inhabitants of this county think we are a community of thieves . . . poor, down-trodden, God-forsaken Sangerfield has her thieves which cannot be caught, her places of defilement which cannot be purified! Why will people send off missionaries to heathen lands on gloriously uncertain pilgrimages when so broad a field near at hand remains uncultivated . . .?" And when it was suggested by the *Utica Herald* that Utica's Deputy Sheriff Ray might be the best person to bring the Loomises to trial, the *Waterville Times* responded that although "Mr. Ray has been called by an evening paper, 'the flower of young America,' . . . if he goes down to arrest the Loomises let him not forget his pistol."

Jim Filkins was encouraged by the rising community sentiment against the Loomises and he therefore undertook further raids.

On November 13, 1858, he recruited fifty men and surrounded the Loomis home. Calling loudly for Wash, Grove and Plumb to come out, he threatened to set the house afire if they did not. Seeing the large number of armed men the brothers emerged, then immediately broke in different directions on the run. Grove reached the shed where his prize horse was kept saddled, mounted it, and rode directly through twenty men surrounding the shed knocking many of them to the ground. With bullets pursuing his fleeing figure, he disappeared down the road. Plumb, meanwhile, bolted for the swamp and reached its safety ahead of his pursuers. Wash alone was surrounded, handcuffed, and escorted to the Madison County Jail in Morrisville by the partially satisfied posse.

Filkins was determined to have Grove join Wash in jail. One week later, following an early-winter snowstorm, Filkins and nine men approached the Loomis farm as first light was breaking the gray sky. Unknown to the officers Grove had been "apprised by letter" of the raid by "a prominent Madison County official" and had left for Albany. Having idolized his older brother, Plumb decided that it would be a good joke on the lawmen if he took Grove's place. As Filkins and his men approached the farm they saw a man dressed like Grove and riding Grove's horse; when the rider failed to halt, the law officers fired and their fire was returned. In the ensuing battle the rider was hit in the wrist and his horse killed, but he was able to run through the snow to the safety of the swamp. According to the *Utica Morning Herald* the "officers tracked him for five miles by the blood which he left on the snow showing he had been severely wounded but they did not come up with him."

The next day it was learned that it had been Plumb, disguised as Grove, who had been the one injured. He had gotten safely to the home of Dr. Medina Preston, son of Clarissa and Stephen Preston and thus his cousin, who had extracted the bullet and hidden him. Later Plumb swore out a warrant against Filkins for attempted murder. The charge was heard by a grand jury but they failed to find cause for indictment. In fact a member of the jury told Filkins that "we came very near to indicting you for *not* killing Plumb." "The only apology I can make," replied Filkins, "is that it was so early in the morning I could not see very well."

Meanwhile, according to the *Waterville Times*, Wash Loomis had been "a tenant of the Madison County Jail, delightfully situated in the village of Morrisville," since his arrest November

13. He was charged with the robbery and the attempted murder of Jeremiah Clark, and for once a judge denied bail. "Wash must be tried this time," he announced; "there is not enough money in Madison or Oneida County to bail him."

Such treatment of a Loomis infuriated family members who were accustomed to special considerations of judges in Madison County. Rhoda Loomis decided to help, and in February, 1859, she sent her son his favorite mince pie. The jailer, either suspicious or himself fond of mince pies, discovered metal files baked into the pie beneath the flaky crust. "Say Wash," he asked, "does your mother put hardware in all the pies she bakes?" "What kind of pie?" Wash asked. "Mince," the jailer replied. "Yes," Wash said, "she always puts in pieces of iron when she bakes mince pies."

By March the Loomises had spread enough money among Madison County officials so that Wash was released on bail. However, as he stepped from the jailhouse, he was arrested by Oneida County law officers on charges of having previously resisted arrest and having assaulted the officers with a deadly weapon. He was taken to the Rome jail but nobody expected him to stay there long. The new Oneida County District Attorney, elected to succeed Jarius H. Munger whom the Loomises had robbed, was Hiram T. Jenkins, the twenty-six-year-old son of a former congressman and a graduate of Hamilton College. Jenkins was said to have inherited his father's intelligence but not his integrity, and was known to be on friendly terms with the Loomises. The *Utica Morning Herald* freely predicted that "as this county enjoys a reputation for being remarkably facile in bailing criminals, it is probable that Wash will soon be out again and that will be the end of the matter." The prediction was well founded, for within a month all charges against Wash had been dropped. He was, in the words of the *Waterville Times*, again "free as the soaring lark, free as the runaway slave when his feet touch the soil of Canada."

The newspaper's comparison of Wash's freedom to that of a runaway slave was not by chance, for it was at precisely this time that Wash Loomis was replaced as the main topic of conversation in Bissell's general store by John Brown. He had been seen openly walking the streets of Peterboro, even giving a public lecture, despite the fact that President Buchanan had offered a reward for his capture. Rumors about John Brown's business in Peterboro swirled giddily among the neighboring villages.

As later became known, the July 4, 1858 attack on Harper's Ferry had been aborted. Brown had recruited a large force, including the men he had trained in Iowa and additional conscripts offered by Harriet Tubman from the three hundred slaves she had led to freedom in Ontario. Then in May, 1858, one of Brown's men turned traitor and revealed plans for the raid to "some prominent members of Congress." Brown wanted to proceed anyway but Gerrit Smith and others financing the raid demanded that it be postponed. Smith went to Boston as previously planned to address the American Peace Society, giving a talk entitled "Peace Better Than War." While there he met with the Boston abolitionists and reaffirmed plans for the delayed raid on Harpers Ferry.

John Brown was sent back to Kansas to make it appear that rumors of a raid were unfounded. While in Kansas he organized a foray into Missouri and freed eleven slaves, leading them across Kansas and Iowa in the middle of winter. Brown's fingers, nose and ears froze as he was pursued by several posses. President Buchanan publicly condemned Brown's actions and offered a reward of two hundred and fifty dollars for his capture. From Iowa, Brown responded by offering a reward of two dollars and fifty cents for the capture of President Buchanan. News of Brown's successful Missouri raid was widely reported. Gerrit Smith, hearing of it, wrote exhultantly to his wife: "Do you hear the news from Kansas? Our dear John Brown is invading Kansas and pursuing the policy which he intended to pursue elsewhere."

Then suddenly, on April 11, Brown appeared in Peterboro. Thanks in large part to Gerrit Smith's continuing efforts at public education, Central New York was seething with abolitionist sentiment. On April 9, the *Oneida Sachem* reported that "William Wells Brown, formerly a slave, delivered a lecture on American slavery at the Methodist Episcopal Church on Monday evening last." On April 11, the newspaper carried a long account of a Savannah slave auction at which "the Negroes were examined with as little consideration as if they had been brutes indeed, the buyers pulling their mouths open to see their teeth, pinching their limbs to find out how muscular they were . . . one man went for $1750 because he was a fair carpenter and caulker . . . one woman went for $1250 . . . the lowest price paid was for Anson and Violet, a gray-haired couple, each having numbered more than fifty years—they brought but $250 apiece." Altogether 436 men, women and children were sold at the auction.

Two days after arriving in Peterboro John Brown gave a public lecture at the local church. According to the report of the meeting in the local newspaper, Brown recounted his Missouri raids to free slaves and gave a "lengthy defence of the duty of liberating slaves by force, quoting from scriptures to sustain his positions." Gerrit Smith was moved to tears, following Brown with a speech in which he said: "If I were asked to point out—I will say it in his presence—to point out the man in all this world I think most truly Christian, I would point out John Brown. I was once doubtful in my own mind as to Captain Brown's course. I now approve of it heartily, having given my mind to it more of late."

There was no question at the time that John Brown was going to carry out the planned raid on Harpers Ferry; rather the questions discussed in April, 1859, at Peterboro were numbers of troops, weapons and the date. It was agreed that if Brown's raid was not immediately successful, at least it might polarize the feelings of people for and against slavery and spark violent confrontations. John Brown and Gerrit Smith were, in essence, hoping to set off a civil war which would ultimately free the slaves.

Their discussions concluded, Brown left on April 14 for North Elba to see his family. It must have been an emotional visit for he knew it would be his last before the raid. From North Elba he traveled to Boston and New York to meet with supporters and raise additional funds. He made the final payment on the thousand pikes he had ordered and arranged for their shipment to Chambersburg, Pennsylvania, just north of Harpers Ferry. Brown then went to Ohio, back to Pennsylvania, and finally to Harpers Ferry with two of his sons. Posing as farmers from New York looking for better land, they rented a farm approximately five miles from the town and began final preparations.

Gerrit Smith stayed in close touch with John Brown during these weeks, sending money as needed and offering advice. When Brown was arrested after the raid a check for one hundred dollars from Gerrit Smith was found in his pocket. Smith was so enthusiastic about the coming raid that he was unable to contain himself, and in August, 1859, wrote a letter to the *New York Tribune* broadly hinting at what was coming. In the letter Smith advised that "intelligent black men in the States and Canada should see no hope for their race in the practice and policy of white men. No wonder they are brought to the conclusion," said Smith, "that no resource is left to them but in God and insurrections. For insurrections then we may look any year, any month, any day." A few days later a southern reader of the newspaper replied in a published letter that Smith was "a monster in human shape . . . there had been no such scheme of damnable villainy conceived since the Devil himself entered the Garden of Eden to bring ruin upon mankind by corrupting our first parents." Prophetically the reader ended his diatribe against Smith: "You ought to be regarded rather as a principal than as an accessory, and be dealt with accordingly." The rival *New York Herald* joined the fray editorially on September 5: "The sage of Peterboro . . . is going into the 'fire, rape and slaughter' business all by himself."

On Sunday night, October 16, 1859, John Brown and eighteen men entered and took control of Harpers Ferry, seizing approximately fifty townspeople as hostages. It was, Brown hoped, the first stage of what would become an uprising of slaves throughout the South. Ironically the only person killed during the takeover was a free Negro working at the railroad depot who refused to halt when ordered to do so by Brown's men. By the following afternoon a few slaves on surrounding farms had been liberated but no general uprising had begun; instead militia units from nearby villages had assembled, surrounded the town, and killed one of Brown's men, a free Negro who was fighting for his still enslaved wife and nine children living thirty miles away. Thus, the first casualties on both sides at Harpers Ferry were free Negroes.

Brown retreated to a group of buildings around the government arsenal and sent out a man bearing a white flag to arrange a truce; the man was immediately shot down. William Thompson, another of Brown's men taken prisoner by the militia, was being held in the Foulke's house. The militia decided to kill him and told him to prepare for death whereupon Miss Foulkes threw herself over Thompson shielding his body. This charitable act was later put into perspective when Miss Foulkes said she did it because she "didn't want to have the carpet soiled." Thompson was taken to the railroad bridge, thrown off, and his body used as target practice.

Rumors reached Washington that Brown had a force numbering between five hundred and seven hundred men. President Buchanan responded by ordering Colonel Robert E. Lee and a company of Marines to Harpers Ferry to put down the insurrection. At dawn on October 18, the Marines stormed the Engine-house capturing Brown who had been seriously wounded. Ten of Brown's eighteen men, including two of his sons, lay dead.

The *New York Herald* reporter reached Harpers Ferry early on October 18 and telegraphed his story. By late that afternoon newspapers linking Gerrit Smith to Brown's raid were already on their way to Central New York: "Apropos of this exciting news we recollect a very significant passage in one of Gerrit Smith's letters published a month or two ago, in which he speaks of the folly of trying to strike the shackles off the slaves by the force of moral suasion or legal agitation, and predicts that the next movement made in the direction of Negro emancipation would be an insurrection in the South. Is this the first act in that programme? And are these white abolitionists spoken of in our despatches emissaries of the peaceful Gerrit?"

Nobody in Central New York had any doubt about the answer to the question, but news for Gerrit Smith was to get worse. On October 19 the *Herald* quoted one of John Brown's surviving sons as having confessed that "parties in the North" had supported the raid, and the following day the newspaper headlined "Gerrit Smith, Joshua Giddings, Fred Douglass And Other Abolitionists and Republicans Implicated." John Brown, it said, "has made a full statement implicating Gerrit Smith . . . [who] appears to have furnished some of the sinews of war." Any doubt as to what was coming next was settled by the *Herald's* editorial of October 21: "Enough, it seems, has been ascertained to justify a requisition from Gov. Wise of Virginia upon Gov. Morgan of New York for the delivery over to the hands of justice of Gerrit Smith and Fred. Douglass as parties implicated in the crime of murder and as accessories before the fact."

John Brown's trial began October 25 in Charlestown. In Peterboro Gerrit Smith was frantically destroying letters and records linking him with Brown, and sent his son-in-law to Boston and then Ohio (where another one of John Brown's sons lived) to destroy incriminating papers there as well. The *New York Herald* sent a reporter to Peterboro where he found people in Madison County talking of nothing else; rumors abounded that Gerrit Smith was about to be kidnapped and taken to Virginia for trial. The Mansion House was guarded; according to one of Smith's biographers "the male occupants of it carried arms by day, and slept with weapons within reach." When interviewed Smith told the reporter: "I am going to be indicted, sir, indicted!" until his lawyer advised him to be quiet. The reporter described Smith as displaying "a hasty, nervous agitation, as though some great fear was constantly before his imagination."

On October 31, John Brown was found guilty. His eloquence during the trial impressed even the most hardened of his captors as he compared slavery to a state of war in which a powerful elite had violently subjugated a defenseless minority. Asked if he had anything to say before sentencing, Brown extemporaneously delivered an address which Ralph Waldo Emerson would later compare to Lincoln's Gettysburg Address:

> "Had I interfered in the manner which I admit . . . in behalf of the rich, the powerful, the intelligent, the so-called great, or in behalf of any of their friends . . . it would have been all right. Every man in this court would have deemed it an act worthy of reward rather than punishment . . . I say I am yet too young to understand that God is any respecter of persons. I believe that to have interfered as I have done, as I always have admitted I have done, in behalf of His despised poor, I did not wrong, but right. Now, if it is deemed necessary that I should forfeit my life for the furtherance of the ends of justice, and mingle my blood further with the blood of my children and with the blood of millions in this slave country whose rights are disregarded by wicked, cruel and unjust enactments, I submit. So let it be done."

John Brown was sentenced to be hanged by the neck until dead in thirty days time.

In the November days following the sentencing a wave of sentiment in support of John Brown spread throughout the North. Henry Thoreau said "he could not have been tried by his peers for his peers did not exist." Ralph Waldo Emerson publicly proclaimed that Brown's hanging "will make the gallows as glorious as the Cross." Walt Whitman, Herman Melville, Louisa May Alcott, John Greenleaf Whittier and others wrote favorably of him; articles in the press, speeches in town halls, and sermons in churches condemned slavery and praised Brown. Victor Hugo advised from Europe that "the execution of Brown might consolidate slavery in Virginia, but it is certain that it would convulse the entire American Democracy. You would preserve your shame, but you would sacrifice your glory."

While many were praising John Brown, others were interested in bringing to justice those who had supported his raid. Frederick Douglass had gone to Canada and was preparing to sail to England, while all the Boston co-conspirators had gone either to

Canada or Europe. Most of the attention, therefore, focused on Gerrit Smith.

The pressure was too much. Following Brown's arrest Gerrit Smith "became more and more sleepless" and "took but little food." He "became suspicious of those about him . . . rambling and incoherent in conversation . . . he demanded to be allowed to go to Virginia to attend his trial." Even the newspaper reporter for the *New York Herald* noted that Smith "is a very different man from what he was twelve months since." Once John Brown had been sentenced to hang, Smith's mental state deteriorated more precipitously.

On November 7, 1859, Gerrit Smith was involuntarily admitted to the New York State Lunatic Asylum at Utica. It had, like the Mansion House, six large columns and was at the time the largest insane asylum in the United States. Its superintendent, Dr. John P. Gray, was a man known for his three hundred pound girth and fine wine cellar, and was becoming known as one of the leaders of American psychiatry. Gray diagnosed Gerrit Smith as having "acute mania," a diagnosis supported by Smith's case record in which he was described initially as "raving, incoherent . . . Talks constantly, recites snatches of hymns, poetry, scriptures . . . Utterly incoherent and does not know those about him . . . Talks about going to hell and political meetings." Gray was a believer in physical causes of mania and suspected that the strain Smith was under had exacerbated a nervous condition already weakened by chronic constipation. As was the custom at the time Gray prescribed dietary measures and patent medicines, and thought the prognosis for recovery good.

Gerrit Smith was still in the Asylum on December 2, 1859, when John Brown, seated in the back of a wagon on his own coffin, rode to the gallows. As he left his cell he handed a note to his guard predicting that "the crimes of this guilty land will never be purged away but with Blood." Simultaneously Henry Wadsworth Longfellow sat at his desk in Massachusetts and wrote: "Even now as I write they are leading old John Brown to execution in Virginia for attempting to rescue slaves! This is sowing the wind to reap the whirlwind which will come soon."

John Brown carried himself proudly erect and did not hesitate at the gallows steps. The crowd was tense; because of rumors of a rescue attempt many extra troops had been brought in to guard the gallows. The commander of the cadet battalion from the Virginia Military Institute was Thomas J. Jackson, later to be known as Stonewall. And one of the militiamen in Company F from Richmond was a young actor and avowed segregationist named John Wilkes Booth. They watched as John Brown paid the ultimate price for his actions.

The mood in New York State, as in all thirty-three states, shifted perceptibly following John Brown's abortive raid and hanging. What had been a festering sore, hatred slowly stirred by an underground railroad and by raids on settlers in Kansas, became instead a bleeding wound. Violence entered the vocabulary of those who would do away with slavery, and violence was in the response of those who would keep it. A sense of inevitability came into the peripheral vision of the nation even as its leaders sought compromise.

One such emerging leader was Roscoe Conkling. As Mayor of Utica since early 1858 he had watched with approval as Jim Filkins commenced raids on the Loomises, then with disapproval as his friend Gerrit Smith was linked to the raid on Harpers Ferry. Conkling shared the abolitionist goals espoused by Smith and John Brown and had publicly called slavery "one of the blackest and bloodiest pictures in the book of modern times." Where Conkling differed with his friend from Peterboro was on the means for achieving abolition. Conkling maintained that Congress was where the abolition of slavery would take place and he criticized Smith for having given up his Congressional seat in 1854. Gerrit Smith, by contrast, contended that justice for the Negroes would only be achieved by extralegal means.

In November, 1859, Roscoe Conkling was preparing to demonstrate the correctness of his position for he had been elected as a Representative to the thirty-sixth Congress. The election had taken place in November, 1858, although the newly elected Congress would not convene for thirteen months. The congressional seat for Oneida County had become vacant when the incumbent Republican, Congressman Orsamus B. Matteson, had been censured by his peers for corruption and forced to resign. Conkling's reputation for integrity and Matteson's endorsement of Conkling's Democratic opponent combined to give Conkling "the largest majority ever achieved for a local candidate in Oneida County." Conkling continued as Mayor of Utica while waiting for Congress to convene. Finally on November 21, 1859, Conkling boarded a train for Washington at the Utica railway station while a "large number of friends took leave of him"; several blocks west of the station his friend Gerrit Smith was being held in the Lunatic Asylum. Conkling was widely acknowledged to be on his way to a leadership position in the nation's capital.

On December 5, 1859, three days after John Brown had been hanged, Roscoe Conkling was officially sworn into the House of Representatives. Within twenty-four hours he had served notice that Congress was to be his battleground for the abolition of slavery and that northern congressmen were no longer going to be intimidated by those from the south. When an aged but still fervid abolitionist, Thaddeus Stevens, rose to tell his southern colleagues that "fifty times they have found weak and recreant tremblers in the North" but there would not be a fifty-first, six congressmen from the south advanced toward him. The formidable freshman congressman from Utica thereupon "planted himself in front of the aged and crippled Stevens, and glared defiantly at the advancing flower of Southern chivalry" until they retreated back across the House floor. Such a show of force was more than a symbolic gesture; three years previously on the Senate floor abolitionist Senator Charles Sumner from Massachusetts had been beaten with a heavy cane until he was unconscious by segregationist Senator Preston Brooks of South Carolina. The passions in Washington reflected the growing divisions within an embittered nation.

Roscoe Conkling did not forget his friend, Gerrit Smith. On December 14 the United States Senate appointed a select committee to investigate whether other persons might have helped John Brown "by contributions of money, arms, munitions or otherwise." Gerrit Smith was listed to be summoned but Dr. John Gray informed Washington that Smith was still too ill to travel. Smith in fact had improved greatly, was no longer psychotic, and able to go for daily walks outside. His recuperation continued and on December 29 he was discharged to return to Peterboro with a promise to Dr. Gray "not to undertake or make any brain effort for six months." Meanwhile Smith's nephew, John Cochrane, who was a member of Congress, and Conkling met privately with members of the Senate committee. Their intervention on Smith's behalf was effective and Cochrane was said to have "received assurances that Smith would not be called up for questioning without prior notice to him." The committee eventually issued an innocuous report finding no conspiracy nor any evidence to implicate Gerrit Smith in the affair.

The main reason for the loss of interest in prosecuting Gerrit Smith was a rising abolitionist sentiment in the North. John

Brown was increasingly seen as a martyr and prophet, and his raid acquired a veneer of respectability. Gerrit Smith, having recovered fully from his psychotic episode, even decided to take the offensive and clear his name; in February, 1860, when three New York State politicians publicly linked Smith with John Brown's raid Gerrit Smith sued them for libel. John Brown had been merely an acquaintance, Smith averred, who visited Peterboro once briefly in 1859. Smith claimed that because of his illness he had "but a hazy view of nearly the whole of 1859." On May 22, 1860, the *New York Herald* printed a three column letter from Smith denying any knowledge of John Brown's raid; charges to the contrary were said by Gerrit Smith to be "among all the meanest, nakedest, and most atrocious lies." Two months later Smith claimed to have a "dread of violence and horror of bloodshed." Political events were moving so rapidly in the nation that people's memories were becoming selectively shorter.

During the spring of 1860 it became increasingly clear that John Brown's death had signaled the death of the United States as it had existed. Victor Hugo, watching from Europe, described the situation on March 30, 1860:

> "Slavery in all its forms will disappear. What the South slew last December was not John Brown but Slavery. The American union must be considered dissolved. Between the North and the South stands the gallows of Brown. Union is not longer possible: such a crime cannot be shared."

On May 18 the fuse ready to ignite a civil war grew shorter when Abraham Lincoln was nominated for President by the Republican Convention in Chicago. "I feel confident that he is in his heart an abolitionist" wrote Gerrit Smith. The Democrats had met a month earlier in Charleston and split into two factions over the slavery issue; Stephen Douglas became the nominee of the Northern group and John C. Breckinridge of the Southerners. It was clear that Lincoln would win easily over the divided opposition and southern states began serious discussions of secession.

In Utica and the villages of central New York there was talk of little else. Congress adjourned, and Roscoe Conkling spoke at a large Republican rally in support of Lincoln in Utica on June 4. Conkling reflected the mood in the nation's capital: "For six long months have I been in a city where political and sectional animosities and partisan hatred, such as the institution of slavery alone can engender, have poisoned the very fountains of good neighborhood, and led men, and even women, to forget the ordinary emotions of good feeling and courtesy."

In Waterville the men gathered in Bissell's general store momentarily forgot the Loomises as national events swept toward a palpable but invisible cataclysm. Hermon Clarke was Bissell's twenty-two-year-old clerk, and to him it seemed as if the world was becoming mad as he listened to the talk of Gerrit Smith and John Brown, Lincoln and secession, even war. He had been raised on a farm outside the village and was considered to be a bright young man. Dressed in a storekeeper's apron he ground coffee and poured vinegar for the customers, anxious to please and get ahead in life. He listened to the discussions of what Lincoln might do and the analyses of Lincoln's speeches to try and predict what was coming. Lincoln had said: ". . . there is even now something of ill omen amongst us. I mean the increasing disregard for the law which pervades the country—the growing disposition to substitute the wild and furious passions in lieu of the sober judgment of courts, and the worse than average mobs for the executive ministers of justice."

The Loomis family, like their neighbors, watched national events unfold and listened to the talk of war. George Loomis had told his family many times that wars were economic opportunities; his own experience in the War of 1812 had confirmed that. As a member of the local militia unit he had marched north to Sackets Harbor on Lake Ontario. The militia units were undisciplined, untrained, and unreliable as military forces. Desertions were a daily occurrence, and special allotments of alcohol frequently were necessary to persuade troops to return to their assigned stations or go into battle. When General Dearborn led a militia unit like that of George Loomis north to attack Montreal the militia stopped at the Canadian border, claiming that their commissions did not require them to proceed beyond state lines.

In Sackets Harbor chaos had reigned: "The town was a scene of confusion and disorder. Drunken militiamen jostled one another in the streets, quarreling, cursing, and polluting the very atmosphere with their oaths and ribald jests." Prostitution, petty thefts, and counterfeit currency were endemic. Farmers throughout the region sold their crops at wildly inflated prices to British troops across the border, just as in Boston merchants openly sold supplies to the British. It was a congenial atmosphere for George Loomis and at the end of the war he returned to Sangerfield a considerably wealthier man than could be accounted for by his militia pay and federal bonus of fifty-five dollars at the end of his service.

As the Loomises prepared to take advantage of the inevitable war, they continued stealing and counterfeiting. Their robbery of homes and stores became increasingly sophisticated, with gunpowder and sledgehammers used to open safes. The raids of Jim Filkins againt the Loomises were becoming annoying to them so in October, 1860, Wash, Bill, and two other gang members assaulted Filkins and warned him to leave the Loomises alone. In the spring of 1861 another assault occurred and indictments against the Loomises were obtained in both instances. As usual, prosecution was delayed and the charges eventually dropped. Roscoe Conkling's successful prosecution of Bill Loomis ten years earlier had been forgotten as the *Utica Morning Herald* reflected the exasperation of many of the community when it editorialized:

> "The Loomises bear a charm of some kind; law is utterly powerless in their case. Though other offenders may be brought to trial, they escape. Never has a Loomis been brought to trial by jury for any of their numerous offenses. The fact is a shame and disgrace to our courts of justice. We have never known a similar instance where law has been thwarted at every turn as in the case of these notorious persons."

On November 6, 1860, Lincoln was elected President. "The normal condition of all the territory of the United States is that of freedom," he declared, and the South prepared for the worst. On December 20, South Carolina held a state convention and voted to secede from the Union. Mississippi, Florida, Georgia, Alabama, Louisiana and Texas followed suit, and on February 4, delegates from the seceding states met to form the provisional government of the Confederate States of America. En route to Washington to assume leadership of the country, Lincoln's train stopped briefly in Utica where he gave a speech. The world watched and wondered what the man from Illinois was going to do.

Roscoe Conkling, re-elected to Congress for a second term, strongly supported Lincoln. The city of Washington, Conkling said, was an "atmosphere with noxious vapors" caused by "ten thousand springs of falsehood and perversion." Conkling characterized outgoing President Buchanan as "petrified by fear, or vacillating between determination and doubt, while rebels snatched from his nerveless grasp the ensign of the Republic."

In New York City the Mayor, Fernando Wood, proposed that the city also secede from the Union so that it could continue its profitable trade with southern states. The Loomises and other vultures of war looked on greedily, waiting for it to begin.

# CHAPTER VII

# War

Word spread quickly on April 12, 1861, when General Beauregard and his forces opened fire on Fort Sumter. South Carolina had demanded the surrender of all federal facilities on its soil since declaring itself no longer part of the Union. President Lincoln's response was to send supplies to the Fort thereby provoking South Carolina's reply. A state of "insurrection" was declared by Lincoln, who then issued a proclamation for 75,000 militiamen and asked Colonel Robert E. Lee to command the Union forces. Lee resigned his commission and joined the Confederate Army instead.

Virginia, Arkansas, North Carolina and Tennessee moved quickly toward embracing the Confederacy as its capital was moved from Montgomery to Richmond, just one hundred miles south of Washington. Jefferson Davis was installed as President. Many Southerners doubted the North would be willing to fight, inundated as it was with "undigested immigrants ruled by money-mad Yankees . . . any army it raised would dissolve like the morning mists once it ran into real soldiers." Surely the North would back down when they realized the South was serious. One prominent Southerner, assuring his listeners that serious fighting was impossible, promised to wipe up with his handkerchief all the blood which would be spilled by the secession of the South.

Northerners were equally confident the South was posturing, waving its bravado like its new flag and with as little consequence. Everyone knew the North had almost four times more eligible males for fighting since many in the South were slaves. In addition, the North controlled most of the country's manufacturing, weapons factories, railroads, shipbuilding, and bank deposits. It would all be settled quickly, wise heads in the North agreed.

In Sangerfield and Waterville public rallies were held and volunteers eagerly enlisted. Many who did so did not necessarily support the abolition of slavery, but did believe that no state had the right to secede. The war, then, was not about slavery as much as it was about preserving the Union. The first regiment of Oneida County troops was ready to leave on May 17, and a second regiment left four days later.

In Madison County parades and meetings were held in most villages, with smartly-clad military men and local dignitaries presiding. A large rally was held at Hamilton on April 23, and six days later the first Madison County contingent left. On May 16 a second company, departing from Peterboro, was addressed by Gerrit Smith who was slowly resuming public appearances following his stay in the Lunatic Asylum. The war was justified because the government must be upheld, Smith insisted. He described himself as a man of peace except when circumstances necessitated bellicose actions; "I have never spoken against putting down traitors," he said. The North must protect itself against "domestic traitors and pirates" who would overthrow it, "for although the passions, prejudices, and perverseness of men beget many forms of insanity, Southern slavery only is capable of driving millions to the mad work of violently overthrowing a government whose partiality toward them and indulgence of them are the only wrong it has done them." Four months later Smith published one of his speeches entitled "No Terms with Traitors" in which he urged "not one word of peace, nor one leaf of the olive-branch, nor one concession however small to the rebels as long as they are rebels." Impressed, Colonel S. T. Smith of the Union Army wrote Gerrit Smith asking for one thousand dollars so that a regiment could be recruited consisting only of soldiers with the last name of Smith; it would be known as the Smith Legion.

One of the earliest volunteers for service in New York State was a thirty-three-year-old engineer named Ely S. Parker. He had trained at Rensselaer Polytechnic Institute in Troy and supervised improvements on the Erie Canal. When war broke out

Parker was working as a federal engineer in Galena, Illinois, where he had become close friends with a clerk in the local hardware store. The clerk's name was Ulysses S. Grant, and he had been a Captain in the Army when he had resigned abruptly in 1854 for drinking on duty; ironically his letter of resignation had been officially accepted by the then Secretary of War, Jefferson Davis.

Both Grant and Parker decided to help the Union, and Grant was given his commission back without difficulty. Parker, however, was told he was not needed. The problem was that Ely Parker had another name, having been known as Hasanoanda by his Seneca Indian brethren. He had initially studied law but was then told that he could not take the New York State Bar exam because he was an Indian. So he went to college, became an engineer, and had been hired by the government. He had kept in close touch with the remnants of the Senecas in western New York, often speaking out against the theft of their lands by the state, and had been elected Grand Sachem of the tribe.

Parker went to Albany and offered to raise a regiment of Seneca and other Iroquois Indians to fight in the Union Army. The Indians would not be needed he was told; they were not eligible for commissions. Undiscouraged, Parker went to Washington to offer his services as an engineer to the War Department. Through Grant's influence Parker was able to talk to Secretary of State William H. Seward who told him flatly: "The Civil War is a white man's war. Go home, cultivate your farm, and we will settle our troubles without any Indian aid." Seward himself had publicly urged the appropriation of more Indian land for settlers, and viewed the Indians as impediments to civilization. A few Northerners urged a more pragmatic approach and argued for using anybody who would fight. Gerrit Smith was one of these: "Common sense teaches us that we should get the Negro to help us if we can, and the Indian also if we can, and the devil himself if we can. I would that we could succeed in getting our harness upon his back and in making him work for us . . . To serve so good a cause as ours would improve even so bad a character as the devil's." In the South, by contrast, many Indians had become slaveholders and were viewed from the outset as valuable allies. Treaties were negotiated between the Confederate government and the Choctaws, Chickasaws, Creeks, Seminoles and Cherokees and these Indians agreed to raise four regiments to fight against the Union.

The Loomis family had six healthy sons between the ages of twenty-five and forty-two when the War began but none of them ever served. It was claimed that Plumb tried to enlist but was turned down by army physicians "because of a bad heart." Since he had already distinguished himself in numerous brawls and midnight raids on neighboring pastures, the purported rejection was regarded with considerable skepticism.

Instead the Loomises turned their bellicose attentions toward Constable Jim Filkins. On May 8, 1962, as the surrounding towns were holding rallies and parades to fill enlistment quotas, Denio Loomis rode up to Filkins' blacksmith shop in North Brookfield with a warrant for his arrest. The papers had been issued by Judge Marsh in Higginsville where Bill Loomis lived and they charged Filkins with assault and battery incurred during one of the raids on the farm. Since the warrant had been issued in Oneida County but served in Madison County, Filkins argued that he had a right to a hearing in the latter.

At that point Wash, Plumb, and Bill Loomis arrived with several members of Filkin's posses shackled in a wagon and said that they were all under arrest. Filkins convinced the Loomises that they should go to the town of Madison to consult with judicial authorities. When Wash instead steered the wagon toward the Loomis farm Filkins jumped to the ground. Grove and Plumb started toward him with clubs but Filkins, armed with a revolver, persuaded them they would have more than assault and battery to worry about if they persisted. As a compromise both sides agreed to go to Waterville. There the magistrate affirmed that Filkins did indeed have the right to examination and bail and ordered the immediate release of Filkins and his men.

Late that night there was a knock on Filkins' door in North Brookfield. Wary of trouble, Filkins asked who was there and was answered by Christopher Mason, an occasional member of his posses. Mason had been a schoolteacher at one time but "had degenerated" under the influence of alcohol. Bribed by the Loomises, Mason had agreed to betray Filkins and when the door was opened to let Mason in Wash, Plumb and Denio Loomis with two other gang members poured through. Filkins fought but had no chance as Wash knocked him down and Denio put handcuffs on him while Filkins' wife and young children screamed in terror. Dumping Filkins into a wagon "in a bruised and bleeding condition," he was "carried over the swamp" to the Loomis home.

Realizing that Mrs. Filkins would summon help, the Loomises

left immediately with their prisoner for Higginsville. Arriving late that night they secured a lawyer to represent Filkins and the next morning went to Judge Marsh's office. Marsh, in the pay of the Loomises, had issued the warrant for Filkins' arrest and now enumerated several more charges against him for crimes said to have been committed in the course of his raids. The intent of the action was to get Filkins jailed for an indefinite period, and for briefly it looked as if the Loomises might be successful. As the magistrate was sorting out the various legal documents, however, a commotion was heard outside the office. A posse of North Brookfield men led by Ephriam Conger had ascertained Filkins' whereabouts and, having ridden most of the night, burst into the room with guns drawn. Filkins should be released on bail they demanded. Judge Marsh looked helplessly at the Loomises, then acknowledged that the visitors' arguments were persuasive and set a modest sum for bail which was immediately paid. Following this incident Filkins obtained indictments in Madison County against the Loomises for assault with a deadly weapon and kidnapping. True to form, however, when the charges finally came to trial Judge Mason, a reliable friend of the Loomises, quashed all but one indictment against Wash. On that charge Wash was found guilty, but Judge Mason dismissed him with a twenty-five dollar fine.

The Loomises' influence over law enforcement officials in Madison County at this time was matched by their control of legal processes in Oneida County. District Attorney Hiram T. Jenkins, who would hold the office for nine yeras from 1859 to 1868, was predictably responsive to Loomis needs. The Oneida County Sheriff was Hugh Crocker who had held the job from 1852 to 1855 and was sheriff again from 1861 to 1864. Crocker was described as "one of Utica's most active and shrewd businessmen" who was "a butcher by trade . . . genial and pleasant in manner and accommodating with all his patrons." Once elected, Sheriff Crocker's patrons included the Loomis family.

An example of Oneida County justice occurred in July, 1861. District Attorney Jenkins' office was a small building in the corner of his yard and the key to the door "hung conveniently nearby" as it had for many years. During the night of July 14 the office was entered by someone who knew where the key hung; two bushels of legal papers were removed, including thirty-eight indictments outstanding against the Loomises. Several of Jenkins' personal papers were also taken including mortgages and bonds. Rather than attempting to prosecute the Loomises for the theft, Jenkins offered Wash Loomis two hundred and fifty dollars for the return of all papers except the indictments and Wash agreed. The Loomises had learned that not only could they destroy indictments with impunity, but they could get paid for doing so.

Meanwhile the news from Washington was not good for a war which was supposed to have been over within three months. The thirty-seventh Congress convened on July 4 and Roscoe Conkling took an active role in passing legislation necessary to finance Union forces. Conkling showed a good understanding of the issues, rising in Congress to note: "I believe every gentleman in this House understands that war is not a question of valor, but a question of money; that it is not regulated by the laws of honor, but by the laws of trade." For his part Conkling was "ready to vote all the money needed to throttle rebellion, to trample to death this painted lizard called secession."

On July 21, while Congress was discussing the financing legislation, the first battle of the War took place at a railroad junction just west of Washington. It was widely believed when the Union troops filed out of Washington that they were marching to glory to crush the southern insurrection once and for all. The various Union militia regiments each wore its own uniform; a New York regiment calling itself the Highlanders wore kilts for dress parade while other regiments wore "gaudy clothing patterned after the French Zouaves—baggy red breeches, short blue coats, yellow or scarlet sashes about the waist, turbans or fezzes for the head." The populace of Washington caught the festive spirit and accompanied the troops toward Bull Run "in carriages, wagons, buggies and on horseback" bringing with them "hampers of food and drink" with which to picnic while watching the rout of the Rebels.

It did not work out that way, and history was to label the day's events as "the momentous fight of the amateurs, the battle where everything went wrong, the great day of awakening for the whole nation." The Union troops did everything they could to break through Confederate lines but the South stood firm, led by General Thomas J. Jackson whose refusal to yield ground in the battle earned him the sobriquet "Stonewall." By late afternoon Union forces had been turned back but as they started for Washington the civilians who had come to watch blocked the roads with their conveyances "creating the father and mother of all traffic jams."

Stray shells and rumors that the confederate cavalry was in pursuit produced increasing panic so that Union soldiers began dropping their weapons and running toward Washington; "Before dark there was complete and unregimented chaos spilling all over the landscape, and hardly anyone who could move at all stopped moving until he had reached the Potomac River." Almost three thousand Northerners had been killed, wounded, or were missing in battle, including many from Madison County such as Captain Otis Tillinghast who had been a graduate of West Point.

Bull Run might have been rationalized as an aberration and forgotten had it not been followed by Balls' Bluff in October. On a steeply wooded hillside thirty miles up the Potomac River from Washington, Union troops under the leadership of Colonel Edward Baker attacked Confederate positions and were beaten back. When Colonel Baker was killed his troops panicked, spilling over the steep cliffs into the water, fighting for positions in boats until they capsized, and retreating in a disorderly rout. Union dead numbered almost eight hundred compared to only forty-eight Confederates.

Colonel Baker had been a prominent Senator before the War and his death awakened Congress to the true magnitude of the task before them. Representative Roscoe Conkling rose to ask for an official investigation of Ball's Bluff, the "event which I believe to be the most atrocious military murder ever committed in our history as a people . . . a blunder so gross all men can see it." When colleagues demurred, saying that such an investigation might undermine respect for Union commanders, Conkling replied:

> "Shall we proclaim indulgence for ignorance and incompetency, immunity for barbarous negligence, silence for military crimes, even though a revelation of the truth would soil the glittering plumage of the highest officer in the armies of the republic? No, sir: whoever is responsible for that fatal field, if he yet lives, ought to be nightly on his knees imploring forgiveness for the mighty murder he there committed."

A Joint Committee on the Conduct of the War was in fact set up, and President Lincoln appointed General George B. McClellan as general-in-chief to replace the aging General Winfield Scott.

Conkling had become a leading hawk in urging vigorous

persecution of the war, and he traveled throughout central New York speaking at rallies. His flamboyant style attracted much public notice, and a regiment from Boonville named themselves the Conkling Rifles. Conkling's political opponents asked why he himself, only thirty-two years old had not enlisted and called him "invincible in peace and invisible in war." Conkling's brother, Frederick, also a member of Congress from New York at this time, had organized a regiment of New York Volunteers and was serving as a colonel. On one occasion when Roscoe Conkling was publicly accused of doing nothing except talking he replied: "I am a workingman, and earn my bread by the sweat of my brow. It does not seem to me that it makes any difference whether this perspiration is on the outside or inside of my head."

Despite Congressional responsibilities Conkling continued to actively practice law in Utica between sessions of Congress. In August, 1861, he defended the Reverend Henry Budge in a sensational murder case in which the minister was accused of slitting the throat of his wife with a straight razor. Conkling, making the argument for suicide, "hired a New York City pathologist as tutor, procured a serviceable cadaver, and went to work to learn anatomy . . . With this new knowledge, Conkling was able to conduct a withering cross-examination of the prosecution's star witness, the doctor, destroying his testimony in a taut confrontation . . . his command of medical jargon was perfect; as a result his overpowering closing speech won an acquittal."

Roscoe Conkling drew more public notice in central New York in October, 1861, when he defended Jim Filkins. The Loomises, determined to get Filkins out of office, had brought new charges against him for assault and battery incurred during one of his raids, and a Madison County judge on good terms with the Loomis family had agreed to bring Filkins to trial. A conviction against Filkins, Wash Loomis reasoned, would thoroughly discredit him and render him ineffectual as a lawman. The prosecutor for Madison County who would argue the case against Filkins was David Mitchell from the village of Hamilton, a man known for his long hair and flamboyant style. Filkins, realizing the consequences of losing such a case, asked Roscoe Conkling to defend him. Conkling was awaiting the reconvening of Congress slated for December 1 and agreed to help Filkins whom he respected for standing up to the Loomises. It would not be the last time that Conkling would come to Jim Filkins' defense in a time of need.

The trial took place in Morrisville and was well attended.

Mitchell eloquently expounded the merits of the Loomis family whom he portrayed as "a noble people incapable of crime who were continually being persecuted" and bullied by Filkins. Mitchell overplayed his hand; his description of the Loomises as law-abiding citizens was so absurd that both courtroom spectators and members of the jury laughed outright. Roscoe Conkling defended Filkins as courageously standing up to an outlaw family which had corrupted justice as they plundered the surrounding farms and villages. Filkins and his deputies were acquitted on all counts, and following the verdict Roscoe Conkling announced: "We have met the Lion of Madison County, the Honorable Mr. Mitchell. He has shaken his mane and threshed his tail, but all of his words were to no avail."

During the later months of 1861, the local activity of the Loomises was sharply increased. No longer concerned about indictments, "the newspapers listed burglaries and robberies daily." Homes were broken into, stores cleaned out, and highway robbery became commonplace. The price of hops was high so large sums of money were circulating in the community. On October 15, Mr. Waldo of Waterville was robbed just outside the village. On October 30, Albert Steele's residence in Bridgewater was burglarized with the loss of two thousand five hundred dollars in notes. On November 10, in South Brookfield, thieves entered the home and office of Judge Ira Crandall, stealing legal records and indictments and even taking a watch from next to Crandall's bed as he slept. On November 21, Menzo Cole of Deansboro was stopped on the road, beaten unconscious, and robbed of nineteen hundred dollars which he had just received for selling his hops. Not all thefts in the area were the work of the Loomises, of course, but most were assumed to be so.

In late 1861 events in the Loomis homestead took a nasty turn which surprised even those grown accustomed to their depredations. Two years earlier Wash Loomis had met Hannah Wright, the daughter of a farmer living near Bill in Higginsville, and had persuaded her to come and live with him. Wash was aware of his mother's fierce opposition to permanent liasons between her sons and their women friends, but Wash, age thirty-eight, was interested in settling down and raising his own family.

From the beginning Rhoda Loomis opposed Hannah, treating her as a servant and doing everything she could to drive her away. Rhoda's opposition increased sharply in 1860 when Hannah became pregnant with Wash's child. A son was born on February

10, 1861, and named Grove Loomis, Jr. after Wash's brother. Wash was away frequently on business and during those periods Hannah had to endure harassment from Rhoda as well as from Plumb and Denio who could be counted on to do their mother's bidding. Those who knew the Loomises well were aware of the increasing tension in the family as Wash's determination to achieve autonomy clashed with Rhoda's resolution to regnancy.

On November 25, 1861, young Grove Loomis Jr. was crawling about the house and Wash had left for an extended trip to Albany and Vermont. Thomas Mott, a gang member who frequently stayed with the Loomises and who was considered to be one of the least scrupulous, entered the kitchen where Hannah was working. Mott carried a double-barreled rifle which was fully loaded. Pretending to be cleaning the barrel, he waited until Hannah was in front of the fireplace, then "accidently" dropped the rifle into the fire causing it to explode. One ball struck Hannah in the thigh causing much pain and bleeding. The *Utica Morning Herald* reported the accident took place when Mott was "cleaning the gun and not knowing it was loaded, put it in the fire to warm it" but everyone knew the truth. Hannah's leg became infected, developed gangrene and she died December 8. No charges were filed, but Mott left immediately to join the Union army before Wash Loomis returned. He was later said to have confided to a friend that he had been paid fifty dollars by Plumb and Denio Loomis to arrange Hannah's "accident."

Wash, still away when Hannah died, received word of the tragedy from a messenger sent by Grove. There was no doubt in his mind, nor anyone else' mind, about Rhoda's role in the affair. Wash had to decide whether to break with his family and leave home, or resume his role as Loomis son and gang leader. Rhoda, almost seventy years old, could not be expected to live much longer and that fact presumably helped Wash make his decision. When Wash returned home he never mentioned Hannah or the "accident," but immediately took young Grove Jr. to the North Brookfield home of Richard Gorton and his wife, who were related to Hannah, to be raised by them. According to a newspaper account Wash asked the Gortons to rear Grove Jr. "in utter ignorance of his parentage, and teach him to call them by the endearing title of father and mother, promising at the same time to aid and assist them in providing for the child."

Hannah's death seriously exacerbated the existing divisions in the Loomis family. Grove and Bill supported Wash even more strongly, while Cornelia, Plumb and Denio allied themselves with Rhoda. Wheeler, as usual, shifted between factions as it suited his needs. Wash resumed his titular leadership but it was not the same; all trust had disappeared and the family was held tenuously together by the common goal of avarice and the common threat of Jim Filkins. Wash would wait patiently for Rhoda to die and would never again trust her.

Discouraged by attempts to get Jim Filkins jailed, in early 1862 the Loomises decided on a new strategy. As a constable Filkins was an elected official, and up for re-election in March. The Loomises set about insuring his defeat by bribing, cajoling, threatening, and persuading the inhabitants of North Brookfield that it was time for a new constable. When election day came and the votes were tallied Filkins had lost by three votes and was no longer constable. The Loomises celebrated; they had found yet another way to remove interference to their operations.

North Brookfield was not the only local town controlled by the Loomises at this time. Sangerfield was even more of a Loomis stronghold, and Filkins claimed that "he could enumerate seventy persons in the town of Sangerfield alone who are either affiliated with the Loomises or stood ready to harbor or bail them. Many were land holders and nearly all were of fair standing in the community." Waterville, on the other hand, had continued to grow as a center of opposition to the gang; W. J. Bissell provided daily exhortations against them in his store and the *Waterville Times* printed anti-Loomis comments in almost every weekly edition.

Bissell and other community leaders in Waterville were angered when they heard that the townspeople of North Brookfield had voted Filkins out of office. In Bissell's store a plan evolved which led to a committee, and then to a formal proposal to Filkins. The citizens of Waterville would like to have Filkins as their constable, they said, if the blacksmith would agree to move to their village so that he would be eligible to hold office. Filkins, anxious to continue his fight against the Loomises, agreed to do so if the business leaders would pledge to fully back a campaign to drive the Loomises out altogether. The pledge was made and one of the two existing constables agreed to vacate his office. Filkins moved to Waterville, was unanimously nominated by both parties, and in a special election became a Waterville constable five weeks after his defeat in North Brookfield. The Loomises were furious, and Denio publicly vowed to shoot

Filkins if he ever came onto their land again. The battle had escalated.

The decision by Waterville business leaders to back a campaign to clean out the Loomises was symptomatic of a growing undercurrent in the community. It was as if the Civil War to the south had reversed normal small-town reticence to interfere in the affairs of neighbors. The trend had been heralded in October, 1861, when Edward Eastman and Edward Montgomery stopped at the American Hotel in Waterville for drinks. Returning to their horse and buggy, they discovered a valuable fur laprobe missing. Inquiries revealed that Loomis gang member Ezra Beebe had been seen in the vicinity of the buggy and Montgomery vowed to get the robe back. "I don't think you'll have much success," Bill Benedict, one of the town constables told him. "Maybe not but remember, Bill, it's a dark night. It might be lighter before I arrive home." That night Ezra Beebe's barn, over the hill from the Loomis farm, burned to the ground. As the barn went down several pistols fell out of holes in the side where they had been secreted. They were later identified as having been stolen from a machine shop which had been robbed in Utica.

It was shortly after this that Wash Loomis walked into Squire Phitt's hotel near Hamilton and spotted Fred Hall, one of Jim Filkins' most reliable posse members. Wash, still recovering from Hannah's death, had become more overtly aggressive and pointed angrily toward Hall: "I'm going to teach you to come to our house with that damned Filkins." Hall picked up a chair to defend himself and waited for Wash's advance. "I'll have no brawling in here," Phitts announced, but Wash continued toward Hall. "I told you I'd have no brawling in here," Phitts repeated. "Get out!" Wash continued forward, pushing past Phitts but he miscalculated the proprietor's resolution. "You asked for it," said Phitts as his fist caught Wash square in the face. As Loomis staggered backward the Squire leaped after him, caught him by the shirt collar and the seat of the pants, and threw him out into the road. "Don't come in here again," added Phitts as he threw Wash's coat after him. Word of the confrontation spread up and down the valley rapidly and was repeated to incredulous listeners. Noboby had ever treated Wash Loomis in that manner.

As soon as he had been officially installed as constable in Waterville, Jim Filkins set about his task. As the *Waterville Times* phrased it, Filkins "was this spring chosen to his office because of his supposed competency to look after certain characters in our vicinity, and our citizens are determined to fully sustain him." Filkins obtained a search warrant and in mid-April, 1862, proceeded to the Loomis homestead accompanied by three assistants.

Only Wash and Cornelia were at home, and they received their visitors cordially. Starting in the cellar Filkins searched the house inch by inch without finding any stolen items. Filkins finally proceeded to the attic where, according to the contemporary newspaper account, "a most rigid examination failed to bring forth anything suspicious, until the officer discovered that a portion of the floor board near the chimney had the appearance of having been recently removed. Upon prying these up a dark chasm appeared, the size or form of which was not discernable, but which was declared by Wash to have been made for the purpose of ready access to the chimney in the event of its burning out and endangering the adjoining wood work. The officer went down stairs for a candle with which to make explorations, leaving one assistant with Loomis and his sister. Wash thereupon speedily descended into the vault and threw out two heavily laden bags which he placed away among some feather sacks in a part of the room that had been fully searched, at the same time attempting to induce the assistant not to mention the circumstance. By this time the officer returned with the light, and Loomis conducted him through the vault where of course they found nothing. As they were about to leave the garret, the assistant called the attention of the officer to the bags." Upon emptying them they discovered "a quantity of boots and shoes," six revolvers, and a lap-robe. The boots and shoes were later identified as having been stolen from a store in North Brookfield, the revolvers had been taken from a pistol factory near Utica, and the lap-robe was the one which had been stolen by Ezra Beebe from Edward Montgomery's buggy.

Wash was arrested for grand larceny and taken before Judge Church in Waterville for arraignment. "Why do you bring this infernal scoundrel before me?" Church asked Filkins. "Why don't you hang him?" The hearing was attended by several spectators including a tailor from Leonardsville who had been robbed several months previously. While watching the proceedings the tailor noticed another man wearing one of his coats and apprised Filkins of the fact. Filkins identified the man as George Peckham, a Loomis gang member from Hamilton, and immediately arrested him. Judge Church, meanwhile, set Wash's bail at five hundred dollars. As soon as he had paid it Wash was rearrested on another warrant charging him with receiving stolen goods, and Wash had to pay another five hundred dollars bail to remain at large.

The following day Filkins was again at the Loomises with a search warrant for stolen sheep. As he approached the house "Plumb and Denio mounted their horses and prepared to get away. 'You need not run,' said the constable, 'I have not got a warrant for you.'" Wash again received Filkins with affected politeness: "I didn't expect you to call again so soon." After producing the warrant Filkins proceeded to examine the sheep in the adjoining pasture and picked out those thought to be stolen. Wash appeared shocked. "You know, Jim," Wash said, "there's a damn sight of inequity in this county. John Hall probably stole those sheep and put them in our flock to cast suspicion on me."

Filkins, enjoying his new job, was determined to keep the Loomises so busy in court that they would have no time for further crimes. Obtaining indictments and serving warrants on them became a fulltime job. On one occasion a warrant for Plumb's arrest was being served when he bolted for the swamp. Albert Root, a member of the posse, cornered Plumb and roughly subdued him with a few kicks added for emphasis. Plumb was furious and, when released on bail, immediately brought charges against Root for assault and threatening his life with a gun. Judge Church in Waterville heard the case, as two witnesses took the stand and described the physical beating and the threats against Plumb's life which they had observed. Plumb then described the beating in detail, claiming that he could see the bullets pointing at him from the barrel of Root's revolver. Judge Church looked skeptical and asked to see the revolver in question. "Tell me, Mr. Loomis, looking at this revolver would you tell the Court whether it is loaded or not?" Plumb scrutinized the gun, then answered confidently: "No, it is not loaded." Judge Church opened the gun, let the bullets fall onto the bench, then rapped his gavel: "Case dismissed."

In Bissell's general store in Waterville the daily forays of Jim Filkins into Loomis territory were much discussed. Bissell was proud of his role in having helped recruit Filkins and, despite the fact that most people did not like Filkins personally, they could not help but admire his courage. Hermon Clarke, politely waiting on customers, listened to the stories and the increasingly open talk against the Loomis family.

Between discussions of Filkins and the Loomises in Bissell's store there was always the war. In the spring of 1862, the talk was still of a quick Northern victory, but farmers coming in to buy seeds and townspeople purchasing food or notions said so with less conviction than six months earlier. Skirmishes regularly extended as far as Colorado and New Mexico, and at Shiloh, Tennessee, a furious battle was fought with thirteen thousand Union casualties. Among the captured Confederate troops was young Henry M. Stanley, seeking fame with an Arkansas regiment; he would achieve it later in Africa seeking explorer David Livingstone. The battle of the two ironclads off the coast of Virginia was also of great interest, the "Monitor" looking like "a tin can on a shingle" and the "Merrimac" like "a barn gone adrift and submerged to the eaves." After hours of mutual broadsides, at times touching each other, both retreated with relatively little damage.

Most attention, however, focused on the action taking place between Washington and Richmond. General McClellan had gathered over one hundred thousand Union troops and was moving inexorably toward the Confederate capital. Yorktown yielded, then Williamsburg, and by May 20, McClellan was within eight miles of Richmond; many persons evacuated the city including the wife of President Jefferson Davis. For a few tantalizing weeks it looked as if the war would be over.

McClellan, however, never made the decision to undertake a final assault on Richmond. Instead he kept asking for more troops despite the overwhelming numerical superiority he already possessed. According to one historian McClennan "always saw a larger Confederate army over the hill somewhere between himself and Richmond. He held on to these delusions even when scouting reports indicated the contrary" . . . he was "one of the strangest military figures of our history." President Lincoln, thoroughly exasperated by him, said that "sending reinforcements to Mc-Clellan is like shovelling flies across a barn."

It was at this time that Julia Ward Howe, wife of the man who had been one of John Brown's staunchest supporters, visited Washington. From her window in the Willard Hotel she could hear Union troops marching along Pennsylvania Avenue as they prepared to join McClellan's forces. In the two years since his death John Brown had become a martyr and symbol of Northern resolution, and Union troops marched to verses of what had become a familiar chant:

> John Brown's body lies a-mould'ring in the grave,
> John Brown's body lies a-mould'ring in the grave,
> John Brown's body lies a-mould'ring in the grave,
> His soul goes marching on!
>
> Glory, glory! Hallelujah!
> Glory, glory! Hallelujah!
> Glory, glory! Hallelujah!
> His soul is marching on!
>
> He captured Harper's Ferry with his nineteen men so true
> And he frightened old Virginia till she trembled through
>     and through
> They hung him for a traitor, themselves the traitor crew,
> But his soul is marching on!
>                                             Chorus.
>
> John Brown died that the slave might be free,
> John Brown died that the slave might be free,
> John Brown died that the slave might be free,
> And his soul is marching on!
>                                             Chorus.
>
> The stars of Heaven are looking kindly down,
> The stars of Heaven are looking kindly down,
> The stars of Heaven are looking kindly down,
> On the grave of old John Brown.
>                                             Chorus.
>
> Now has come the glorious jubilee,
> Now has come the glorious jubilee,
> Now has come the glorious jubilee,
> When all mankind are free.
>                                             Chorus.

Mrs. Howe was troubled by the image of John Brown, whom she
had known well, being used to march into battle so she sat down
and composed what seemed to her verses more appropriate for
the marching song:

> Mine eyes have see the glory of the coming of the Lord;
> He is trampling out the vintage where the grapes of wrath
>     are stored;
> He hath loosed the fateful lightning of His terrible swift sword;
> His truth is marching on.
>
> Glory, glory, Hallelujah!
> Glory, glory, Hallelujah!
> Glory, glory, Hallelujah!
> His truth is marching on.

It was called the "Battle Hymn of the Republic" and she sold it to the *Atlantic Monthly* for four dollars.

General McClellan's army never got closer to Richmond than eight miles. As the spring sun dried Virginia's fields, General Robert E. Lee took command of Southern forces and began an offensive. While General J.E.B. Stuart dazzled Northerners with cavalry sorties, and General Stonewall Jackson harrassed Union forces to the west, Lee began a Seven-Day Campaign which pushed McClellan north. It was expensive, costing twenty thousand Confederate casualties to sixteen thousand for the Union, but Richmond had been saved.

President Lincoln was deeply disappointed by the failure of McClellan's campaign and immediately issued a call for more troops. In Utica a large rally to support the war was held on July 14 and this was followed by smaller rallies in almost every village in Central New York; Sangerfield on July 24, Morrisville on July 29, Peterboro on August 7, etc. The rallies were advertised to "express undiminished confidence in the justice of our cause" and featured local leaders and elected officials as speakers; Roscoe Conkling and Gerrit Smith both participated. Referring to the Confederate enemy as well as to Northerners who were undermining Union efforts, Conkling noted that "there is a multitude of harpies, which no man can number, preying upon the vitals of the Commonwealth." Young men were urged to enlist in the cause to save the Union and money was raised to pay enlistment bonuses. Such bonuses averaged about fifty dollars a person at the time, but since pay in the Army was only fifteen dollars a month the bonus was a major incentive.

At the Sangerfield rally the enlistment quota was met without difficulty. One of the volunteers was Hermon Clarke who decided his country needed him; he did not care much for President Lincoln nor about the plight of slaves, but he believed strongly that the nation must remain one. Mr. Bissell said he would be sorely missed at the store but assured him his apron and job would be waiting when he had put the Confederates in their place. On Monday morning, August 4, Hermon Clarke joined thirty-five other young men at the American Hotel in Waterville and, to the music of the Waterville Brass Band and the Sangerfield Drum Corps, they went off to war.

The departure of increasing numbers of young men from villages like Sangerfield, Waterville and North Brookfield became more noticeable as the weeks passed. Women and children had to assume more responsibility for the harvest, especially hops which had to be picked at precisely the right time. Energies went into maintaining farms, with no manpower left over to clear new fields, dig new wells, or plant new orchards. Occasional voices began to be raised in the North wondering whether the war was worth it all. On July 30, 1862, a Cincinnati newspaper first used the term "Copperhead" to denote northern Democrats who were questioning the war; the name derived from the Indian heads cut from copper pennies which they wore in their lapels.

Hermon Clarke and his group joined other Oneida County recruits at Rome and, after brief training, the regiment proceeded to Washington. The city was in chaos at the time with General Lee threatening it with Confederate forces while internally crime was so rampant that a special police force had been established. "In 1862 that force made 22,207 arrests, most for disorderly conduct, petty larceny and prostitution. Politicians and city officials inevitably blamed [Negroes] but the fact is that far more Irish were arrested than Negroes."

Clarke's company was assigned to a small fort on bluffs overlooking the Potomac River just north of Chain Bridge, and from there he wrote home regularly. "The river is beautiful below us," he wrote his family, "and the sunsets are splendid. The Ohio and Chesapeake Canal runs by here under the hill, on which the rebels lately fired into a boat or two."

Hermon Clarke had been in camp only a few days when he wrote that "we heard cannonading in the direction of Manassas and beyond the Chain Bridge. It ceased during the night, but began furiously at daybreak yesterday morning. It was a continual boom, boom, boom, all day till dark, and you have probably ere this received the particulars of a terrible battle between Jackson and our army." General John Pope and his Union forces had become entangled between Lee and Jackson's Confederate forces at the Second Battle of Bull Run. The North suffered fifteen thousand casualties in defeat and Hermon Clarke wrote of seeing "long lines of soldiers passing along the roads in their retreat from Manassas . . . thousands of them have encamped for several days immediately opposite us . . . The city has been in a perfect fever. Union families were hurrying across the Chain Bridge while we were there to escape rebeldom."

There was talk that Jackson and Lee were preparing to attack Washington when Hermon Clarke wrote that "we have slept on our arms for several nights in consequence of the rumor of rebels crossing the river above us . . . Our guns from the three forts bear on the fords and shallow places near where Jackson is by some expected to cross." Jackson's forces in fact had gone to Harpers Ferry, capturing an immense cache of Union equipment, while Lee's forces were moving toward Antietam. There, on September 17, Northern forces confronted him in what would be the bloodiest single day of the war—twelve thousand casualties on each side.

At Bissell's general store the daily casualty list in the *Utica Morning Herald* was scanned and Hermon Clarke's letters read; the men wondered aloud what had gone wrong. In late May Richmond was about to fall but now, less than four months later, the Confederate Army was threatening Washington. According to one historian "never before or afterward was the Confederacy so near to victory as it was in the middle of September, 1862." Abroad, the English and French followed the fortunes of the South with great interest and wondered whether it might be time to recognize the Confederacy's independence. William E. Gladstone, Chancellor of the Exchequer, made a public recommendation to his English colleagues on October 7: "There is no doubt that Jefferson Davis and other leaders of the South have made an army; they are making, it appears, a navy; and they have made what is more than either—they have made a nation. We may anticipate with certainty the success of the Southern States so far as regards their separation from the North."

Following Antietam, anti-war sentiment in the North became more audible. In New York State the leading Copperhead was Horatio Seymour, Roscoe Conkling's brother-in-law who was campaigning to regain the governorship. Seymour believed that states had the right to secede from the Union and "honestly thought that the war was a ghastly mistake." Conkling remained a leading war hawk and publicly called Copperheads "hypocrites" and a "swarm of sharks and pestilent beings." Such divisions within families were not uncommon; Stonewall Jackson's sister worked for the Union and sent a message to her brother saying that she would "take care of wounded Federals as fast as brother Thomas would wound them," and Mary Todd Lincoln had four brothers fighting for the Confederacy.

As the 1862 elections approached they increasingly took on the mantle of a referendum on the War. Northerners were growing tired of promises followed by defeats, promises followed by lengthening death lists, and promises followed by rising prices and taxes. The Republicans and Roscoe Conkling were associated with these, while Democrats like Seymour promised peace. Conkling campaigned hard to retain his seat in Congress but the mood of Oneida County was moving against him. Conkling's problems were exacerbated by the increasingly open rift with his influential brother-in-law, a rift made worse by Conkling's polite estrangement from his wife, Julia, and increasingly public proclivities for other women. Conkling's acerbic style had also earned him enemies within the Republican ranks in Oneida County, enemies whose opposition to Conkling was characterized by the *Utica Herald* as "personal in the lowest and meanest sense." Together Roscoe Conkling's political liabilities exceeded his assets in late 1862, and when the votes were counted on November 4, Conkling had lost his seat in Congress to Democrat Francis Kernan, the man who had taught him law, by ninety-eight votes. Horatio Seymour and many other Democrats won handily as voters registered their disgust with the War.

President Lincoln heard the message clearly and the following day removed General George McClellan. General Ambrose E. Burnside was given command of the Army of the Potomac and immediately directed them south toward Richmond. On December 13, Burnside's 106,000 troops met Stonewall Jackson's 72,000 Confederates at Fredericksburg and suffered a humiliating Union defeat—12,700 dead and wounded for the North compared with 5,300 casualties for the South. Some Union Army units mutinied as rumors abounded that Lincoln's entire cabinet was about to resign.

Hermon Clarke remained optimistic although his letters home to Waterville reflected the increasingly harsh conditions of the winter. He mentioned meat which had become rank, worms in the bread, and six inches of snow which "drifted around the tents making it somewhat cool for those who slept on the outside." On December 28, following the humiliating defeat of the Union Army at Fredericksburg, he wrote home as follows:

> "Yesterday afternoon I went over towards the Capitol to a hospital. They had just buried 14 men that died the day before. There were five in the dead house that had died since morning. There were 250 arrived at that hospital yesterday morning from Fredericksburg, and there was a large dry goods box full of feet and hands they had taken off from the wounded. That will made one homesick if anything will."

# CHAPTER VIII

# Rape

If the war was going poorly for Hermon Clarke and the Union Army, it was going very well for the Loomis family. Clarke and his fellow soldiers from Waterville were aware of events at home for their families wrote them the details; even Mr. Bissell had written Hermon in November, 1862, telling him how much he was missed in the store and giving him the latest news on Jim Filkins' pursuit of the Loomises.

The market for stolen horses had never been better. The Confederate cavalry consistently outshone the Union whose losses of men and horses grew daily. In a single raid in October, 1862, General J.E.B. Stuart had stolen five hundred Union horses near Chambersburg, Pennsylvania, and driven them behind Confederate lines. Prices paid by the Union for horses rose weekly, and Central New York's newspapers reflected the Loomises' response to the market:

> January 30, 1863: "On Friday night last Charles Champ-
> lin's horse was stolen from the Central Hotel in Utica.
> Suspecting that the thief was a member of the Loomis gang,
> he went to a livery and procured a fast horse and a com-
> panion and started southward. Losing track, he went to
> Waterville and procured the services of dare-devil Con-
> stable Filkins. The party finally started for Wash Loomis'
> house, being reinforced by two other plucky men, making
> four in all. Arriving in the night they were stationed at the
> four doors of the house, the Constable at the front one. He

125

made a vigorous knocking which was soon replied to by
Wash Loomis, from an upper window, yelling out, 'What in
hell is wanted?' He was told that he had better come down
and open the door or it would be smashed in. Down went
the window, and while waiting for the door to be opened,
the Constable thought it a good opportunity to look around
the concern and accordingly he went to the barn, and was
about to open the door, when up went the window again,
and Wash yelled out, 'What in damnation do you want
there? I have a stallion there worth $7,000, and he is all
perspiring, and I have just had him out exercising him—
don't open that door.' In a moment after, Wash rushed out
of the house with a big club, followed by another man with a
gun, and still another man with a pistol. They made directly
for the Constable, who warned them not to strike or fire a
shot, or he would blow their brains out. Wash then made a
break for Charley [Champlin], and wanted to know who he
was, and what was his business. Charley told him his name,
when he was immediately recognized by Wash, who said:
'Do you suppose I would harbor anything of yours? Why we
used to go to school together, but I can tell you where your
horse is. The fellow who has it, is a fool; he can steal, but he
don't know how to hide. He lives in the second house, away
down the road.' The detectives immediately went to the
house, knocked the door down, and took the fellow out of
bed. They went to the barn and found the horse about used
up and the sleigh buried under a snow bank."

—*Utica Telegraph*

February 6, 1863: "Oscar Babcock, residing two miles east
of Sangerfield Center on the turnpike, had a horse, cutter,
and harness stolen on Sunday last. The animal was a dark
brown mare, a smallish pony with left hind foot white, scar
under the fetlock of right hind foot four inches long, a part
of mane short, star in forehead, switch tail, and will be five
years old in the spring. The cutter was old-fashioned, swell-
body, one front panel broke in and the dash broke off,
yellow running part striped with black, brown box striped
with red. A reward of fifty dollars is offered for the return of
the property and conviction of the thief; or twenty-five
dollars will be paid for the return of the property stolen."

—*Waterville Times*

May 28, 1863: "The horse which was stolen about two weeks ago from Mr. George A. Peck of Marshall has been recovered through the energy and shrewdness of Officer Filkins. The horse was stolen by two young men, supposed to have been Jack Keenan and Laverne Beebe, both well-known as thieves [and Loomis gang members] . . . They were tracked for some distance by Filkins and were found to have traded the horse off at Pittsfield, Otsego County to one E. Van Etting, a Yankee notions peddler, who gave them $30 to boot. Peddler then tracked about 100 miles in direction of Deposit and was located on last Thursday afternoon at Franklyn, Delaware County with the horse, which was identified and given up."

*—Waterville Times*

July 3, 1863: "The notorious Bill Loomis of Oneida County was arrested at his home last Sunday night by Deputy Sheriff Matthews of Canton, St. Lawrence County, on a charge of stealing a horse from a man in Canton. The sheriff with his prisoner stayed at the Bostwick House, Lowville, last Monday night and on Tuesday morning went on their way to Canton. Loomis made considerable resistance when arrested, fighting until he was overcome by the superior strength of the sheriff."

*—Lowville Journal*

On one occasion a sheriff followed Big Bill Rockwell leading a string of stolen horses from the Finger Lakes region to Nine Mile Swamp. Another gang member was trailed to Vermont and arrested, and still another was arrested and jailed in Illinois.

An increasingly common means used by the Loomises to dispose of the stolen horses was to take them to Higginsville, load them on Bill Alvord's "thief boats" in the Sidecut Canal, and send them down the Erie Canal where they were sold in Albany to Union Army buyers. On the routes to northern Pennsylvania and southern Ontario the Loomises stole and sold horses with virtual impunity, for many of the judges and law enforcement officials were on their payroll. The Loomises were now regularly stealing the same horse two or more times, selling it to a farmer and returning a few nights later to steal it again and sell it farther down the road.

As Hermon Clarke and his fellow soldiers from Waterville read their mail it was not the Loomis' horse stealing which made them most angry. The truly odious activity from their point of view was encouraging and sheltering deserters from the Union Army. Desertions were common on both sides during the Civil War, averaging about ten percent of the troops. The rate varied widely from regiment to regiment and was a source of great embarrassment. On November 4, 1862, the *Utica Daily Observer* published the names of thirty-six soldiers who had "skedaddled," as it was called, from Clarke's Oneida County regiment.

The Loomises both encouraged deserters and provided them with shelter. For example in September, 1862, Ezra Beebe met two young soldiers from Brookfield in a Waterville saloon and persuaded them to desert to work for the Loomises. He would hide them, he promised, on his farm and they would make a lot of money. Approximately two weeks later Jim Filkins tracked Jack Keenan, another gang member, to Beebe's farm. Entering the house by the back door early in the morning "he discovered Beebe and Keenan sound asleep" and "had handcuffs on their exposed wrists before they leaped up." Upstairs Filkins found the two deserters. Filkins returned to Waterville with all four prisoners in tow.

The extent to which the Loomises were harboring deserters became clear in February, 1863, when Filkins and three others raided the Loomises looking for stolen horses. According to the *Waterville Times*: "When the loud knocking was made on the door, there was a great stamping and shuffling heard inside, and on looking in the window no less than a dozen deserters were discovered with military clothes upon them, and Wash himself was afterwards seen with a soldier's overcoat on. The house is evidently a rendezvous for these scamps, and it were well if the locality could be rummaged, and a lot of these worse than rebels arrested." Later in 1863 Grove Loomis was arrested and indicted for "harboring, concealing and employing deserters"; as usual, however, he was released on bail and the charges eventually dropped.

The problem of deserters was widely discussed in central New York at this time. Roscoe Conkling, having returned to Utica and his private law practice following the adjournment of the thirty-seventh Congress, was appointed by the federal government to prosecute a deserter named Charles Hobson. Hobson claimed that states' rights took precedent over federal rights and that he therefore could not be prosecuted by the federal government. The case was of national interest because of its implications for state and federal legal jurisdiction and it went to court in July, 1863. Conkling disliked deserters almost as much as he disliked Copperheads, and argued eloquently for the federal prerogative. Conkling won, and deserters and those who harbored them were put on notice.

Conkling accepted defeat for re-election in 1862 as a temporary setback in his political career. Anticipating the 1864 congressional elections, he saw only one man, Erastus Clark, as a potential rival for the Republican nomination. Calling in one of his many political debts, Conkling approached the secretary of state of New York and suggested that Clark be appointed to a high position in Albany therefore removing Clark from Utica. The secretary of state agreed, and in his memoirs recorded Conkling's profuse thanks: "Sir, a thing that is quickly done is doubly done. Hereafter, as long as you and I both live, there never will be a deposit in any bank, personally, politically, or financially to my credit which will not be subject to your draft." Conkling had formalized the separation from his wife at this time, having bought her a large house overlooking Utica while he continued living in a room at the Baggs Hotel.

At the Loomis homestead the estrangement between Wash Loomis and his mother had also been formalized. Wash, Grove and Bill increasingly operated independently and at a distance, most of their energies concentrated on the thriving horse-stealing operations. Most thefts took place many miles from the homestead where Wash's success in bribing local law officers was becoming legendary. Rhoda, by contrast, used Plumb and Denio to work with gang members in surrounding towns, stealing from homes and stores and occasionally robbing wayfarers. It was as if there were now two Loomis gangs, and on any given day one often did not know what the other one was doing.

Jim Filkins continued his campaign against the Loomises during these months but it became increasingly apparent that obtaining indictments was not enough. Wash, for example, had been indicted in April of 1862 for grand larceny and receiving stolen goods. When his trial was scheduled for August Wash's attorney, Daniel C. Pomeroy of Utica, asked District Attorney Hiram T. Jenkins to postpone it:

"Friend Jenkins:
   Will you consent that the indictments against G.W. Loomis go over to the next term of court? I don't believe he

can get ready. Please let me hear from you by return mail.

> Yours truly,
> D.C. Pomeroy"

Friend Jenkins did agree, and then postponed it again until January, 1863. By this time Jenkins had reduced the charges to one count of larceny for stealing revolvers for which the evidence was meager. When the trial finally took place Wash obtained a unanimous verdict of not guilty.

Such miscarriages of justice were discouraging to those trying to bring the Loomises under the law. Legal prosecution, no matter how strong the evidence, appeared to be futile. Because of the war it was also becoming increasingly difficult to raise a posse; there simply were not enough eager young men around willing to risk the Loomis' revenge. Perhaps most discouraging, however, was the increasing fear that the Loomises inspired in their neighbors because of their reputation. "You'll smoke for this" was not an idle threat by the Loomises but meant the loss of a barn by arson. Ephraim Conger learned this after he helped reclaim a stolen wagon from the gang, Morris Terry after he "made disrespectful comments of the Loomis family," and Henry Crandall after he demanded the return of some stolen cows. Arson suspected of being of Loomis origin had become so widespread in the area in 1863 that most men increasingly felt inclined to mind their own business when the name Loomis was mentioned.

Not so the *Waterville Times*, which became progressively more outspoken as the Loomises succeeded in getting one indictment after another quashed. On February 20, 1863, under the caption "Another Theft Traced to the Loomis' Door," it described the theft of merchandise which was "tracked directly to the Loomis' yard where nearly everything that is stolen near here is tracked. For years it has been attempted to bring the gang to justice through process of law but without success. The law proving an utter failure as a means of stopping the depredations and outrages of this vile gang, and no man's life or property being safe while it is within their reach, what is to be done? We think there is but one way to go in order to put a stop to it, which is, to use the California remedy; give them so many hours in which to leave the state, and if not gone at the end of the time specified, a judicious lynching." One week later, under a caption which simply said "As Usual," thefts of an overcoat, buffalo skin and whip were described; they had been taken from a schoolhouse "where a singing school was being held." The thieves were traced to the Loomises. "It is a shame that the scoundrelly gang is permitted to continue their depredations on people as they do. The country ought to be rid of them in *some* manner." The Loomises laughed, and Wash sent a note printed in the *Waterville Times* of March 6 saying: "There is not one word of truth" in the accusations of the paper.

Sentiment in the North for abandoning the war increased significantly in early 1863. General Burnside, trying to restore morale following the Fredericksburg defeat, decided to lead Union forces across the Rappahannock River in a surprise attack on General Lee's left flank. Three days of steady January rain turned the unpaved roads into a sea of mud and Burnside's forces ground to an ignominious halt. One officer in the "Mud March," as it would be known, issued a request for "50 men 25 feet high to work in mud 18 feet deep." The fiasco was too much for Lincoln who replaced Burnside with General Joseph Hooker. Hooker was a West Point graduate known for his self-confidence and attention to details. He told President Lincoln it was not a question of whether he could take Richmond, but simply when. Later in the war Hooker's provisions for army troops recovering at a hospital near Washington included arranging for visits by young women to entertain the troops; Hooker's name thereby became enshrined in perpetuity in the activities of the ladies.

The staggering casualty rate among troops on both sides of the war was taking its toll, averaging four hundred and thirty deaths a day. Desertions continued to increase, and were estimated to have reached one hundred thousand soldiers among Union regiments by late 1862. Volunteer quotas were becoming increasingly difficult to fill and discussion in Washington turned to conscription. Finally on March 3, 1863, the Conscription Act was passed by Congress calling for the enlistment of all able-bodied males between twenty and forty-five years of age unless they could obtain a substitute or pay three hundred dollars in lieu of service.

Hermon Clarke attended the Congressional hearings and wrote to his father expressing skepticism that the draft would work: "I have been to Washington twice . . . I was in Congress the 3rd of March until after midnight; it was a great show . . . How much is it going to increase the forces to inforce [sic] the conscription? I think the men are few who won't pay $300 before they will come." Clarke undoubtedly was thinking of people like the Loomis men who could easily afford to pay the fee.

Many others thought that the Conscription Act was unfair as well and draft riots broke out in Wisconsin, Kentucky, Pennsylvania, New Jersey, and New York. The riots in New York City began in July when crowds, shouting about having to furnish "poor man's blood for a rich man's war," grew to seventy thousand people and proceeded to burn "the draft office on Broadway and a dozen more buildings . . . They looted and burned several homes of wealthy families on Lexington Avenue." The anti-war sentiment of the rioters metamorphosed into anti-Negro hatred as they chased "young black children all the way to the East River and let them drown." One Negro man was "castrated . . . then tossed into the East River where he drowned" while on Clarkson Street " a young Negro was hanged and men danced and sang around him while a fire roasted his flesh." By the time Union troops arrived to quell the riot an estimated three thousand persons had been killed. President Lincoln, however, adamantly refused to rescind the draft.

The war was becoming nastier everywhere. In Richmond there had been bread riots in April and looting by a crowd of a thousand women and young boys; because of shortages and inflation the price for a half-pound loaf of bread had risen to twenty-five dollars. The riot was finally ended when the mayor got up before the crowd and read a proclamation entitled the Riot Act, telling the crowd it would be fired upon if it failed to disperse. Hunger in the South was a major problem; when Hermon Clarke's regiment marched through Virginia in May, 1863, Clarke wrote home to Waterville that "the women and children are nearly starved. It is a pitiful sight to see them."

Armed mobs dominated much of the fighting in the West, such as Confederate guerrilla bands which raided Missouri and Kansas. One such band, led by W.C. Quantrill, included Jesse James and the Younger brothers, and it killed two hundred civilians in Lawrence, Kansas, in August, 1863. Years later when a Prussian general was asked why he did not study the war tactics of the American Civil War, he replied that the war had been fought principally by armed mobs.

While some Northerners were growing increasingly tired of the war in 1863, others called for a redoubling of efforts. Roscoe Conkling became increasingly critical of his brother-in-law, Governor Seymour, attacking his Copperhead sympathies and his handling of the New York draft riots. Conkling spoke at large

Republican rallies in the villages of Oneida on October 24 and
Camden on October 31, and became a leader of a committee to
encourage volunteer enlistments.

In Peterboro Gerrit Smith echoed Conkling's hawk-like sentiments, and offered to contribute three thousand dollars to equip
Negro troops whose use had finally been approved by President
Lincoln. In July he sent a thousand dollars to victims of the New
York draft riot, and the following month offered to personally
pay three hundred dollars to every drafted soldier from the town
of Smithfield. He also helped organize the local chapter of the
Loyal National League in New York, an organization devoted to
"unconditional loyalty to the Government of the United States
. . . unwavering support of its efforts to suppress the Rebellion."
In May, 1863, both Smith and Roscoe Conkling addressed a
state convention of over two thousand League delegates in Utica
and "reiterated the doctrine that the rebellion must be suppressed." Even Frederick Douglass returned to the speaking circuit, giving a talk in Syracuse on "Rebellion, its Cause and
Remedy."

General Joseph Hooker commanded one hundred and thirty
thousand Union forces and wanted an opportunity to prove himself in battle. At Chancellorsville in early May, 1863, he got it
and was soundly defeated by Lee and Jackson. The North suffered over fifteen thousand dead, wounded or missing but the
South's losses were greater for they included Stonewall Jackson.
Lee realized that his forces could not continue to sustain heavy
losses indefinitely because of the shortage of manpower and
decided that it was time to take the offensive. The Confederate
Army started north toward Gettysburg.

The Union Army caught up with Lee's forces on July 1, initiat-
ing a fierce, three-day battle. Brothers were literally fighting
against brothers, in one case on the land of the farm on which
they had grown up. The casualties on both sides were appalling—
28,063 for the Confederates and 23,049 for the Union. Hermon
Clarke's Oneida County regiment was deep in Virginia preparing
to move toward Richmond but a Madison County regiment was
at Gettysburg and sustained 306 men killed, wounded or missing
within a single hour. When dusk finally fell on July 3 General Lee
was retreating through the rain to Virginia.

Waterville was still assimilating the impact of Gettysburg on
July 22 when, at midnight, there was a knock on the Filkins' kitchen door. Filkins was preparing for bed in the single bedroom

which he shared with his wife and four children immediately off the kitchen. He reached for his revolver and approached the door warily for his life had been threatened more times than he could remember. Just two months earlier, in fact, he had received an anonymous warning which had been printed by the *Waterville Times*:

> "Dear Sir:
>   As a friend to you and all mankind I set down to write to forewarn you of danger. That gang has offered one of their associates a good sum of money to kill you at some convenient time, and he says he doubts whether they will pay him if he should do so. He is a daring and bold robber. I dare not sign my name."

Filkins called out the kitchen window and asked who was there. "I'm Mr. Clark's hired man," a voice replied. "Last evening he came by Van Dee's and saw Jack Van Dee at home and asked me to come up here and let you know." Van Dee was a member of the Loomis gang that Filkins had been trying unsuccessfully to arrest. Filkins recognized the voice as that of Plumb Loomis and stepped back to make sure his revolver was fully loaded. At that moment the quiet of the night was shattered by the firing of a double barreled shotgun as slugs poured through the kitchen window and into the room. Shotgun pellets tore through Filkins right arm between his wrist and elbow and also penetrated his thumb and wrist on his left hand. Sarah Filkins screamed as Filkins started for the bedroom bleeding heavily. As he reached the bedroom two more blasts came through the bedroom window shattering the blinds and tearing away the lower part of the sash. Visitors the next day counted fourteen shot holes in the mantel and forty-seven more having passed through the bed curtains. The bedroom door was filled with buckshot. Filkins lay quietly on the floor losing consciousness as neighbors came running to see what was happening. The dark forms of several men were seen running away from the house. Miraculously neither Sarah Filkins nor the four children had been hit.

When Jim Filkins regained consciousness he was being treated by Drs. George W. Cleveland and George W. Bailey. Both his arms were tightly bandaged and he was told that it would be some time before he would be using them. He said he was sure that it had been Plumb Loomis who fired the first shot and guessed that the Beebes—Ezra the father and Laverne the son—

were also involved. He sent for Bill Benedict, the other constable, and told him to go over to the Beebes to see if he could find a double-barreled shotgun which had recently been fired. If he found nothing there he might go to the Loomises and look around. Benedict said he would go nowhere, and in fact not a man could be found who would leave the village. The citizens of the town were thoroughly terrified.

Jim Filkins recovered more rapidly than expected and within weeks was actively seeking evidence to present to a grand jury. The people in the village, feeling guilty that nobody had had the courage to pursue the case immediately, took up a collection and presented Filkins with a purse of two hundred dollars. Filkins eventually collected enough evidence to secure indictments against Plumb and Denio Loomis, Ezra and Laverne Beebe, and Thomas Mott, but before they could be brought to trial District Attorney Hiram T. Jenkins postponed the case.

The attempt to murder Jim Filkins signaled a new phase in Loomis family activities. Heretofore an attempt had been made to cloak the family with a veneer of respectability, however thin. Wash and Grove especially had argued for maintaining the facade of being law-abiding citizens and for denying illegalities. The attack on Filkins, probably instigated by Rhoda, meant that the facade had been dropped. The Loomises were overtly challenging the laws and declaring themselves above them.

One wonders, in retrospect, how much of the attack against Filkins was a consequence of continued Loomis intrafamily warfare taking place next to Nine Mile Swamp. Less than one month before the attack Grove Loomis had moved his seventeen-year-old girlfriend, Nellie Smith, into the Loomis home to live with him. Nellie was from a respectable family in the village of Madison and said she agreed to live with Grove "because he wanted me to and because he promised to marry me if I would go." It had been just eighteen months since Wash's mistress had been "accidently" killed in the Loomis kitchen; Rhoda's dislike of all women who had designs on her sons was well known. Grove's decision to bring Nellie to live with him was another challenge to Rhoda and her authority. As she always had done, Rhoda was prepared to do whatever was necessary to reassert that authority. Attacking Filkins, which was so contrary to the modus operandi favored by Wash and Grove, was one way to do so.

The suspicion that Loomis lines of authority had broken down received impetus six weeks after the attack on Filkins when

Wheeler Loomis was arrested for rape. A man walking on a road near Peterboro found a young woman lying by the roadside, hands and feet tied with ropes and mouth gagged. She was Esther Parks, a fourteen-year-old widely known to be mentally retarded and who had been missing from home for three days. She had been abducted by two men, she said, who had taken her money and then raped her. Wheeler Loomis, then thirty-two years old, was named as one of the men.

Nobody in Sangerfield or Waterville was surprised at the charges against Wheeler for he had always been regarded as the least scrupulous of the Loomis sons. He had previously been arrested for rape but the Loomises had offered the girls' father nine hundred dollars to drop charges. The father did so, then the Loomises refused to pay him; the judge, being a friend of the Loomises, refused to reinstate charges. Wheeler had shifted allegiances in family disputes between his mother and Wash, but it was generally believed that his older brother had kept him in line.

The rape of a young, retarded girl elicited much community animosity against the Loomises. Wheeler was taken before Judge Crandall of South Brookfield, a judge known for his antipathy to the Loomises, who decided to refer the case to a grand jury. The following night Judge Crandall's office was broken into and papers stolen, but he had already mailed the needed documents to the court. Esther Parks then disappeared and could not be found to appear before the grand jury. Testimony of her father, mother, and a physician were sufficient to secure an indictment, and Esther was finally located at the Loomis home where she was being held to prevent her from testifying. When released she was so terrified that she went to live with the Sheriff's family for several months so that she would not be kidnapped again. Wheeler was released from jail on October 6 after his family paid two thousand dollars in bail. The following day he left for Canada, thereby forfeiting bail, and remained there for the rest of his life. It was thought by many that the Loomises were glad to be rid of him.

The Loomises were always looking for ways to discredit Jim Filkins and in September, 1863, they tried a new strategy. In July, shortly before he had been shot, Filkins had arrested Ezra Beebe and Frances Van Dee and charged them with robbing a store of eight hundred dollars in clothes and other merchandise. Miss Van Dee was the sister of gang member Jack Van Dee and had a moral reputation in Waterville that was less than sterling. At the time of the arrest Filkins took her directly to the jail where he made her strip, suspecting correctly that she was hiding stolen goods under her skirts at that moment. However, Filkins failed to call in a woman to chaperone while he conducted his search, and Frances Van Dee filed a suit against Filkins for improperly forcing her to expose herself to him. In terms of his reputation, conviction in such a suit might seriously damage Filkins' career as a law officer.

The case came to trial in September. Frances Van Dee retained as her lawyer Sewell S. Morgan while Filkins prevailed upon Daniel Ball. The courtroom was crowded with spectators as Sewell Morgan, referring to his client as "Franky," described the affronts she had undergone during the "exposure of Franky's body to Filkins' offending eyes." Frances Van Dee sat demurely at the table looking properly indignant.

When Sewell Morgan had finished presenting the case against Filkins he sat down smiling. Daniel Ball, a Waterville lawyer who was widely respected, rose and looked slowly from Frances Van Dee to Sewell Morgan and back again. " 'Gentlemen of the jury,' he said, 'my opponent has spoken familiarly of the plaintiff as "Franky" and dastardly of Filkins. I agree that any man who would strip a woman naked and search her person breaks all laws of decency. Yet, gentlemen of the jury, before we are finished with this case of the exposure of this woman's person, we're going to prove to you that the private parts of this woman are the most public places in town!' A ripple of amusement grew louder as the spectators began to shout and cheer Ball's words." The judge, much perturbed by the disturbance, banged his gavel to try and restore order. Meanwhile Frances Van Dee could be seen hurriedly conferring with Sewell Morgan. When the uproar had subsided "Morgan rose to his feet, mopping his brow with a large bandanna. 'Your Honor,' he said, 'my client does not wish to press the suit against Mr. Filkins. She prefers to drop the case.' "

During the later months of 1863 prospects for a Union victory improved but the continuing costs for both sides were staggering. At Chickamauga in two days of fighting the North sustained 16,169 casualties and the South 18,274. Hermon Clarke's regiment was seeing action in South Carolina and he described life in letters home:

> November 7, 1863: "Fifty [men] were on picket one day and relieved by the other fifty the next. While on duty there were

four to six men on post. None was allowed to sleep, to sit
down or to lie down. If a man was seen even leaning against
a tree he was arrested and hung up by the hands."

December 7, 1863: "The northeast winds here are terribly
cold. There have been some very hard storms at sea."

In the December letter Hermon also offered an opinion of his
neighbors at home—Copperhead and war profiteers—who were
undermining Union Army efforts. "I tell you we will soon end the
fighting here and if the traitors north don't keep quiet we will fix
them . . . I tell you [this is] the feeling of the soldiers."

It was not only the Loomises whom Hermon Clarke had in
mind as war profiteers, but also a newly emerged group of
"bounty jumpers." The draft continued to be very unpopular
and counties tried to fill enlistment quotas with volunteers whenever possible. In order to accomplish this, money was raised
locally to pay enlistment bonuses which had reached six hundred
dollars in Oneida County and seven hundred dollars in Madison
County. "Men enlisted, accepted the bounty, deserted, enlisted
elsewhere under different names, got another bounty, deserted,
enlisted elsewhere . . . The business was organized, and necessarily it had the cooperation of many bounty brokers and military
officers." In some cases bounty brokers drugged or forcibly com-
pelled men to sign enlistment papers; in Syracuse a case was
publicized in which an officer, home on leave, was drugged,
enlisted as a private, and sent to the 192nd Regiment before he
could make anybody believe who he was.

The Loomises, lured by the quick profits of bounty jumping,
prevailed upon gang members to repeatedly enlist and desert,
harboring them at the farm in the intervals. They were merely
making their profit from the war, they argued, like everybody
else was doing. Gideon Welles, Lincoln's Secretary of the Navy,
had appointed his brother-in-law as exclusive purchasing agent
for Union ships and the brother-in-law had pocketed $95,000 in
kickbacks. Simon Cameron, Lincoln's Secretary of War, was
fired when it was found that he was purchasing guns from private
contractors for $22 each while the government was manufactur-
ing the same gun for less than $14. John C. Fremont, Lincoln's
commander of the Department of the West, was charged with
"favoritism, corruption, and widespread speculation in contracts." Government sutlers, who provided army camps with
food and clothing, were notoriously corrupt. And a small group

of investors in the railroads, including Thurlow Weed, were said to be making extraordinary profits from federal subsidies. Why, asked the Loomises, should they not make a modest profit as well?

Many of the Loomis' neighbors, including those who had been friendly with them before the war, became progressively angrier at them as the fighting dragged on. Prices were rising while wages were falling; coffee, tea and sugar were in short supply while the prices of coal, beer and whiskey had doubled. At the same time the list of dead and wounded accumulated in the towns around Nine Mile Swamp, and neighbors became increasingly sensitive about which families had contributed their share to the war effort and which had not. The healthy men in the Loomis family were becoming increasingly conspicuous as they were becoming increasingly wealthy.

By May, 1964, Hermon Clarke's regiment had returned to Virginia. General Ulysses S. Grant had been put in charge of the Union Army which was edging south toward Richmond. The Confederates under General Robert E. Lee stood in the way and on May 5 and 6, 1864, the two armies met in densely thicketed woods in what would become known as the Battle of the Wilderness. It was, in Grant's estimation, the most vicious fighting of the entire war; the dense woods precluded use of the artillery and much of the combat was hand to hand. To make matters worse it had been an extremely dry spring so the woods caught fire from time to time burning alive the wounded as they frantically tried to crawl to safety. Hermon Clarke's regiment was part of the fighting; some said that those who survived the Battle of the Wilderness were never quite the same. In a letter home Clarke described one fight in which "there were about 400 killed" and "the battlefield took fire and burned the wounded, about 70 Rebs and 10 of our men." Altogether Union casualties at the Wilderness were 18,000 against 7,700 for the Confederates.

Despite such losses General Grant continued pushing his troops toward Richmond. Hermon Clarke's letters told those listening at Bissell's general store what the attempt to end the war was costing in human terms:

> May 11, 1864: "The fighting was severe. At daylight it com-
> menced again, but soon stopped to bury the dead. We
> buried about 50 Rebs. How many they buried we don't
> know. I don't know how many we lost, but there were a
> great many wounded that we saw. I tell you it was sickening

to go along the woods and see the wounded, some knocked all to pieces, some bleeding to death and suffering in every form. It was so hot that a dead man would turn black in a few hours."

The *Utica Daily Observer* listed casualties from the local regiment almost daily; on May 25, 1864, it named 16 killed, 63 wounded and 9 missing from the battle of Drewry's Bluff.

Hermon Clarke was also learning that it was a strange war, with brief periods of comraderie between opposing armies interrupting the spasms of slaughter. He described this in a letter home:

June 23, 1864: "Our lines are from 50 to 100 yards apart. We stand up and look at them and they at us. Occasionally a man goes out half way and one of the Rebs comes out. They shake hands, talk, etc. Our fellow gives Johnny some coffee, and Johnny gives our fellow some tobacco. This occurs a number of times a day." Furthermore "there is an agreement between them that there shall be no firing on picket [duty]"; on one occasion "our post was not 10 yards from the Reb post. They were friendly enough to tell us if we made a mistake and got too far into their lines."

The use of Negro soldiers in the Union Army had begun in 1863 although initially they received only half the pay given to white soldiers. By mid-1864 Negro troops constituted fifteen percent of the Union forces and were playing an important role in the fighting. Hermon Clarke welcomed their help:

July 23, 1863: "The Niggers charged on our left and did well. Some of them came where we were and attempted to kill our prisoners. I didn't see but one killed; he was a fine looking fellow. A great bushy Nigger came up to him, knocked him down, and ran his bayonet through his heart. Our boys turned on the Niggers and kept them back."

When Negro troops received too much public attention, however, Hermon Clarke showed resentment: "I see the New York papers give the credit of the battle [on the] 15th to colored troops. Well, I think two-thirds the number of whites would have done the work." Hermon Clarke's true sentiments regarding the people he was theoretically fighting to free were probably expressed by another member of his regiment whose letter was published in the *Utica Daily Observer*:

> "The radicals serenaded Gen. Wadsworth the other night, and he made a speech, in which the everlasting nigger played the principal part. It was nigger at the beginning, nigger in the middle, and nigger at the close . . ."

Not only had Negro troops been approved for use in the Union Army, but manpower was in such short supply that Indians were also given commissions in 1863. Ely S. Parker was one of the first, and joined his friend Ulysses S. Grant who at that time was commanding Union forces at Vicksburg. Altogether the Indians who fought for the North numbered 3,530 and of these almost one-third were killed. Many more Indians fought for the Confederate side with Stand Watie's regiment of Cherokee Mounted Rifles distinguishing themselves in several battles. In 1864, Watie was promoted to brigadier general and put in charge of an Indian Cavalry Brigade.

At the same time as some Indians were fighting in the Civil War, others farther west were being systematically slaughtered. The commander of the Colorado militia, Colonel John M. Chivington, publicly advocated the killing of Indian children—"nits make lice" he had said. On November 29, 1864, Chivington's troops came upon a peaceful Cheyenne encampment at Sand Creek, Colorado, and proceeded to butcher 105 women and children and 28 men, scalping each of them. Torture and mutilation were reported to be widespread with Chivington's own men testifying to the horrible scene. The massacre was later condemned by the Federal govenment.

Throughout the remainder of 1864 Grant's Union Army continued to push slowly toward Petersburg and then Richmond. Hermon Clarke was part of that campaign and throughout the summer and fall he continued to write home to Waterville:

> July 13: "We are allowed about 3 hours in 24 for sleep while in the rifle pits, the rest of the time on duty. The average killed and wounded in our Regt. is about 4 per day. So far one out of four has been killed instantly, and there will be more than half that go to the hospital [to] die."

> August 2: "Sixteen from our Brigade died of sunstroke before 3 P.M. and others were severely injured by heat."

In his August 2 letter Clarke also described the Union attempt to take Petersburg by digging a tunnel beneath the city and blowing it up. The action was, in Grant's words, a "stupendous failure" and cost another four thousand Northern casualties.

August 22: "Men here receive letters every day [telling them] that their families are suffering for want of money, but we can't get the pay, for the Government says it hasn't got the money. It requires a mighty sight of patriotism to keep a man's spirit up under such circumstances."

October 3: "There were about 275 men of our Regiment [who] went in and we lost over 120 killed, wounded and missing . . . A spent ball hit me on the shoulder but didn't go through my blouse. A piece of shell struck my gun and broke it. The gun saved my leg."

October 28: "Andrew Rowell [Herman Clarke's lifelong friend] was mortally wounded in the first volley - a piece of shrapnel struck him in the head, a ball in the shoulder, and another in the leg. He is no doubt dead before now; I saw him put in an ambulance. He was insensible when I last saw him."

November 13: "I would like to have those men who are so anxious for a vigorous prosecution of the war witness such scenes as we did on the 29th of September and the 27th of October. Men wounded in every manner imaginable. Some dead, others dying - giving their last message to some comrade. Some cursing the war that deprived them of a leg or an arm and made them cripples for life, and in the same breath praying for their families who were suffering and, they know, must always suffer by reason of it."

Incredibly, in a single month General Grant's Union forces lost 60,000 men.

Notwithstanding the war, 1864 was an election year and on June 7 the Republican Party renominated Lincoln for President. There was considerable opposition to the nomination, and Thurlow Weed told Lincoln frankly that his re-election was "an impossibility." The Democrats, meeting in Chicago on August 29, nominated General George McClellan to oppose the man who had once fired him. McClellan castigated Lincoln's conduct of the war and Lincoln's chances for retaining the Presidency were widely regarded to be negligible.

On September 22, the Republicans in Oneida County met in Rome to nominate a candidate to try and win the congressional seat back from Francis Kernan. Conkling had done his homework and anticipated the nomination. There was opposition, however, by Republicans who claimed that Conkling's political appointments "had been for private ends . . . to build up a personal party." Just at the point where the opposition to Conkling was in danger of spreading, one of Conkling's close supporters brought out a letter from President Lincoln saying that "no one could be more satisfactory to me as the nominee in that District than Mr. Conkling." Conkling thereupon received the nomination.

Leaving nothing to chance, Roscoe Conkling spent the next six weeks touring Oneida County and visiting "nearly every hamlet and crossroads" including Waterville and Sangerfield. He attacked Kernan for having failed to support the war effort. Meanwhile in the South, General Sherman had captured Atlanta and was marching toward the sea, General Sheridan was winning victories in the Shenandoah Valley, and General Grant was making progress against Lee's forces in northern Virginia. Union morale soared as the prospect of victory became increasingly brighter. A vote against the Republicans became a vote against the Union. When the votes were counted on November 9, Roscoe Conkling had easily regained his seat in Congress and Abraham Lincoln had won re-election as President.

The Loomises, too, realized that the end of the war was near and increased horse thefts to take advantage of the Union Army market while it still existed. Their profits had never been higher nor their power greater. Much of Central New York was no longer subject to county, state or federal laws, it seemed, but only to Loomis laws. The list of sheriffs, judges, district attorneys, state legislators and other public officials who had accepted bribes from them grew longer each month and extended well across state lines into Pennsylvania, Vermont and Ontario, Canada. When Laverne Beebe was arrested in Ontario near Niagara Falls, for example, Filkins obtained an agreement from Canadian authorities that Beebe would be held for sixty days so that extradition papers could be arranged. Less than three weeks later Beebe was freed with no notification whatsoever to the Americans.

Despite Filkin's continuing efforts, other attempts to combat the Loomises were sporadic and ineffectual. Late in 1864, for example, a local protective association was formed in North Brookfield. Amidst great secrecy several prominent village leaders convened a meeting at the Baptist Church to discuss how the nightly thefts and barn burnings might be curtailed. The meeting was well attended, by-laws for the association had just been passed and each member was being assessed one dollar in dues. At that moment the doors swung open and in walked Wash and Grove Loomis. "'We have heard that you are forming an organization to stop the thieving and horse stealing going on in our neighborhood,' Wash gravely remarked. 'Grove and I think it is a fine plan and we want to join.' He tossed two one-dollar notes on the table. 'Here's our money,' he said. The brothers walked from the room laughing." That terminated the protective association.

During the fall of 1864, while the Union Army inched toward Richmond and Hermon Clarke wrote home weekly describing the casualties, while Roscoe Conkling went from village to village campaigning for Lincoln and the Republican Party, the effrontery of the Loomis family achieved new heights. On September 23, law officers from Madison County located several items stolen by the Loomises and took them to North Brookfield for safekeeping so they could be used to obtain indictments. The stolen goods were locked in a barn behind the Exchange Hotel, owned and operated by Deputy Sheriff Ephraim Conger. Late that night the barn was set afire destroying all the evidence as well as horses, hay and grain; it was only with great effort that the hotel itself was saved.

A second fire followed on October 10. The Madison County Circuit Court had convened at the Morrisville Courthouse, a two story baroque structure with four columns and cupola, that was the pride of the town. Several indictments had been obtained against Wash, Grove and Plumb Loomis as well as other gang members who were scheduled to go to trial. On the night before the court session was to begin the courthouse was set afire in the middle of the night. Volunteers came quickly and towed the pumper from the firehouse to the scene of the fire. The hose was unrolled but as water began to be pumped it was noted that the water was coming out the sides of the hose in several places. On closer examination it became clear that the hose had been cut with an axe. Wash Loomis, in town for the court session, was at the scene to help put out the fire and "seemed to be utterly astonished when someone told him that the hose had been cut." "It's a damned outrage and I would like to help hang the man who did it," Wash told those around him. The courthouse burned to the ground destroying everything inside. The *Madison*

*Observer* speculated that "it was the work of an incendiary who went about his fiendish business in so thorough and systematic a manner to fail in accomplishing his detection." The village Board of Supervisors offered a reward of one thousand dollars for information leading to the apprehension of the perpetrators but to no avail. A new courthouse eventually was built at a cost of $16,000.

Slowly and inexorably Confederate troops were pushed back as winter set in. Hermon Clarke wrote home that "while we lay in our camp before Richmond the weather was very cold. One man in the 3rd New York, the regiment next to us, froze to death on the night of December 31st." In the North people waited expectantly for the war to be over. Lincoln and his aides began making plans for the postwar period, and at his inauguration on March 4, 1865, the President called for "malice toward none, with charity for all . . . let us . . . bind up the nation's wounds." Vice-President Andrew Johnson was visibly intoxicated for the occasion.

On April 3, Union soldiers finally entered Richmond as Jefferson Davis and his cabinet fled south. Two days later Lincoln visited the city and was briefed by General Grant and his staff. Ely S. Parker, who had become Grant's military secretary, took the opportunity to apprise Lincoln of the pressing needs of American Indians.

The final act in the drama was played at the village of Appomattox Court House on April 8. Grant and Lee met to discuss terms for the surrender and a resident of the village, Wilmer McLean, offered his home for the occasion. Ironically McLean had moved to Appomattox Court House because his previous house at Bull Run had been damaged in the 1861 battle and he wanted to get away from the war.

When General Lee arrived he shook hands with Grant, then with each member of his staff. When he got to Parker he looked startled, perhaps wondering momentarily whether Grant had a mulatto on his staff. Then realizing that Parker was an Indian, General Lee looked at him and said: "I am glad to see one real American here." "We are all Americans," Parker answered kindly.

Grant and Lee chatted about old army days until Lee brought up the subject of surrender. The two discussed terms, and Grant jotted notes into a book. After they had agreed on the terms Grant handed the book to his chief aide-de-camp to make an official copy for Lee's signature. The aide-de-camp, apparently flustered by the gravity of the occasion, began writing but his hand was shaking so badly he could not continue. He handed the book to Parker and suggested that he write it, which he calmly did. An Iroquois Indian had thereby written the official terms of surrender to end the Civil War and free the Negroes.

## THE LOOMIS HOME

*Built in 1825 with special architectural features such as double-panelled walls and false floors for concealing contraband, the Loomis homestead was the headquarters for the largest family crime syndicate in 19th century America.*

## NINE MILE SWAMP

*As it looks today from the hill behind the Loomis home, the swamp was used to hide hundreds of stolen horses as well as Loomis Gang members being sought by the law.*

### WASH LOOMIS
*Bright, articulate and personable, he was the leader of the largest family outlaw gang in 19th century America. His mistress was murdered on his mother's orders and he in turn was murdered by an officer of the law.*

### GROVE LOOMIS

*Considered to be an expert on horses and women (in that order), he was the most daring member of the Loomis gang. Vigilantes brutally beat him and set him afire, but he survived.*

### PLUMB LOOMIS

*One of the worst of the Loomis gang, he was eventually hung by a mob of vigilantes, but narrowly escaped death.*

### CORNELIA LOOMIS

*She rode with her brothers, participated in a wide range of family crimes, and carried on an affair with another Loomis gang member.*

*Keith's Hotel in Brookfield. On July 8, 1858, Plumb Loomis, being held for arraignment, escaped from the upstairs window and jumped on the back of a waiting horse.*

*Waterville home of Constable Jim Filkins where on July 22, 1863, Plumb Loomis and two associates shot Filkins through the bedroom window. Over sixty shot holes were counted in the room the next day. Filkins was wounded, but not killed.*

## GERRIT SMITH

*Wealthy landowner and abolition-
ist who lived near the Loomises,
his regular guests included John
Brown, his niece Elizabeth Cady
Stanton, Frederick Douglass,
Horace Greeley and Henry Ward
Beecher.*

Matthew Brady photo, courtesy of the
National Portrait Gallery,
Smithsonian Institution

Courtesy of the Ellen L. Peletz and the Madison County Historical Society

### MANSION HOUSE

*Gerrit Smith's 28-room house in Peterboro, just 15 miles from
the Loomis farm. Here was planned John Brown's 1859 raid on
Harpers Ferry as well as the first Women's Rights Convention
held in Seneca Falls in 1848.*

*The Morrisville Courthouse which was burned to the ground by the Loomises on October 10, 1864 in order to destroy indictments against them. In an act of insolence extraordinary even by Loomis standards, Wash Loomis started the fire and then showed up at the scene offering to help put it out.*

*Bissell's general store in Waterville, the center of opposition to the Loomis gang, as it looked in 1865 when the Sangerfield Vigilantes Committee began meeting secretly in the storeroom upstairs.*

*Cort Terry, left, Henry Bissell, right, are thought to have been members of the Vigilantes Committee who helped Constable Jim Filkins murder Wash Loomis.*

*The Park Hotel as it appeared in November, 1865, where three
Loomis gang members confronted Constable James Filkins
and threatened to kill him four weeks after Filkins had
murdered the leader of the gang.*

*The American Hotel in Waterville, a favorite place for locals to discuss the latest Loomis depredations. In 1866 three genera-tions of Loomises (mother Rhoda, daughter Cornelia, and a 12-year-old grandson) were brought here on route to the Utica jail after being arrested for possession of counterfeit bills.*

## ROSCOE CONKLING
*A fearless opponent of the Loomis gang, as Oneida County District Attorney in 1850 he obtained the first conviction of a member of the Loomis family.*

John F. Jarvis photo
Courtesy of the National Portrait Gallery, Smithsonian Institution

## ROME COURTHOUSE
*Here on June 3 and 4, 1867, Roscoe Conkling, then United States Senator, wrote the final chapter in the Loomis saga by getting dismissed the indictments against Constable James Filkins for murdering Wash Loomis. Conkling subsequently became one of the most powerful politicians in Washington.*

# CHAPTER IX

# Scalping

Joy and relief spread along the valleys of Central New York with news of the Confederate surrender. One out of every six Union soldiers had been killed; more Americans had died in the war than would die in World War I and World War II combined. New York State alone had suffered over fifty thousand deaths, and it was a rare family which did not personally know at least one young man who would not come home. In Utica "a great and spontaneous outpouring of people gathered in Baggs Square" to celebrate the end of the war. "Loud calls were made for Roscoe Conkling" but Conkling had already left for Washington. Having been appointed as a member of an official fact-finding committee by the Secretary of War, Conkling was one of the first Union officials to enter Richmond after its fall.

In Bissell's general store Hermon Clarke's recent letter was passed around as if to help understand what the fighting and deaths had been about. He described the reaction of Negroes as Union troops entered their towns: "It was interesting to see the colored population. So happy a crowd I never saw: families standing on the sidewalk shouting 'We are free! We are free!'— kissing one another and running to their neighbors, kissing them. The biggest thing I ever saw. In several instances I heard the old Negroes say, 'We have prayed for this for years and years, and now you have come! Bless God and the Yanks forever.'"

There was still sporadic fighting by isolated Confederate units; the last Confederate general to surrender, Cherokee Brigadier

General Stand Watie, did not lay down arms until June 23. But attention turned toward reconciliation and plans for the South, and on April 13, General Grant arrived with his staff in Washington to discuss these plans with Lincoln. The President outlined programs and urged generosity, not vindictiveness, as the most effective balm for the nation's wounds. The following day, Good Friday, Lincoln met with Ely Parker to discuss the plight of the American Indians; after the meeting Parker left for New York while Lincoln joined his wife for a play at Ford's Theater.

John Wilkes Booth, the Southern sympathizer who had witnessed John Brown's hanging five years previously, had become increasingly embittered as the Confederacy went down to defeat. The previous year he had organized a scheme to kidnap Lincoln and take him to Richmond but it had come to naught. Justice would be served, Booth vowed, and he stole into Lincoln's theater box firing a bullet directly into Lincoln's head. Within hours the President was dead.

The shock waves of assassination shook the body of an exhausted nation. The war was over but killing continued, a torn afterbirth to a difficult delivery. How much more blood had to be shed, people asked. Ely Parker was especially bitter about Lincoln's death: "You white men are Christians and may forgive the murder. I am of a race which never forgives the murder of a friend." On April 26, Booth was cornered in a barn in rural Virginia and shot to death. The same day the train bearing Lincoln's remains en route to Illinois stopped in Utica for twenty minutes to allow the citizens to pay their last respects; Roscoe Conkling was a member of the official escort committee.

For the Loomises the war's end meant a search for new markets for the stolen horses. There is no evidence their activities slowed, though they were increasingly forced to go farther from Sangerfield to find horses of quality. On April 30, 1865, Denio Loomis stole the horse of Hiram Cowen from a farm west of Syracuse; few good horses remained within a fifty mile radius of the Loomis farm in any direction.

Indictments against the Loomises continued to accumulate despite their friendship with many law enforcement officials. Delaying court actions and keeping gang members out of jail took increasing amounts of Loomis' energy and money as lawyers, judges and sheriffs demanded ever more for their services.

Several weeks after the Morrisville Courthouse fire a rumor circulated that some of the indictments against the Loomises had not been in the building when it burned but rather had been next door in the county clerk's office; this was a brick building with iron doors and thus impervious to arson. Wash Loomis tested the validity of the rumor by requesting copies of all indictments outstanding against the Loomis family, and was given copies of several of them.

On May 10, 1865, the same day that Jefferson Davis was being captured in Georgia, the county clerk's office in Morrisville was broken into by forcing open a window. According to the account in a local newspaper, "the intruders, as it was evident from the condition of the office the next morning, proceeded deliberately to collect all the loose papers and documents, which they put into the stove and burned. The property destroyed included all the lawyers' papers, the old deeds and mortgages, the court papers and the recorded deeds and mortgages left there during the past six weeks. It is supposed that this wholesale destruction of valuable records was perpetrated with the object of disposing of certain indictments and other law papers concerning parties charged with crime, and suspicion rests upon several notorious persons whose antecedents warrant the belief that they may have been engaged in these proceedings." Every outstanding indictment against the Loomises in Madison County was destroyed, and the statute of limitations in many precluded new indictments being obtained. Also destroyed were indictments against other gang members including one against Ezra Beebe; Wash Loomis assessed Beebe one hundred dollars for services rendered.

Jim Filkins and his supporters in Waterville were dismayed by the news from Madison County. Aware that other indictments were outstanding against the Loomises in Oneida County, Filkins journeyed to Utica to meet with District Attorney Hiram T. Jenkins and ascertain progress toward bringing the Loomises to trial. Jenkins informed Filkins that a *nolle prosequi* had been entered in all cases and that none of the charges would be prosecuted, including the indictments against Plumb and Denio Loomis for assault with intent to kill Filkins in the July attack. Incredulous, Filkins asked Jenkins why he had done such a thing. "Well, Sheriff Crocker came to me in the December term of court saying that it was his last term and he had an agreement with the Loomises to see them clear of everything before he went out of office. He wanted to make his word good and asked me to help him." Not a single indictment remained against the Loomis family in either Madison or Oneida Counties, and the talk in

Bissell's general store was of little else. In Utica, however, Jenkin's dropping the indictments caused remarkably little comment and he was renominated as District Attorney without opposition.

Release of Union troops from the army was a slow process, and it was not until June 18 that Hermon Clarke's regiment arrived at the Utica train station. The coaches were mobbed by families and friends as the Utica City Band played "Home, Sweet Home." A formal banquet was prepared in the station and Roscoe Conkling rose to officially welcome the soldiers:

> "Three years ago fear was everywhere. No home was safe; strong men bowed themselves; our Government tottered; our flag was derided and dishonored on land and on sea, and foreign nations were casting lots for our vesture. Then it was, at the country's call, that you left fireside and home for the camp, the trench and the hospital - then it was that you went out to defend on far distant battle-fields the life and glory of your country. You have done your whole duty. You have made marches more dreadful than battles. You have conquered in fights which will be historic forever. You have belonged to the most glorious army which ever assembled on earth . . ."

Conkling, impatiently awaiting the convening of the thirty-ninth Congress so he could return to Washington, had just accepted assignment from the Secretary of War to be the special prosecutor of Major John A. Haddock, deputy provost marshal in charge of army recruitment for western New York State. Haddock had been charged with graft and corruption in keeping part of enlistment bounties for himself—"he is in collusion with bounty brokers and prostitutes his official position to personal ends," it was charged. The trial lasted four months and was increasingly publicized as it exposed shameful debris from the war. Conkling, in a summation, displayed controlled fury against those who had profited from the war:

> ". . . the Rebellion, now ended, seems to have been appointed to illustrate, in manifold ways, the shame not less than the glory of humanity. A vessel tossed and groaning in a gale, a crew heroically manful, and a myriad of sharks following the ship - such is a faithful emblem of our condition during the mighty convulsion which has just subsided. The nation was in the last peril of existence. The continent quaked under the tramp of uncounted host, eager, from

general to private, to suffer all, and dare all, for the salvation of the Government of their fathers. But with them came knaves, titled and even shoulder-strapped, a darkening cloud of vampires, gorging themselves upon the heart's blood of their country. Shoddy contractors, bounty gamblers and base adventurers found their way even into the army."

Haddock was found guilty, court-martialed, and fined ten thousand dollars.

Throughout the North at this time there was intense discussion regarding what to do with Jefferson Davis and other leaders of the Confederacy, most of whom had been put in prison. Many, like Conkling, urged prosecution and retribution while others, like Gerrit Smith, counseled leniency. In a speech in New York on June 8, 1865, Smith said:

"The South, by plunging the nation into this horrid War, committed the *great* crime of the age. The North, under persistent urgency of press and pulpit to punish the South for treason, is in danger of committing the *mean* crime of the age . . . My position is simply, that there shall be no punishment of the South for the Rebellion—or, to use another word, no punishment of her for treason."

Smith had a vested interest in urging that there be no punishment for treason, for the *Chicago Tribune* had just published a story reiterating previous accusations that Smith had been instrumental in helping John Brown's raid and thereby precipitating the war. The newspaper's attack on Smith was devastating, including the accusation that he had intentionally taken "refuge in a lunatic asylum" to avoid prosecution. "Gerrit Smith," it said, "stands indebted to his sire for a feeble intellect and a large fortune."

Smith, enraged, went to Chicago threatening suit unless the newspaper printed an apology. The *Chicago Tribune's* reply was to print another story about Smith saying that such a suit by Smith would prove not only that Smith had been insane "but that he had never been cured." Smith thereupon sued the newspaper for fifty thousand dollars in damages and the *Tribune* replied publicly: "We have never seen Mr. Smith in an insane asylum, but we expect to before he recovers his $50,000." The suit dragged on for almost two years before finally being settled out of court by the newspaper which printed an apology for implying that Smith had feigned insanity.

Roscoe Conkling's prosecution of Major Haddock and Gerrit Smith's suit against the *Chicago Tribune* provided lively entertainment for the men collecting daily in Bissell's general store in Waterville. The more immediate topic, however, was what to do about the Loomises. Inspired by their success in eliminating all existing indictments, the gang launched a local crime wave throughout the summer and fall of 1865. Robberies occurred nightly over a wide area as stores, factories, offices, tollhouses, and homes were all looted. Increasingly, the Loomises were not participating in the thefts directly but acting as a collecting point for the stolen goods and disposing of them through their extensive criminal network. Cornelia Loomis continued to be an active participant in the scheme, and in December, 1865, she was indicted for receiving stolen goods.

Many of the older men at Bissell's claimed ignorance of what to do since all legal remedies against the Loomises had failed. Hermon Clarke had returned to his place behind the counter, and many of his contemporaries with whom he had fought frequented the store. They had learned many lessons in the trenches of the war, and had read about the Loomis' activities in letters they received from home month after month as the fighting went on. When the older men asked what should be done with the Loomises, the veterans of the Battle of the Wilderness and Drewry's Bluff did not hesitate to offer suggestions.

The *Waterville Times* also kept up its editorial barrage against the gang, increasingly often making reference to the "California solution" as a possibility. Occasionally other local weeklies took up the cry. In October, 1865, the *Norwich Union* printed a letter from a man accusing the Loomises of not only stealing his buggy but also of poisoning a horse being used in pursuit of the thieves. There were echos of the Civil War in his suggestion that "we had better get up a jury of Sherman's Boys headed by 'Judge Lynch' and go out there and clean the Loomis ranch out."

Sometime during the summer of 1865 a secret organization, the Sangerfield Vigilantes Committee, was formed. Jim Filkins was a member. Charles Green, the President of the Waterville Bank, was also a member as was Green's brother-in-law, Alexis Seymour. W.J. Bissell, Morris Terry and a few other community leaders who had spoken out against the Loomises also joined. The meeting place was the storeroom over Bissell's store where Hermon Clarke went daily to get store supplies. Clarke was probably a member, along with John Garvey who had also fought for the Union. Morris Terry's son, Cort, and young Hank Bissell, both eighteen, were included in the discussions as they evolved.

Meetings of the Vigilantes Committee consisted of discussions of options for dealing with the Loomises. Since legal approaches had proved futile, talk centered on extralegal approaches. Returning veterans of the war had brought back views of expediency previously missing from farming communities like Waterville and Sangerfield. As it was to be later expressed in a Nevada newspaper justifying a vigilante undertaking:

> "We are not quick to advise a resort to unlawful methods even to obtain justice. But there are times in the history of nations, States, communities and individuals when a revolution is necessary. There is a struggle for mastery between the right and the wrong, the good and the bad, which breaks forth beyond the bounds of ordinary procedure."

By early October a plan had been agreed upon.

On Monday, October 30, the *Utica Morning Herald* carried news of another disaster with loss of life—a "Terrible Steamboat Accident" caused by a boiler explosion in a boat on the Hudson River. Seven persons had been killed immediately and seventeen others seriously scalded. The paper described the scene in detail: "Forward, near the engine room bulkhead, lay the dead, first a mother and her two little children. Next a mother and child, whose husband and father lay at the other end of the saloon suffering fortunes inexpressible." In another column the paper announced a local meeting of Republicans in Waterville that evening and discussed the Republican meeting scheduled for Wednesday night in Utica at which Roscoe Conkling was scheduled to speak.

At two o'clock in the morning on October 31, 1865, four dark figures moved quietly through the night toward the Loomis home. It was the time of year when cold winds blow from the west, presaging the coming winter, the trees bare of all except occasional maple leaves. Corn stands in some fields awaiting a final harvesting, while milkweed pods open wide to shed white fingers to the air. Night comes early to Nine Mile Swamp.

There were at least seventeen people sleeping at the Loomises that night, including Rhoda, Cornelia, Wash, Grove, Plumb, Denio, and Wheeler's young son, Charles. Sleeping in upstairs rooms were gang members Lorenzo Bixby, Eli Tilby, John Stoner, George Day, George Jones, Charles Bird, and Frank

Kent. Elizabeth Calkins, a woman Rhoda Loomis had taken out of the poor house and who was used as a servant, slept by herself. Louise Gates, a young woman from Utica who was Wash's new mistress, slept with him, while Nellie Smith shared Grove's bed.

What happened that night can be told in the words of the people in the house, recorded the following day at a coroner's inquest. Louise Gates described how it began:

> "I was awakened about 2 o'clock by a rap on the bedroom window of the room I occupied, and someone called 'Wash.' Wash arose, went to the window and said, 'What do you want?' The voice at the window said come to the back door, 'I want to speak to you a minute;' Wash turned around, opened the door and went out.
>
> Then pretty quick I heard footsteps in the middle kitchen; they were not the footsteps of Wash; somebody came to the bedroom door and Wash followed him and said, 'Filkins, I don't want you in there, come out, there is nothing there you want.'
>
> Filkins came into the room, had a lighted candle in his hand, and he looked under the bed, then held the light up and looked in my face; then turned and went to the door, and said, 'No, there is nothing here but a woman.'
>
> Then he said, 'Wash, I want you.'
>
> Wash turned around and walked with Filkins to the back kitchen door, which they shut; the bedroom door was still open; then I heard a dreadful jar that shook the house all over; somebody then opened the back kitchen door, passed thru the middle kitchen and went upstairs; this was immediately after the jar."

At the top of the stairs was a room in which Lorenzo Bixby and two other gang members slept. Bixby recalled:

> "I then heard heavy boot tramp on the kitchen stairs coming up into the room where I was; I then saw a light at the head of the stairs.
>
> I raised my head and saw three men standing at the head of the stairs; two of them stopped at the head of the stairs and the other came directly to the bed where I slept and held a lantern down near my face.
>
> I said what do you want? He said ugh; he then stepped in the door of the room adjoining the room where I slept and said 'Grove'; I heard Grove say, 'Yes'; he then turned around and held his light to the face of the man that lay next to the alley on the other bed; he then held the lantern

by the face of the other man in the bed, and changed what I took to be a revolver from his right hand to his left hand and rapped on the door again with his right hand and said, 'Grove!' The same voice within said 'Yes!' In a moment I heard the door unbolted and Grove came into the room where we were.

The man at the door said, 'Well, Grove, I have come to see you in the night;' I suppose I know who that man was; he is a man who has been represented to me as James Filkins; Grove said: 'Yes, all right.'"

Grove described what happened next:

"I opened the door and went out; Filkins was standing close to the door; he took me by the collar; I said, I will go with you Mr. Filkins; he said 'I know you will' and handled me rather roughly at first and then we walked downstairs; two or three men were standing near the head of the stairs; they stepped aside and let us go down first.

They had guns in their hands; Filkins had no gun, but had a lighted candle in a candlestick; one of the others, I think, had a lantern; they followd us downstairs into the middle kitchen; he still held on to my collar; I said, 'Let me see Washington for a moment'; We were near by his bed-room; I started to go toward the door and he pulled me back by the collar roughly and said to me 'He is not there, go with me and I will take care of you.'

We then walked into the back kitchen, and the others fol-lowed and closed the door behind them; Filkins walked on along towards the northeast outside door of the kitchen. He stepped along to his overcoat which was hanging up near the door and felt in the pockets, and said, where are my handcuffs. I said Mr. Filkins, you don't need handcuffs, I will go with you. He said, I think you will. He was feeling in his own pockets when he asked where the handcuffs were. Instantly he struck me six or eight times in the head as fast and hard as he could. I staggered against the side of the room.

He said, 'Knock him down'; they then struck me two or three times, I did not fall. He then struck me five or eight times with a slungshot. He had a revolver which he fired a time which missed me. I think the charge passed into the fireplace. He then struck me twice with the revolver and broke his revolver in two.

I then fell, and he jumped on me two or three times on the side and stomach and the others I think kicked me at the same time on the head and neck.

Filkins then said he is dead, lets burn him up. At that he
and they pulled down two or three coats and put them on
me, and also a bag of oats and a fur collar, and threw on
some camphene or something out of a bottle over me and
set fire to it."

Before he fell Grove had been screaming "Murder! Murder!"
and most of the remaining members in the household bolted out
of bed. Nellie Smith had cautionsly followed her lover and Filkins
down the stairs, and recalled:

"I hear Grove holler murder; I went to the door and
opened it a little ways; Filkins came to the door with his
revolver in his hand, pointed it at me and said, 'Come
another step and I will shoot you, it is no place for you in
this kitchen tonight,' and closed the door; then I heard
Grove cry, for God's sake don't kill me; I went to the door
again, opened the door and saw Filkins have Grove bent
forward and pounding his head with a revolver; the tall man
came to the door, pushed me back and closed it.

Cornelia was then coming out of the north room; I said to
Cornelia; 'They are murdering Grove in the back kitchen,'
We pushed the door open - she and I; Grove was lying on
the floor; Filkins was jumping on him; I heard Filkins say
that he was dead and they would burn him; I turned and
ran to call the folks; I went back again; Grove lay on the
floor burning; Cornelia and I ran to the door; Cornelia got
there before I did. We pulled off from Grove two overcoats,
and threw them into the fire-place. I can't say as the other
two men were in the room when Filkins was jumping on
Grove; I did not see the two men, after the tall one closed
the door; I think Filkins left the room just as I opened the
door and saw Grove burning; Grove's head was on a bag of
oats, and camphene or kerosene seemed to have been sprin-
kled on the bag and coats; after we extinguished the flames
on Grove, I went to him and spoke to him.

I says to Grove: 'Have they killed you dead?' He made a
noise, so that I knew there was life in him."

Meanwhile Rhoda Loomis had followed Nellie Smith and Cornelia into the room where Grove lay. His clothes were no longer
on fire but his "head was bloody, his face was swollen, and his
eye was black." Surveying the scene Rhoda saw her injured son
and also the coats burning in the fireplace. According to Rhoda's
testimony given the following day at the inquest she turned her

initial attention to the burning coats rather than to Grove:

> "I went to the fireplace to take it [a coat], and [Cornelia] said, Mother, don't take it out; it is all kerosene; I let it be on fire a minute or two, and then took it out; there was a fur collar buttoned on it; I have not seen it since; neither coat nor collar; the upper part of the coat was burned most; I did not take the coat out of the room; I don't know whose they were; there was a strong smell of kerosene in the room; the gray coat is the one that Grove had on at the time."

Upstairs Plumb and Denio had been awakened by the commotion. Plumb described gang member George Day coming into his room and shouting:

> " 'They are killing Grove down below.' I said to him who or what; he said it is Filkins, haven't you heard him. Denio was with me in bed; he had not got up at this time. I said to George, run downstairs; he said no, I durst not. About that time I was dressing; George had on his pants, his coat on his arm, and shoes in his hand. I went down into the middle kitchen, going down by the front stairs. Cornelia was then trying to open the door into the back kitchen; she had got it open a little way. She said run back, don't come this way any further, they will kill you. I started further that way when the Smith girl said, go back they are killing Grove. I started to go back, and as I was going I looked around. Cornelia had got the door open about two feet; I heard someone of whom I had a glimpse, and whose voice sounded like Filkins' say, 'It's no place for a woman here, keep back or I will shoot you or kill you.'
>
> Cornelia then said, Grove is dead, the house is afire, run as fast as you can. I ran for the front door and met Denio coming downstairs with a pair of rubbers in his hand; he had his clothes on. We went into the front yard, Denio said let's go to the house, they are all at the barn. I said, let's go away this way (north); I ran directly to Mr. Edward Mason's house across lots. I went to Mason's bedroom window and waked him; told him the house was all on fire."

Plumb and Denio remained in hiding at the Mason's house for several hours until they were certain that it was safe to return home.

Although there had been at least nine grown men in the house in addition to Wash and Grove when Filkins and his accomplices arrived, none of them made any effort to help. Even after Plumb and Denio had departed the others remained in their beds despite cries and shouting from the kitchen. While Rhoda Loomis was salvaging the burning coats from the fireplace, Nellie Smith tried to revive Grove by pouring "some spirits" down him. To the astonishment of all Grove revived, "complained of pain in his head and stomach," but got upon his feet and asked for his hat." Despite the brutal beating he had sustained Grove had important matters which had to be attended to. According to Nellie Smith's testimony:

> "Grove put his hat on and went out of the northeast door; he went up to the shanty where the horse was and unlocked the door. I did not go with him. He came back and said to me: 'If you see any signs of fire run up and cut the halter and let the horse loose.'"

Grove then got a ladder to put the fire out in the barn, but finally passed out as he went to get water.

Cries of fire finally brought the remaining gang members from their bedrooms and they went to work to put the fire out. Rhoda tried to save the more valuable stolen goods which had been hidden beneath the floor of the barn while others tried unsuccessfully to free the other horses. Louise Gates, meanwhile, was frantically searching for Wash and imploring others to look as well. After looking in the woodhouse, according to her testimony, she cried:

> "'Where is Wash? Where is Wash? Why don't they find Wash?' Then I went back to the house and went and set in the bedroom and cried. I don't know how long I stayed there."

Once the fire was out Lorenzo Bixby found Wash underneath the woodhouse, "insensible" and "covered with blood." On hearing Wash's name Louise Gates came quickly from her room, "looked at him a few minutes" and "stayed with Wash most of the time after this till he died."

Dr. Medina Preston, Wash's cousin, was summoned from Sangerfield and arrived at dawn. He said there was nothing that could be done, and returned about noon when "life was almost extinct." Under the most favorable circumstances, he testified the following day, Wash "could not possibly have recovered."

Wash Loomis died early in the afternoon with his family gathered around. Grove had regained consciousness but, on Dr. Preston's orders, was to remain quiet. Wash's death was immediately reported to Judge Cleveland in Waterville who asked his brother, Dr. George W. Cleveland, to perform an autopsy. Wash Loomis' wounds were described as follows:

> "At the large transverse wound immediately at about the point where the perpendicular wound connected with it, was a fracture of the skull extending downward, and to the right three inches and a half; two and a half inches of the upper part of this fracture was opened one-eighth of an inch, another fracture starting from the same spot, extended towards the left ear which I traced two inches or more; another fracture starting from the same part, ran directly to the crown of the head, 1½ inches; this last was comminuted; the others were simple fractures; both tables of the skull were fractured; discovered no foreign substance in either of the wounds; these wounds were the cause of his death."

In fact the blows to Wash's head had not only fractured his skull in several places, but had also laid back his scalp. It was, some later commented, as if he had been scalped by attacking Indians.

It was a sensational news story, carried prominently by the *New York Tribune* under "Mob Law in Oneida County." Subheadlines told the whole story: "An objectionable family mobbed —All the barns and eight horses burned—Two men horribly beaten and not expected to recover—No arrest made—Great excitement." The *Utica Morning Herald* headlined a "Startling Murder in Sangerfield" and confirmed the details of "the rumors upon the street which first gained currency about noon yesterday, to the effect that a murder had been committed in the town of Sangerfield . . . When we arrived in Waterville to endeavor to investigate the facts, we found the murder the all-absorbing theme. Knots of men were discussing the circumstances upon street corners . . . the details of the terrible tragedy furnished the only theme of conversation." Other stories were relegated to the bottom of page one, including an account of the signing of a treaty with the Arapahoe, Cheyenne, Apache, and Kiowa Indians on the Plains; "the Kiowa gave up three white women and children held prisoner for eight months. Presents were distributed to the Indians after the treaties were signed."

On Friday afternoon, November 3, Wash Loomis' funeral was held in the Congregational Church in Sangerfield. Family, friends, enemies, and the merely curious filled the church to capacity. The Reverend Marshall of Madison preached the sermon, described by the *Waterville Times* as "very appropriate and impressive." The Loomis family found it scathing, and years later Grove Loomis made arrangements for another minister to preside at his funeral to insure that the Reverend Marshall would not be given a second chance. Wash had been just forty-two when killed, the head of the largest family outlaw gang in the United States. After the funeral he was placed in the ground next to his father.

The coroner's inquest was convened the day after Wash's killing to ascertain whether there was legal cause to proceed with actions against those responsible. Testimony was taken from everybody in the house at the time of the murder and the inquiry was concluded on November 4. The coroner found probable cause that James Fiklins and "unknown others" had been responsible for the murder, and a warrant for Filkins' arrest was issued.

The evidence against Jim Filkins was overwhelming. Several members of the Loomis family identified him as being at the murder scene. Furthermore during the coroner's inquest it was revealed that Filkins had bought kerosene for his lamp the night of the murder, that a pair of handcuffs belonging to him had been found at the Loomis farm, and that the ivory-handled pistol used to beat Wash to death had belonged to Filkins. Nobody in Central New York had any doubt about the identity of the murderer. Barring some anamorphosis of justice, prevailing wisdom on the streets of Sangerfield and Waterville held that Constable Jim Filkins was headed to jail for excessive zeal in performing his duties.

If the Loomises had let the legal process follow its appointed course, that is almost certainly what would have happened. The Loomis leadership, however, had died with Wash Loomis and even before Wash had been buried factionalism and discord had taken over. Nellie Smith, speaking for Grove, wanted to know why none of the other men had come to his rescue while he was screaming and being beaten. Louise Gates bitterly attacked everyone for failing to challenge the intruders when they first arrived; if they had, she said, Wash would still be alive. Plumb and Denio stood accused of cowardice for running to the neighbors and hiding; Rhoda defended them by saying she had ordered them to do so. Bill Loomis, arriving from Higginsville, appeared devastated by Wash's death and disgusted with his entire family. The other gang members seemed to be most interested in distancing themselves from the Loomises; getting murdered by law officers in the middle of the night was not, they said, part of their contract.

The strategy which evolved at the Loomises in the days following Wash's death was apparently planned by Rhoda. An expert at bribing public officials and exploiting men's vulnerabilities, Rhoda had only a hazy conception of legal institutions as they were designed to operate. Grand juries, judges, and district attorneys existed in her mind only as objects to be corrupted; the idea that they might also serve a legal purpose, and in this case work to achieve justice for Wash's death, simply never occurred to her.

Rhoda's plan was to get Jim Filkins jailed as soon as possible and to insure that he remained there. With Filkins out of the way the family could then return to their profitable ways, even without Wash, with virtually no interference. For Rhoda getting back to business was the first priority. A grand jury was scheduled to meet in Utica on November 13, but if the preliminary hearings on the murder could be delayed for a few days then the case would not be ready for this grand jury but would be put over until the next grand jury in February. Filkins, meanwhile, would have to sit in jail with no opportunity to obtain bail.

On Monday morning, November 6, a preliminary hearing on the case was scheduled by Judge Cleveland in Waterville. Filkins appeared with his lawyer, Daniel Ball, and made clear that he was available at any time and ready to proceed. Oneida County District Attorney Hiram T. Jenkins, always willing to help the Loomises in times of need, was conveniently absent so the hearing was postponed. A second hearing was scheduled for November 8, with identical results; Judge Cleveland, exasperated, issued subpoenas for the Loomises and threatened to issue one for District Attorney Jenkins as well.

On the afternoon of November 8, Plumb Loomis appeared in court and asked that the preliminary hearing be postponed for a few days. Judge Cleveland denied the request and ordered Plumb to give immediate testimony. Plumb excused himself to use the bathroom, then fled from the building. An hour later Judge Cleveland received a telegram from District Attorney Jenkins asking that the hearings be set aside. Cleveland, now furious at the intentional delays and collusion between the Loomises and District Attorney, issued subpoenas for all witnesses and ordered constables to bring them to court. Two members of the gang— Lorenzo Bixby, who had been in the house the night of the murder, and Nathan Gates—were found and forced to testify. Bixby was especially uncooperative, claiming almost total amnesia for the events of his life. The *Utica Morning Herald* reported that Bixby "did not know his father's business or who his neighbors were. Similar testimony reads of idiocy, but with keen, sagacious, and crafty appearance to stamp him as concealing his past history." The folllowing day Denio Loomis and Louisa Gates were brought to court and forced to testify.

Still not satisfied Judge Cleveland dispatched two constables and two assistants to serve subpoenas and bring the witnesses to court. The four went to the Loomis house at daybreak on Monday, November 13. As described in the *Utica Morning Herald*: "Elizabeth Calkins was discovered in an outhouse, but on perceiving that she was discovered started for the house hotly pursued by Constable Sanford. Old Mrs. Loomis seized Sanford by the arm and held on until the girl had disappeared within the door. Guards were stationed outside, and a thorough search made of every visible room from cellar to garret, but some secret hole had received her and the constable, after two hours fruitless examination, came away crestfallen." The newspaper, in summarizing the judicial hide-and-seek taking place in Sangerfield, stated flatly that "the most important witnesses had not been produced but had been kept concealed."

Apparently fearful that Judge Cleveland was going to conclude his investigation in time to give the case to the grand jury, the Loomises changed their strategy. On November 13, the same morning that Constable Sanford was chasing Elizabeth Calkins from the outhouse, District Attorney Jenkins took the case directly to the grand jury being convened in Utica. One factor influencing his decision may have been his friendship with Judge William J. Bacon, who instructed the members of the grand jury as follows: "The [Loomis] case will probably be brought before you, and if so, it is the duty of the jurors to give the case a careful hearing and upon proof furnished you ascertain the authors of the murder. It is your duty to make a presentation to this court by indictment. Mob law cannot be justified. A good citizen might be sacrificed by the same rule on another day. Such proceedings cannot be upheld in a law-abiding community. If the grand jurors do their duty, the law is adequate to meet all offenses"

For two days District Attorney Jenkins paraded Loomis family members, who had suddenly become available, and their friends before the grand jury. Filkins was not asked to appear nor even informed of the proceedings. At the end of the testimony the jury could not reach a conclusion. During the course of the testimony two gang members—George Jones and Charles Bird—were mentioned who, it was claimed, had been in the house at the time and had direct knowledge of Filkins and the murder. The grand jury asked to hear from these men. District Attorney Jenkins said they could not be found, but in place of their testimony he had some sworn affidavits which he would introduce as evidence. Mr. C. O. Southworth of Rome, a partner in the law firm representing the Loomises, then was introduced and read the testimony of Jones and Bird which clearly pointed to Filkins as the murderer of Wash Loomis.

On Saturday, November, 18, the grand jury handed down five indictments against James L. Filkins—murder, assault with intent to kill, and three counts of arson. The newspapers reported that the jury had been unanimous in their verdict despite the fact that grand jury proceedings were supposed to be secret. Apparently reflecting a sentiment prevalent in the community, the newspaper added: "Mr. Filkins, we understand, is a respectable man, and will be able to prove an alibi. The witnesses relied upon by the prosecution will be amply impeached as entirely unworthy of belief under oath, or otherwise."

Filkins, who had remained free on his own recognizance, learned of the indictment when he read the newspaper on Monday, November 20. Furious that he had not been informed by District Attorney Jenkins, he immediately set out for Utica accompanied by his lawyer, Daniel Ball. Filkins and Ball realized that both the facts and the judicial process were stacked against them. They therefore went directly to the law office of Roscoe Conkling and asked for his assistance.

Conkling, still basking in the publicity he had received for successfully prosecuting the Haddock case, was waiting for the new Congress to convene on December 4. His reputation had never been higher and speculation was widespread that he was destined for offices above that of congressman. The defense of Jim Filkins must have seemed a hopeless task since the evidence against him was overwhelming. Yet Roscoe Conkling agreed to take the case with no hesitation, going to court that very day on Filkins' behalf.

One can only speculate on Conkling's motivation as he left no documents pertaining to the case. He certainly had followed the events of recent months closely, including the Loomis crime wave

of the summer and fall. It had been over fifteen years since Conkling, as a young District Attorney, had successfully prosecuted
Bill Loomis and obtained a conviction; in the intervening years
no member of the Loomis family had been convicted of more
than a petty crime. Instead they had taken evidence from the
pocket of one district attorney, robbed the offices of a second,
and burned down the Morrisville Courthouse. They had, in
short, made a mockery of justice.

Conkling was certainly also aware that the Loomises had profited enormously by the Civil War. Not only had they not fought
for the Union, but they had harbored deserters even as they
reaped their financial harvest. The Loomises were, in phrases
Conkling had used in the Haddock trial, part of the "darkening
cloud of vampires, gorging themselves upon the heart's blood of
their country." And, like Haddock, they must be brought to
justice one way or another.

It is also probable that Roscoe Conkling admired the courage
of Jim Filkins. Blunt, rash, aggressive, self-righteous, inclined to
expediency in the name of justice—these were qualities that
Roscoe Conkling could understand. Equally probable is the fact
that Conkling was drawn to the case by a personal dislike of
Hiram Jenkins. Conkling had just turned 36—in fact on the same
day Wash Loomis was killed—and Jenkins was 32. Both men had
had well-known fathers who had been dedicated to public service, both were Republicans active in local politics, and both
were lawyers. Jenkins now occupied the District Attorney's job
once held by Conkling, and in Conkling's eyes it must have
seemed that Jenkins had disgraced the position. Not only had he
dropped all outstanding indictments against the Loomises but
here Jenkins was again openly abetting the Loomises in their
attempts to get Filkins into jail. Nothing urged Roscoe Conkling
to battle more forcefully than the smell of corruption in public
office. In a speech in later years Conkling described corruption of
public officials as "the pestilence that wasteth at noon day, what
shall be said of that? Corruption, with its stealthy creep, its
leprous touch and its deadly breath—corruption which has rotted
and wasted so many fair fabrics—will that mark us for destruction too, as the sea-bird blasts the tree on which he builds his
nest? . . . Crying, flagrant, dangerous abuses challenge attention
in this great State through all its length and breadth."

On the afternoon of November 20, 1865, Roscoe Conkling and
Hiram Jenkins faced each other for the first time in a court of

law. "Not guilty," was Filkins' response when Judge Bacon asked how he would plead to the five indictments against him. "Now that you have pleaded," District Attorney Jenkins asked, "what are you and your counsel prepared to do?" Before Filkins could answer, Roscoe Conkling rose and faced Jenkins: "I am prepared to say at once what I will do upon knowing the course proposed by the prosecution," he said challengingly. "I find that for some reason the findings of the grand jury have been encumbered by an extraordinary number of indictments, and a statement has been put forth in the public prints as to the vote by which the indictments were found unanimously, which, even if it were true, was in violation of the law, and calculated to prejudice the accused; and if in addition to all this, objection was to be made to allowing bail, the defendant had better submit to the disadvantage and inconvenience of a trial at once, without time for proper examination, rather than be committed to jail until a future term of court."

Jenkins was flustered, not having anticipated Conkling asking for an immediate trial. He wanted to deny bail to Filkins at any cost. Jenkins responded: "I am not willing to be put in the position of asking for a delay so that the defendant can make that a ground for being let to bail," he said, "but I shall oppose bail being granted." Judge Bacon then acknowledged that the matter of bail would have to be decided by the court. Conkling pressed the issue: "I would move at once that the defendant be let to bail," he said. Thereupon Daniel Ball submitted a statement to the court in support of the request:

> "Mr. Filkins has been ready from the first to respond to any summons. He has asked for an examination and the magistrate has attempted to hold it, but the Loomises have baffled and thwarted it by concealing witnesses and preventing their attendance and by various other devices. Mr. Filkins has voluntarily appeared at all times and had started for Utica as soon as he heard that he was indicted."

District Attorney Jenkins countered by making a lengthy summary of what took place at the coroner's inquest and before the grand jury, concluding that "in cases of murder the Court can grant bail only when, upon the evidence of the grand jury, the guilt of the defendant was not probable." He cited several cases of law to support this conclusion.

Conkling was back on his feet having anticipated Jenkins' arguments. "Your Honor," he said, "I wish to close my argu-

ments for the motion I have presented by maintaining the following propositions." And he launched into a long exposition of
English law, dissecting Jenkins' argument point by point with
abundant case references to support his attack. Most important,
he said, "a defendant is never to be punished before trial, and
bail is never refused or made grievous in amount, except the
object be to prevent escape of the accused. Whenever the Court is
satisfied that the appearance of the defendant at his trial will be
secured by his giving bail, it is the duty of the Court to accept it."
Conkling then pointed out several inconsistencies in the testimony before the grand jury cited by Jenkins, and rested his case.

Judge Bacon conferred with other court officials. He wanted to
be helpful to District Attorney Jenkins but Conkling, re-elected
to Congress and rapidly becoming an important political power,
was not a man to be alienated unnecessarily. Besides Conkling's
arguments were legally persuasive. Judge Bacon therefore stated
the decision of the Court:

> "The jurisdiction of this Court as to bail for felonies
> extends to murder as well as to other crimes. The object of
> bail is to secure the attendance of the accused and, when-
> ever this object can be obtained and insured by acceptance
> of bail, it should not be refused. In many cases the facts are
> such as to render it unsafe to release the defendant from
> custody. In a recent case ten thousand dollars had been
> fixed and, although the other members of the court think
> this amount rather large in the present case, we have agreed
> upon it."

Roscoe Conkling had won the first round.

# CHAPTER X

# Lynching

Due largely to the efforts of Roscoe Conkling, Jim Filkins spent only four days in the Utica Jail. On Friday, November 24, twenty-eight men from Sangerfield, Waterville, and nearby towns drove to Utica and together put up ten thousand dollars in bail for his release. An unseasonal snowstorm made traveling difficult; according to the local newspaper "had not the roads been in terrible condition, some twenty more gentlemen would have gone out to sign the bail bonds, making about fifty in all."

The large number of men furnishing Filkins' bail was not, according to the newspaper, because a large sum of money was needed. "Almost any one of the gentlemen would alone have stood the bail" but "for several reasons" it was decided to utilize a large number of them. "In the first place, the people of this community have strong faith in Mr. Filkins' entire innocence and believe that there is a deep plot to get him out of the way so that depredations upon property may be carried on in greater safety. Secondly, his townsmen desired to make an expression of this faith and belief. Thirdly, it was understood that the gang of incendiaries and thieves who infest this locality had declared that any person who should become bail for Mr. Filkins must take the consequences, and as his bailor, a Deputy U.S. Marshall has had his barn and hop kiln burned to the ground since he signed the bail bond, it was probably thought best to adopt the suggestion of the old saying, 'In union there is strength.' Fourthly, they desired to show that the sympathy of the town was with their fearless, guiltless, and law-abiding officer and citizen rather than with law-breakers and outlaws. Yet, notwithstanding the staunch belief of the people of this town in Mr. Filkins' innocence, they strongly condemn the murder of Wash Loomis, and desire the arrest and punishment of the perpetrator of the lawless and wicked act." Some of the men signing Filkins' bail bond had recruited him to Waterville and actively backed his efforts. Others on the list, however, were said to have "previously been allied with the Loomises."

The Loomises response to Filkins' release was outrage. Grove and Bill let it be widely known that the family had placed a one thousand dollar bounty on Filkins' head. One man was said to accept the offer, take a down payment, but then thought better of it and fled to Canada. One evening shortly after Filkins' release, gang members Tom Mott, George Day and George Jones entered the Park Hotel in Waterville, ordered dinner, and announced they had come to kill Filkins. When Filkins entered the room they drew their guns but did not shoot. Filkins turned, calmly walked out of the room, went home and got his gun. By the time he returned the three men had had second thoughts and departed for the Loomis homestead.

Other Loomis associates were also incensed by the murder of Wash. One story, not verified by local records, claimed that Big Bill Rockwell came from western New York specifically to seek revenge. Cornelia, it was said, knew the identity of Filkins' accomplices and showed Big Bill where each lived. "On that same night numerous farmers' barns in that locality burned down. By a queer coincidence, every farmer whose barn had been destroyed had been a member of the posse that was responsible for Wash Loomis' death."

At Bissell's general store talk among the men was tinged with apprehension. The war was over, yet news everywhere told of continuing violence. In November, Henry Wirz had been hanged, the only Confederate war criminal so treated. He had been a Swiss physician who had become head of Andersonville prison in Georgia and had been charged with the murder of prisoners of war. When sentenced Wirz exclaimed: "I'm damned if the Yankee eagle hasn't turned out to be what I expected, a damned turkey buzzard." Mississippi had passed the Black Codes denying Negroes the rights to attend white schools, bear arms, testify against whites, serve on juries, or hold large meetings; a Chicago newspaper responded that "the men of the North will convert . . .

Mississippi into a frog pond before they will allow such laws." In December the first meeting of the Ku Klux Klan had been called by Jim Crowe and five other former Confederate army officers. And in the west the federal army had begun using machine guns, patented by a physician named Richard J. Gatling, against the remaining insurgent Indians. People in Waterville wondered what the next violent act might be.

The answer came December 6 at the home of Dennison and Phoebe Crandall. An elderly couple, they lived alone on a farm south of Leonardsville ten miles from the Loomises. Dennison was sixty-five but hearty, and widely known to keep large sums of money in the house. On December 5, he withdrew two thousand one hundred dollars from the bank in Leonardsville.

Joe Crandall was a nephew of Dennison and Phoebe Crandall, and an active member of the Loomis gang. On the afternoon of December 6, Joe Crandall set out from the Loomis farm with two associates, Isaiah Belfield and Shadrack Curtis. They carried masks so that they would not be recognized. The three arrived at the Crandall farm "about early candle light, probably between 5 and 6 o'clock"; donning their masks one remained outside while the other two entered the kitchen.

Phoebe Crandall was cooking dinner and screamed at the intruders. That brought Dennison from the other room and he was told to give them his money and bonds or be killed. "You'll not have them," he replied, whereupon one of the robbers swung at Crandall with a club. According to a contemporary newspaper account Crandall immediately "leaped forward and landed a stiff blow to the outlaw's stomach. While the robber clutched at his middle, Crandall seized him and tripped him, throwing him to the floor. The other masked man drew his pistol, but Crandall hit him with a chunk of wood again and again until he dropped to the floor and grovelled like a beaten dog. The first outlaw, having recovered from the blow to his stomach, leaped on Crandall, but the farmer threw him aside like a sack of wheat, got him on his back and beat at his face with his hands. The second outlaw joined the fray and, as Crandall rose to meet him, the first outlaw drew his pistol and fired. The farmer staggered as the ball lodged behind his ear. The two outlaws leaped on him and bore him to the floor. Blood streamed down the side of his face. 'Let me go,' he panted, 'and I will get you some money.' He broke loose, ran into his bedroom and slammed the door behind him. Though the room was in darkness, his hands found what they were searching for, a long flail stick which he had nicknamed his 'headache stick.' The door was pushed open slightly and a pistol was thrust into the room. Crandall struck the hand with his stick. He swung the door open to face the burning eyes of the first out-law. He raised his stick to ward off an attack, but the stick caught on the door-casing. The outlaw raised his pistol and fired point-blank at Crandall's face. Though the ball struck the farmer slightly below the eye, he did not fall, but advanced toward the outlaws, who retreated toward the stove. At this moment a third masked man appeared in the kitchen. Coolly, he raised his pistol and shot Crandall through the back of the head. As the aged farmer staggered across the room and fell headlong, his wife screamed. The outlaw shot her, too."

Despite having been hit in the head by three bullets, Dennison Crandall rose once more when he heard his wife scream. The trio then attacked him with "clubs and billets of wood (apparently from a woodbox that was near) cutting the scalp through in several places, some of them several inches in length, irregular in shape, besmearing the walls, ceiling, doors, and floor with the spattering blood until he finally fell to the floor when they undoubtedly pounded his head until they supposed him entirely dead."

Incredibly, Dennison Crandall regained consciousness two hours later. Slowly getting to his feet he "groped his way about the room, obtained a match and lit a candle. As the light filled the room he looked about him. Upon the floor, cold and stiff in death, he found the body of his wife." The house had been ran-sacked in an attempt to find the money but, as Crandall learned later, the purse was still safely hidden in his straw mattress. Crandall "got a lantern, lit it, and started across the fields directly to the house of his brother, George V. Crandall, about half a mile distant in a northwesterly direction, where he arrived about eight o'clock . . . His footsteps could be traced by his blood the whole distance."

When George Crandall opened the door he did not recognize his brother. "It was a ghastly and terrible sight to behold, his head apparently pounded to a jelly, cut and mangled, the wounds of the pistol balls all bleeding profusely, blood running from both ears and from his nostrils and mouth, his clothing covered with blood." According to the doctor who examined him, the first bullet had hit him "near the top of his forehead, cutting through to the skull bone, cutting out a round crease and glancing off; another hit him higher up on his head, making a similar wound. The other ball entered about three-fourths of an inch directly under his right eye, penetrating some two and one-half inches on a level with the base of the brain, inclining downwards and inwards, where it yet remains."

Dennison Crandall remained conscious for only a few minutes after arriving at his brother's house. "I fought them the best I could," he said; "I could stand the bullets, but not the clubs." The *Utica Morning Herald* called the murder of Phoebe Crandall "One of the most atrocious and revolting murders that was ever perpetrated in the county."

Community reaction to the Crandall murder was both outrage and fear. Nobody knew who had done it but the assumption was widespread that the Loomises had been involved. As was later learned, following the murder Belfield and Curtis stayed on at the Loomises, while Joe Crandall, disguised in a bonnet and dress, had been driven out of town by Denio Loomis. Nellie Smith reported that she heard Cornelia Loomis scornfully tell them: "It's a pretty big crime for so little money. If I had committed so big a crime, I would have got more money." Dennison Crandall, miraculously recovering from his wounds, offered a one thousand dollar reward for information leading to the murderers of his wife. Nobody was certain whether he could identify the assailants.

Although it had been only a few weeks since Wash Loomis' death, it was clear to those who knew the family that a leadership vacuum had descended upon the homestead. The brutal Crandall murder was cited as evidence of it. Wash would never have permitted such an occurrence, it was said, not because he was against murder but because the brutal murder of an old woman evoked so much community animostiy. Wash's concerted efforts over the years to turn neighbors into friends had been successful, and his personal charm had repeatedly disarmed even the most vengeful of Loomis detractors in surrounding villages. Now Wash was no longer there to plan, to urge moderation and patience, to placate offended officials and sheriffs. Wash had been an outlaw, all right, but he had been an outlaw that a man could trust. Following the Crandall murder one could hear tinges of nostalgia in some of the voices in Bissell's general store whenever Wash Loomis' name came up.

Grove Loomis recovered very slowly from his brother's murder and his own brush with death. He spent increasing amounts of time with his horses, showing little interest in the family's activities. Some said he did not trust them anymore. Bill actively pursued a court suit against Filkins for causing Wash's death but otherwise remained in Higginsville, while Wheeler showed no inclination to return from Canada with the rape charge outstanding.

That left only Plumb and Denio to carry on, and Rhoda and Cornelia urged them to do exactly that. To curtail activities, Rhoda argued, would signify weakness to their enemies. The most fitting tribute to Wash, she said, was to aggressively carry on the Loomis family tradition. Neither Plumb nor Denio had leadership qualities, however, which meant that Rhoda had to rely increasingly on other gang members, most of whom she personally disliked and treated with overt contempt. Rather than the well-ordered criminal activities which took place under Wash's direction, each man increasingly went off in his own direction to plunder and terrorize.

As she had done at times in the past when money was needed, Rhoda decided to return to the distribution of counterfeit, an activity she and George Loomis had found so profitable in the early years of their marriage. She arranged, therefore, for delivery of a large quantity of counterfeit bills to the Loomis farm.

Rumors of the delivery reached Jim Filkins, who despite being under indictment for murder had resumed his responsibilities as an officer of the law. A few community leaders in Sangerfield and Waterville had raised questions about the propriety of having a constable who was under indictment, but then, nobody else seemed interested in taking the job. Filkins, suspecting that he would not be particularly welcome at the Loomis home following his most recent visit, assembled a party consisting of four law officers from Madison County and two others from Oneida County for a raid.

Rhoda Loomis received them surprisingly cordially, telling them they were free to search the premises as they pleased and offering them beer from a small keg in the cellar. Several drinks later the officers were losing interest in the raid when one of them noticed an irregularity in the keg. Filkins agreed, took the keg outside and split it with an ax. A false bottom of the keg was full of counterfeit bills. A search of the cellar turned up several other kegs with a similar mix of beer and bills totaling over eleven hundred dollars. Upstairs Filkins began a search of a room in which

Charles Loomis, Wheeler's twelve-year-old son who was visiting from Canada, was staying. Several packs of counterfeit money were found, at which point young Charles picked up a rifle and pointed it at Filkins. "Damn you," Charles swore, "I'll shoot you if you take my money." Filkins seized the rifle and marched the boy downstairs.

Cornelia, meanwhile, was observed trying to hide something under her dress. The officers attempted to take it but, according to a newspaper account, Cornelia "ran like a deer, up one pair of stairs and down another and through several rooms at the time of the arrest, giving the officer a smart race." Finally the object was seized as she tried to throw it out a window. It was a gold watch and chain which had been stolen two years before.

Three generations of Loomises—Rhoda, Cornelia, and young Charles—were put in a sleigh for transport to Utica for booking. Possession of counterfeit bills and postal currency was a federal offense and thus beyond the jurisdiction of county officials. En route the group stopped at the American Hotel in Waterville where, according to the *Utica Observer*, "the old lady created much amusement for the bystanders by her tantrums and the inimitable 'chin music' with which she regaled officer Filkins. She utterly refused to walk, and had to be carried to and from the carriage. Cornelia objected to being arrested by officer Filkins, drawing herself up proudly and declaring she was of 'high blood' and intimating the said officer might get shot if he was not careful."

Although all three Loomises were released on bail, Filkins and his associates continued to make life difficult for the family. A subsequent raid netted "a silver-plated harness . . . which was stolen from Race and Company's livery in Binghamton in September" and later another raid turned up "a horse, wagon and harness stolen from a livery stable in Oswego last May." The *Waterville Times* carried accounts of these raids, together with the Loomis' response to the accusations: "We are good, honest citizens and Filkins lies about us like a damned thief." On one of her appearances in court Cornelia wore an unusual bombazine dress which Filkins knew had been stolen, so he drove to the Loomis house to arrest her. As he neared the house Plumb ran from the side door carrying a bundle and headed for the swamp. Filkins pushed open the front door and "there stood the fair Cornelia with neither cape on her shoulders or dress on her back. We turned from this spectacle of beauty unadorned . . ." When she had finished dressing she was arrested and taken to Waterville.

The Crandall murder had turned most remaining Loomis supporters against them, but the issuance of the "New York Prison Association Report" in early 1866 solidified community opinion. Reprinted in all local newspapers with editorial comment, the Report described the increasing organization of criminals into gangs and warned that "if this tendency to aggregation and organization continues to increase for the future as it has for a few years past, we shall soon have organized bands of associated depredators in all the counties of the State." It then went on to depict in detail the Loomises:

> "There is a family residing in Oneida County, who according to common fame, have followed the profession of thieving for nearly twenty years. They have grown rich by their unlawful practices. Their children are educated in the best and most expensive seminaries. They dress genteelly, their manners are somewhat polished, and they appear tolerably well in society. Their operations are carried on through the counties of Oneida, Oswego, Otsego, Madison, Chenango, Schoharie, Delaware, and Sullivan. They have numerous well trained confederates in all those counties, who are ready by day or by night, at a moment's warning, to ride off in any direction for the sake of plunder or for the concealment or protection of associates who are in danger of falling into the meshes of the law. These men have been indicted times without number in the above mentioned counties, but none of them have ever been convicted, nor have any of them ever been in jail for a longer time than was sufficient for a bondsman to arrive at the prison. It is generally believed that there are farmers, apparently respectable, who belong to the gang and share in its profits. Whether this be so or not, it is certain that whenever bail is needed, any required number of substantial farmers will come forward and sign their bonds, without regard to the amount of penalty. These men, as might be supposed, exert a great political influence, and it is well understood that they are always ready to reward their friends and punish their enemies, both in primary conventions and at the polls. Although, as we have said, they have been repeatedly indicted, yet the number of their indictments bears but a small ratio to the number of their depredations. It usually happens that any one who is particularly active in bringing any of the gang to justice has his barn or dwelling soon after burned, or his horses are missing from the stable, or his

sheep or cattle from the pasture. These things have happened so often that people are careful how they intermeddle in the matter of seeking to bring them to justice. If a person so intermeddling happens to have a mortgage on his property, it is apt to be very soon foreclosed. If he has political aspirations, thousands of unseen obstacles interpose to prevent the fulfillment of his hopes. If he is a trader, his customers fall off. If he is a physician, malpractice is imputed to him, or other malicious stories are circulated to his discredit; and at length matters come to such a pass that his only recourse is to leave the county. All who make themselves conspicuous as their opponents, are in some way made to feel the effect of a thousand blighting and malign influences, which paralyze their energies and blast their hopes of success. Although the law has been powerless when exerted against the gang, they have been in the habit of using its energies with great effect against those who stood in their path. We are told, with great circumstantiality, by men worthy of all confidence, of numerous instances where the forms of law were used to punish innocence and shield robbery under their skillful manipulations.

The Prison Association Report elicited much interest in Waterville and the surrounding towns. It was widely discussed, even displacing for a time talk of news from Washington. There skirmishings between Congress and President Andrew Johnson had become increasingly bitter since the thirty-ninth Congress had convened in December, and Roscoe Conkling was on the front lines of the fray. Because of his previous two terms in Congress, Conkling had been named to the Joint Committee on Reconstruction popularly known as the "Committee of Fifteen," which was charged with setting terms for readmission of southern states to the Union. President Johnson favored leniency while Congress wanted signs of repentance by the wayward states before allowing them to again be seated in Congress.

All pretense of civility on the Potomac disappeared on February 19, 1866, when President Johnson vetoed the Congressionally passed extension of the Freedmen's Bureau. This was the organization which was to guarantee the rights of freed Negroes; the President suggested that the Negroes did not need government assistance and should instead manage "through their own merits and exertions." Three days later President Johnson, apparently inebriated, gave an extemporaneous public speech in which he accused the leaders of Congress of being "traitors" and claimed that they were plotting his assassination.

Congress struck back by overriding Johnson's veto and denying readmission to the Union for the President's home state of
Tennessee. When David T. Patterson arrived in Washington as
Senator from that state, Roscoe Conkling rose in Congress to
oppose Patterson's admission. Such men Conkling said, "cannot
by an oath purge themselves of treason . . . Sir, I say it is amaz-
ing; I say this whole scene tonight is a sad commentary."

Conkling, like many other people in the North, wanted a
measure of revenge. In a speech he invoked the war dead—"three
hundred thousand men sleep in bloody shrouds"—to justify
delaying readmission of southern states. He also called for the
punishment of Jefferson Davis, languishing in a prison in Richmond and whom President Johnson refused to bring to trial.
Conkling reminded his listeners that "Old John Brown is the only
man who ever expiated treason on an American gibbet." Shall
the reward for treason, Conkling asked, be "wholesale pardon
. . . for traitors whose hands and faces are dripping with the
blood of murder?"

As had happened in the past, Roscoe Conkling's truculence
and sarcasm made him as many enemies as friends, and in the
spring of 1866 these qualities were more prominent than usual.
First he attacked Representative Raymond of New York for
allowing a "malicious and venomous" article against Conkling to
be printed, then ridiculed Representative Schenck of Ohio for
"that celebrated pelvic gesture by which the gentleman makes
himself forcible . . . my friend's manner is rather appalling."
Most seriously, however, he tangled with Representative Blaine
of Maine in an ongoing clash of egos and invective. Conkling
publicly called Blaine a liar and a bully, and said that Blaine's
"zeal outruns his discretion, which perhaps is not the first occurrence of that kind in his life." Blaine was equal to the battle, rising in Congress to note:

> "As to [Conkling's] cruel sarcasm, I hope he will not be
> too severe. The contempt of that large-minded gentleman is
> so wilting; his haughty disdain, his grandiloquent swell, his
> majestic, supereminent, overpowering, turkey-gobbler strut
> has been so crushing to myself and all the members of this
> House that I know it was an act of the greatest temerity for
> me to venture upon a controversy with him."

Others called Conkling "vain as a peacock, and a czar in arrogance" and claimed that he "would at any time sacrifice right to

benefit his party."

Conkling's public battles provided entertainment for the daily gatherings at Bissell's general store as men discussed the news. Slavery had been abolished and Negroes declared citizens by the newly-passed Civil Rights Bill. In fact everyone in the United States was now considered to be equal except for women and Indians. The latter were being systematically exterminated from the Plains to make room for more settlers. The Superintendent of Indian Affairs tried vainly to protect their interests, writing to Washington: "For a mighty nation like us to be carrying on a war with a few straggling nomads, under such circumstances, is a spectacle most humiliating, an injustice unparalleled, a national crime most revolting, that must, sooner or later, bring down upon us or our posterity the judgment of Heaven." In Central New York the remaining Oneida Indians were in the news at this time because the New York State Legislature had announced in February, 1866, an investigation of "the treaty of 1788 and agreements of the State with the Oneida Nation of Indians" to determine whether the Indian land had been taken fraudulantly. Nothing came of the investigation.

April brought spring to the Nine Mile Swamp and with it new kinds of problems for the Loomises. The large stand of maple trees behind the Loomis homestead had been tapped for many years, and collecting and boiling the syrup was an activity in which all family members and visiting associates participated. In 1866 many Loomis gang members were away avoiding indictments, so the Loomises hired extra labor to help with the sugaring. One evening Rhoda Loomis served for dinner pancakes with the freshly-boiled maple syrup. Immediately following the meal everyone became violently ill with vomiting, diarrhea and abdominal cramps. Dr. Medina Preston, summoned from Sangerfield, treated everyone with purgatives and took samples of the food to determine the cause of the problem. He later offered an opinion that the maple syrup had been poisoned.

Most people in Waterville agreed that one of the prime suspects in the Crandall murder case was Laverne Beebe, who had disappeared immediately following the crime. In May, 1866, Jim Filkins received word from law authorities in Iowa that Laverne Beebe, his father Ezra Beebe, and Tom Mott had been arrested there. Filkins applied to New York Governor Reuben E. Fenton for extradition papers but Fenton reminded Filkins that he himself was still under indictment for murder and therefore could not leave the state without permission. Eventually it was decided that Deputy Sheriff Asa Stone of Madison would be in charge of returning the prisoners and Filkins would accompany him.

Stone and Filkins went to Iowa and were returning with their three prisoners by train. In Pennsylvania Laverne Beebe and Mott went to the toilet. Beebe jumped from the window of the moving train and successfully escaped. As Mott was climbing out the window, however, the train lurched causing him to hit his head on the window; he was found unconscious on the floor by Filkins and Stone. Later Filkins publicly accused Deputy Sheriff Stone of incompetence for failing to keep the prisoners in handcuffs and allowing one of them to escape.

Arriving home the afternoon of Saturday, June 9, Jim Filkins was told by his wife, Sarah, that a man had stopped that morning with important information. Several members of the Loomis gang for whom Filkins had outstanding warrants had arrived at the Loomises' the previous night with stolen horses. One of the wanted men was said to be Bill Alvord.

Filkins did not even unpack his bag but, in his own words, "left Waterville for the Loomises' about ten o'clock Saturday night, with Constable Sanford of Waterville. Inquiring along the way, I learned that there were other parties at Loomises' that Deputy Sheriff Conger of North Brookfield had warrants for. Sanford and I went down to North Brookfield and informed him of the fact; Conger and Constable Hibbard of North Brookfield then accompanied Sanford and I and four other men that formed our party to the Loomis house, in the southwest part of the town of Sangerfield. All of us surrounded the house a little after daylight Sunday morning. Mrs. Rhoda Loomis, the mother, was at the back door feeding ducks; as soon as she saw us she halloed out to the men in the house, 'Here's Filkins and a lot of men.' We then entered the house and went up stairs; seeing that the Loomis party had gone up in the garret, Conger and I started to go up the garret stairs together, Conger a little ahead. At this time some one, I cannot positively say who, stood at the top of the stairs with a gun, and said, 'Go back, G-d d--n you, or I will shoot you through!' Conger advanced, and the unknown man struck him with the gun, inflicting an ugly wound in the head. I now, being some fifteen feet from the unknown man, shot at him with a revolver; do not know whether I hit him or not, but I aimed for his breast. The man now attempted to strike Conger again, and I shot at him a second time, taking aim at his head; do not know whether I hit him or not. Some one then fired a gunshot down the stairs; do not know that any one was hit. As Conger and I started to go downstairs we met a stranger, who, upon being asked his name, gave it, but I now forget it. I asked him if old Bill Alvord was up stairs. He said there was some one there they called Bill, that he came from Canada with him a night or two before; Conger put handcuffs on the Canadian. As Conger with his prisoner and some of our men went out of the house towards the road, the party in the garret fired upon them several times; the prisoner was hit in the shoulder and breast with buckshot, wounding him considerably though not dangerously. Another man named Lord was also shot. Conger and his party then went away for help. I stayed there with the others to watch the house; soon we saw a man come out of the house with a gun and start for the woods. We followed him, and he fired at us with a Minie repeating rifle. He fired at us several times as we followed him, and at last hit me, inflicting a wound in the arm and one in the leg. I do not know who the man was. I do not remember much after this." Two large pigs, a horse and a cow were killed in the shootout.

Filkins, unconscious, was put in a wagon and taken back to Waterville to be treated. One bullet had caused relatively little damage passing "through the anterior fleshy portion of the right thigh, traversing a direction of about six or seven inches." The other bullet had "entered the outer side of the left forearm about two inches below the elbow, passed out the inner side of the forearm traversing a distance of about five inches and fracturing the radius in its course." He was operated on by Drs. G.W. Bailey and G.W. Cleveland who removed "five pieces of bone from his arm." When interviewed by a reporter from the *Utica Morning Herald* the following day, Filkins "was evidently in great pain and only talked with much effort. Indeed it was with difficulty we gained the statement, his speech being interrupted from time to time by the intensity of his sufferings."

The "Canadian" who was taken into custody was Shadrack Curtis whose "coppery skin, piercing black eyes and thick black hair cut square at his shoulders hinted of Indian blood." He had been one of Phoebe Crandall's assailants but that was not known by the officers at the time. The man who hit Conger with the gun and then shot Filkins was Bill Alvord, but he was also severely wounded. After the raiding party left, Alvord was brought back to the house and put in an upstairs bedroom. He was unconscious and vomiting blood.

Dr. Medina Preston was summoned, and treated the wounds. Rhoda Loomis then dressed Alvord in woman's clothing and tied a sunbonnet on his head anticipating the return of the lawmen. Shortly thereafter three constables from Brookfield arrived to search the house. Finding a seriously sick "woman" in an upstairs bedroom they asked what was wrong. Rhoda Loomis "shook her head sadly and said her sickness was occasioned by the shaking given her a day or two ago by Sheriff Conger." The constables were suspicious but left. In Sangerfield and Waterville rumors were rife that Alvord had been killed by Filkins' bullets and that the Loomises had secretly buried him. A few days later Grove Loomis drove Alvord to a secret hiding place where he could recuperate from his wounds.

Having now been shot by the Loomises on two separate occasions, Jim Filkins was a local hero. The *Madison County Observer* reported that he was recovering slowly "and in the course of three or four months will probably be able to take to the warpath once more." Utica newspapers covered Filkins' progress on a daily basis, and four days after the shooting published an interview with Plumb Loomis in which he averred that "none of the Loomis family fired upon Filkins, Conger or the others, and that there were no strangers at the house Saturday night." To this the newspaper appended: "All of which statements the reader may accept with as many grains of allowance as he chooses." The citizens of Waterville and Sangerfield, said the newspaper, were "discussing the affair by crowds upon the street corners, at the hotels, and we doubt not wherever else one or two were met together." No mention was made of the fact that Filkins was still under indictment for Wash Loomis' murder.

Filkins had taken out a five thousand dollar life insurance policy with the Travelers Insurance Company following the first attempt on his life. From Hartford the president of the company wrote the local agent and the letter was published in the *Utica Morning Herald*:

> "No apologies were needed for having insured Mr. Filkins, knowing that the Loomis gang were not pleased with his ways. We only regret that the insurance was not larger, and if he had succeeded in killing the whole gang we would cheerfully have made him a pensioner for life. If the authorities of your county, after 20 years experience, cannot

provide a safe residence from that Loomis family, we beg of you to insure all constables, and the Travelers Insurance Co. will provide for them.

"Never hesitate to insure a plucky fellow like Filkins for fear some scamp may kill him. If we could heal him as easily as we can pay him, our joy would be full. The custom of this company is to pay only on maturity of the claim. In this case, however, you are authorized to draw on us at sight, either weekly or monthly, (as may suit his convenience) for the amount of his compensation, twenty-five dollars per week."

In the week which followed the shooting of Filkins, meetings were held in the room over Bissell's store. Similar meetings were convened in North Brookfield, Hamilton, Madison and Morrisville. Jim Filkins was still incapacitated but others were ready to carry on his work. Some people said the solution to the Loomis problem had been suggested by a State Supreme Court Justice who despaired of legal remedies. Others said it had come from Deputy Sheriff Ephraim Conger who had been asked to serve additional warrants on the Loomises. Still hurting from the blows of Alvord's pistol sustained during the raid Conger is said to have picked up his gun and announced: *This* is the only warrant I will serve on the Loomises."

By late Saturday afternoon, June 16, the yard of the Exchange Hotel in Morrisville was filled with carriages, Men were gathering from Stockbridge, Peterboro, Canastota and Oneida, and all were armed. When one young man asked what was happening he was told that everyone was going to Sangerfield to arrest Plumb Loomis for stealing a cap. The men left Morrisville at dusk, and met with similar groups coming from Madison and Hamilton. On the other side of the Loomis farm Ephraim Conger had collected men in North Brookfield, and still others were setting out from Waterville. Altogether there were over one hundred of them, and their weapons included firearms of all descriptions, a keg of gunpowder, and a stout rope.

The leadership of the mob included virtually every law officer in Madison County and many from Oneida County as well. The majority of the men in the mob had been recently discharged from the army; they had lived with violence and death, and were probably attracted by the potential for its company again. As they rode in the dusk they recounted the crimes of the Loomises; many of the men had lost sheep or horses, and a few had had their barn burned. The need for revenge was expressed in a thousand inarticulate ways; this impluse is always close to the surface but in 1866 the social fabric covering it was even thinner than it is today. As one observer has noted: "The fact that civilized men and women adhere to a social contract requiring them to settle disputes in courtrooms instead of at the corral before sundown does not mean that the impulse toward revenge has been eradicated—any more than the institution of marriage implies the disappearance of sexual impulses directed toward anyone other than one's lawful spouse."

Shortly before dawn, as amorphous gray-green shapes began to separate from the night, the groups met at a prearranged point a mile from the Loomis home. Ephraim Conger had bribed someone to poison the Loomis dogs during the night, so as the raiders approached no alarm was given. The men had completely surrounded the house when they were seen by Rhoda who "gave fight like a cornered panther" and "threw herself on the first men to reach the doorstep."

Grove, Plumb, young Charles, and Cornelia Loomis were all at home, along with John Stoner, John Smith, Esther Crandall (Joe's sister), Elizabeth Hawkins, and Plumb's girlfriend, Adeline Glazier. Looking out the windows at the small army of besiegers with guns leveled at the house, the Loomises surrendered without a fight. Sheriff Stone announced that they had come to arrest Plumb on the petit larceny charge of stealing a cap, and handcuffs were placed on Plumb and Grove as all the occupants were herded into the yard.

Any semblance of order rapidly disappeared. Two storekeepers who were present began taking an inventory of the house's contents, but as they did so men ran from room to room looting everything that could be carried. Suddenly smoke was seen coming out a window; Rhoda ran upstairs and threw water on the fire which had been started in a closet, then seized a bed which had been set afire and smothered the flames. A third fire had been set in the cellar which grew rapidly out of control. Cornelia joined her mother carrying furniture and other objects out the front door. As soon as they went back inside the crowd took the things around to the side of the house and threw them back into the rapidly increasing flames. Nothing was saved except a few beds which the crowd permitted them to keep, saying: "Let the poor cusses have a bed to sleep on."

When it became clear that the entire house was going to burn,

Cornelia ran upstairs one last time and threw her trunk out the window. Before she could reach it the men had it open and the contents divided; included was eight hundred and thirty-six dollars. Rhoda Loomis at the last minute tried to save gallon jugs of maple syrup and honey, handing them out the door to the men and asking them to place them by the road. They did so, smashing each jug in the process.

When the house was fully ablaze the men stood around it laughing. Talk now turned to what to do with the Loomises themselves. Suggestions were plentiful, including putting them back in the house to burn, or putting them in the shed with the keg of powder and blowing them up. In the midst of this young Charles bolted through the crowd and up the hill; nobody bothered to chase him. Sheriff Stone of Madison County, who had previously been District Attorney, talked quietly with his son, Deputy Sheriff Asa Stone, and Deputy Sheriff Conger; after that he sauntered slowly down the road and out of sight.

Young Asa Stone took charge, and ordered John Stoner brought to the maple tree which stood between the house and the road. A rope was quickly thrown over a branch and secured, and a noose fashioned for Stoner's neck. To the cheers of the crowd Stoner was raised off the ground and suspended for a few seconds. When lowered he indicated a willingness to tell everything he knew, including the fact that Bill Alvord had been the one who shot Filkins the previous week.

Plumb was brought forward next. As one of the most disliked members of the Loomis family, it gave the crowd great satisfaction to watch the noose being placed around his neck. Plumb was thirty-two years old but still often linked with Denio as one who took orders from his mother. He had been called a coward by many for running away and hiding the night Wash had been killed, so he had something to prove. He expected to be killed by the mob and was determined to die bravely. According to a contemporary account he "stood up straight while they adjusted the noose. Then he said quietly: 'If I confess you'll kill me, and if I don't confess you'll kill me. So kill me anyway.' Someone in the crowd shouted, 'How honest have you been in life, Plumb?' 'Honest from the cradle to where I now stand,' Plumb replied. As he looked out on the crowd he saw several men who in the past had helped the Loomises.

"When his feet swung clear of the ground his body threshed wildly and his face contorted until it seemed as if his eyes were

ready to pop from their sockets. His tongue thickened and pro-
truded between empurpled lips. Urine ran down his legs, soaking
through his pants. When his struggles lessened Stone spoke to
the men holding the rope. They let it slacken and Plumb fell to
the ground, where he lay gasping for breath. At length he stirred
and finally sat up. 'Are you ready to talk now?' demanded Conger. Plumb closed his eyes and shook his head. 'When was the
man Alvord here?' Stone demanded. 'I ain't seen Alvord for five
years.' 'Who shot Filkins last week?' 'A brother of Tom Mott.'
'Who fired my hotel at Sweet's Corners?' Conger shouted. When
Plumb refused to answer, he was suspended from the maple limb
again. His body twitched and then went limp. The Loomises
turned their heads away.

"Rhoda fell to her knees and lifted her face to the sky. 'Is there
a praying man here?' Rhoda asked. There was no reply from the
crowd. 'I've never prayed before,' she said. "But I'm going to
pray now.' Her lips moved. 'Almighty God . . .' At Conger's
orders Plumb was lowered to the ground and the noose removed
from his neck. The rough rope had torn through the tender flesh.
Someone brought a bucket of water and doused him with it. 'Are
you going to talk now,' Conger demanded, 'or have we got to
finish the job?' 'What do you want to know?' Plumb gasped. His
voice was little more than a whisper. 'What do you know about
the Crandall murder?' 'I don't know nothing about it.' 'When
did you last see Bill Alvord?' 'Last Sunday.' 'Who shot Deputy
Filkins?' 'Tom Mott.' 'Who was the man Filkins shot on the garret stairs?' 'Bill Alvord. Filkins shot him twice. The reported sick
woman in our garret was Alvord. Grove took him away last Saturday.' 'Where was Alvord taken?' demanded Stone. 'I don't
know,' Plumb answered. 'I don't know.'

"Deputy Stone, infuriated at Plumb's slow, elusive answer,
nodded to the men holding the rope. He placed the noose around
the outlaw's neck for the third time. 'Don't hang me again,'
Plumb groveled into the grass. 'Shoot me and get it over with.'
'Talk fast then,' Conger demanded. 'Who burned my hotel?'
Plumb closed his mouth sullenly. Seeing that this form of questioning and the two previous hangings had not broken his spirit,
Stone ordered him hanged for the third time. Plumb did not
struggle. His feet were barely off the ground when he went limp.
He was held there for a few minutes before Stone ordered him
lowered. He sank forward on his face. Conger turned his body
over and placed his ear to Plumb's chest. He smiled grimly at

Asa Stone. 'He is still alive.' 'Bring me another bucket of water,' Stone directed. He seized the pail and again drenched Plumb. This time he was revived with great difficulty. He appeared willing to answer. 'Alvord shot Filkins,' he whispered. 'He was here a few days, but Grove took him away. Tom Mott fired the barn of Mr. Terry's in Waterville last fall and Mr. Conger's buildings at Sweet's Corners some time ago. We paid Mott to do it. Yes, Alvord was shot twice last Sunday morning by Officer Filkins. Mott and those others you have papers for are away now, but we'll help you find them if you let me go. Spare our lives and, if you'll permit us, we will strive henceforth to be honest, peaceful and law-abiding citizens.'

"'Send Grove here,' Conger demanded. Grove was hustled forward. His face was pale and drawn. All of his superb arrogance had departed. 'What do you want with me?' he asked. 'You saw what happened to Plumb,' Stone said grimly. 'If you don't want a sample of the same, you had better talk.' 'Everything my brother has told you is the truth,' Grove admitted. 'We can't be blamed for what the men who hung around here have done. If you will give us the chance, we will help you bring them to justice. We will no longer harbor outlaws and criminals.'"

The crowd had quieted, apparently satisfied with the hangings and subsequent confessions. Sheriff Stone walked back into the yard and a decision was made to take Plumb to Morrisville on the petit larceny charge. The remainder of the family were released and told that they had thirty days to be gone; if found in the area after that time the "would forfeit their lives." Several men took torches and set fire to each of the remaining barns, sheds, and finally the hophouse. One man turned loose Grove's prize black stallion before torching its shed. A steady southeast wind fanned the flames, devouring what remained of the Loomis homestead as the crowd drifted slowly down the road. According to the newspaper, "the family, after the occurrence, were sitting at the roadside on the fences with scarcely anything left but that they had upon them."

# CHAPTER XI

# Trial

"Great excitement prevailed," was the way Mrs. Edward Mason's diary began on Sunday, June 17, following the hangings and fire at the Loomises. She lived just down the road from the Loomis farm, and on Tuesday she wrote: "People continue to visit the ruins. It is thought over two thousand people visited the ruins." And the following day: "Hundreds [of people] with a knife take a chip from the limb Plumb was hung upon. Some seem as eager to get a chip as people did of the willow at [the] head of Napoleon's grave."

Reporters for the *Utica Morning Herald* joined the throngs of curiosity seekers: "We reached the Loomis place yesterday about three P.M. All the way thither from Waterville we met people returning from the ruins; indeed, whatever rose to the dignity of a vehicle of any kind at Waterville and vicinity appeared to be pressed into service. At the place itself, teams were hitched at all eligible places, and the people, full two score at that time, were looking with evident interest at the scene before them. All that remained of the Loomis house was the charred and blackened cellar walls, a pile of bricks in the center, which appeared as if it might have answered for a chimney and timbers still burning showed with what intensity the flames raged. The fence situated some feet in front alone remained unscathed. Across the way, an equally desolate scene marked the spot where once stood the hop house." The people at the scene could talk of nothing except what had happened, and what might happen. As the reporters picturesquely phrased it: "Madame rumor was around yesterday. We met her many times."

The Loomis family had been stunned as they watched the fruits of their years of labor rising in smoke. Given some of the suggestions which had come from the crowd, however, they were relieved to be alive. Even as the last of the mob disappeared down the road, Grove organized those present. John Stoner, who was recovering rapidly from his hanging, was sent to Hastings Center and Higginsville to inform Denio and Bill what had occurred. Grove himself left for Hamilton and Oriskany Falls to warn other gang members.

The first priority for Rhoda and Cornelia was shelter, and a neighbor, Decatur Welsh, offered to take them in. They accepted and were interviewed in Welch's living room by newspaper reporters later in the day. The reporters noted that "Mrs. L. did not express herself as particularly pleased with the affair which deprived her of a home. Still her conversation was calm, intelligent, and not particularly vindictive." Rhoda was still playing the role of gracious lady, dignified and aristocratic, even as her home had been burned to the ground and one of her sons hanged until almost dead. Cornelia had learned well from her mother and presented the same calm demeanor. The reporter wrote: Miss Cornelia Loomis does not impress a stranger unfavorably. She speaks with apparent sincerity and candor about the transactions of Sunday morning."

Sympathy for the Loomises, however, was limited. A few persons raised the question of due process, or the specter of mob violence engulfing the innocent along with the guilty. The *Utica Morning Herald*, under a headline of "Mob Law in Sangerfield" noted that "men, forgetful of what is just and proper, have been found thus willing to override law and destory that love of order, a respect for which is the bulwark of a community's safety." More representative of community sentiment was the entry in Mrs. Edward Mason's diary for June 19: "Mr. Welch notified if he did not have Mrs. Loomis and Cornelia removed from his home before sunset his house would be burned over his head before morning." Or the editorial in the *Waterville Times* which compared the vigilante action with the action of the colonists in the Revolutionary War:

> "The act committed last Sunday morning was illegal, we admit, but it no more deserves the name of a mob or the condemnation of the people than did the revolution by

which our forefathers rid our land of British tyranny and robbery. The cases, except in magnitude, bear a similarity to each other. Both were appeals to force, by respectable, virtuous and well-disposed citizens, in disregard of existing laws, to rid themselves of unbearable oppression and wrong which all legal means had failed to reach . . ."

Word of the raid reached Roscoe Conkling in Washington where he continued to be embroiled in debates over Reconstruction and skirmishings with Congressman Blaine. The Filkins trial had finally been scheduled by the court for August 27 so Conkling was very interested in the events in Sangerfield. Congress adjourned July 28 and Conkling returned immediately to Utica. The final raid had finished the Loomises it was said, and they were no longer a problem. Furthermore it was not certain what the reaction of a jury might be to the acts of vigilantism; sympathy for the Loomises would make it difficult to get Filkins off on the charge of having murdered Wash Loomis. After studying the case Conkling concluded that nothing was to be gained by going to trial yet so he requested and received a postponement until November. Roscoe Conkling had other reasons for wanting to postpone the Filkins case. Not only was he up for re-election for his congressional seat in November, but he was considering running for the Senate seat from New York which would become open in January. Although congressmen were elected by popular vote, senators were still appointed by state legislatures.

At the Republican convention in Rome on September 8, Conkling was renominated for his congressional seat unanimously. His acceptance speech was a bitter attack on President Johnson whom he characterized as "on his deceitful errand, with an imperial condescension, a supercilious patronage which seems to ape Louis Napoleon . . . frenzied with power and ambition . . . Andrew Johnson and his policy of arrogance and usurpation will be snapped like a willow wand." Four days later at a mass meeting in Utica, Conkling attacked President Johnson in a two-and-one-half hour speech for which he was wildly cheered. While others were preaching compromise and trying to find a way out of the bitter stalemate between the White House and Congress, Roscoe Conkling threw wood onto the flames and called for more confrontation.

The Loomises, meanwhile, had shown themselves not quite as powerless as people had hoped. Not only were they not gone from the area within thirty days, but they were displaying remarkably little evidence of learning from their recent exposure to community justice. They had rebuilt a house high on the hill near the pinnacle at the site where George Loomis had constructed the original homestead, and gang members were slowly drifting back to swell their ranks.

Within two months of the raid the Loomises appeared to be back in business. In August, Denio was arrested for horse theft. Filkins, still awaiting trial for murder, personally made the arrest and took Denio to jail. Shortly thereafter a boot and shoe store in Waterville was burglarized with five hundred dollars worth of merchandise stolen; the stolen goods were eventually traced to the Loomises. In October, a seventeen-year-old boy named John Comstock was arrested for breaking into a home in Sangerfield; he was said to be living with the Loomises and the *Waterville Times* commented: "Despite the retribution visited upon this villainous gang, it seems they are determined to continue their depredations on the property of others until they get a hanging which will last them forever."

Without Wash's leadership, however, the gang was but a shadow of its former self. Grove was still bitter about his family's failure to come to his aid the previous October and thoroughly frightened by almost being hanged, while Plumb remained in jail. Rhoda kept urging gang members to undertake acts of lawlessness but Denio was the only son remaining to listen to her. Things would get better, she promised, as soon as Filkins went to jail for having murdered Wash.

Wash's legal acumen was missed even more than his leadership. This became evident when Plumb was found guilty of the petit larceny charge and sentenced to thirty days in jail with a three hundred dollar fine. The Loomises said they did not have any money so Plumb was sentenced to another sixty days in jail. A lack of money was in fact the most desperate problem facing the Loomises. Although they owned land in Hastings Center and elsewhere, all their cash, gold, and valuables had disappeared with their home. Property taxes were due on their land but the Loomises said they could not pay them. Other families were ordinarily given an extension in such circumstances but nobody counseled leniency for the Loomises. Accordingly on November 22, 1866, an official notice was posted in Waterville announcing auction of Loomis land for nonpayment of taxes. On January 5, the auction took place in the American Hotel and three hundred and fifty-five acres were sold. It would never have happened, people agreed, had Wash Loomis still been alive.

The search continued for Bill Alvord, wanted for shooting Filkins. On September 20, it was announced that Filkins had located "the desperado lying in jail in Wayne County [Pennsylvania] on a charge of horse stealing . . . Mr. F. [Filkins] easily recognized him as the man who shot him. The scoundrel was made to take off his clothes when an examination revealed the fact that Officers Filkins and Conger hit him each of the three times that they shot at him when they were on the garret stairs. The marks found on him showed that one ball passed through his shoulder, another through his arm, and the third across his breast, each inflicting an ugly wound . . . Justice will probably soon overtake him now."

Alvord had other ideas. Before he could be transferred back to Oneida County he escaped by removing "the fastening which held the bar over his cell door, then unlocked the remaining doors with a skeleton key." Another search ensued and he was located in jail the following April, this time in New York's Auburn State Prison. He had been arrested for grand larceny; at the time of his arrest he had, according to a newspaper account, been "calling himself John Brown."

In the November election Roscoe Conkling easily won re-election to his congressional seat. For the men gathered in Bissell's general store it was not Conkling's congressional race which drew their attention, but rather another congressional race. Elizabeth Cady Stanton, Gerrit Smith's niece, had declared herself to be an independent candidate for Congress. Women had no right to vote but there was no legal barrier, Mrs. Stanton argued, to their running for office. She thus became the first woman political candidate for national office in the United States and garnered a total of twenty-four votes.

The Filkins trial was scheduled for the November court term but Roscoe Conkling again asked for a postponement. A key defense witness was missing, said Conkling, having gone "to Mexico or Idaho to the gold mines and has not been heard from since." Conkling assured the court that the witness would be available for the February term so the case was put off once again.

In fact Roscoe Conkling had no time for the Filkins case. The Republicans had carried New York State as well as the national elections, and many of the candidates for the New York State Legislature for whom Conkling had campaigned had won. Conkling calculated he had a reasonable chance to win the appointment to the United States Senate.

The Legislature was scheduled to meet in January to make that appointment. Conkling's competition included the incumbent, Judge Ira Harris, an undistinguished Senator best known for his use of patronage. In Washington it was rumored President Lincoln had once said he never went to sleep at night without first looking under the bed "to see if Judge Harris was there wanting something for somebody." Another man who wanted the Senate seat was Horace Greeley, publisher of the New York *Herald Tribune*. Greeley was "an odd genius with a great bald head fringed with a ridiculous set of whiskers"; Conkling had labeled him as "grotesque but harmless."

Bribery and corruption in the selection of senators was commonplace and Conkling described the Albany scene in a letter to his wife: "Great sums of money are among the influences here . . . The gamblers say I can have $200,000 here from New York [City] in a moment if I choose, and that the members are fools to elect me without it; only think of it!" But Conkling assured her: "I have resolutely put down my foot upon the ground that no friend of mine, even without my knowledge, shall pay a cent, upon any pretext nor in any strait, come what will. If chosen, it will be by the men of character, and if beaten this will be my consolation."

Conkling's race for the U.S. Senate was watched with great interest by the denizens of Central New York. The Loomises hoped he would become preoccupied with affairs in Albany and Washington and forget about Jim Filkins. Filkins was certain that Conkling could be counted on to help extricate him from his legal difficulties; Filkins had acted, after all, in the spirit of Roscoe Conkling's public exhortations. When the Legislature met on January 10 the voting was extremely close for four ballots until Conkling finally defeated his opponents on the fifth. Roscoe Conkling was to be the new Senator from New York and one of the powerful Republicans in the state. He had the ability to influence the appointment of literally hundreds of state officials.

Filkins' trial was scheduled for February yet once again Conkling asked for a delay which was granted. Conkling had to get back to Washington to complete the remainder of his term as congressman. The pressing business was Reconstruction and the intransigence of President Johnson and these took precedence over Filkins' trial. On March 2, over the veto of the President,

Conkling and his fellow Republicans passed a Reconstruction Act dividing the South into five military districts under federal control and making ratification of the Fourteenth Amendment a condition for any state gaining readmission to the Union. The vote of Negroes was to be guaranteed and protected; twenty thousand military troops were sent to the South to supervise the registration of seven hundred thousand Negro voters. The Freedmen's Bureau was authorized five million dollars to set up educational facilities for Negroes. The fulfillment of John Brown's dream had begun.

The thirty-ninth Congress adjourned on March 3 and the fortieth Congress convened the following day; nobody wished to leave President Johnson in charge of Washington for even a single day. In the new Congress Roscoe Conkling was sworn in as Senator; five days later in his first Senate speech he urged the provision of food for areas of the South said to be starving. The first session of the fortieth Congress lasted just four weeks but during that time Conkling demonstrated his oratorical and political skills. By the time he returned to Utica in April he had attained national stature. The *Chicago Republican* described him as "the youngest man as well as the youngest Senator on the floor [but he] is already the leader of the Senate." The *Washington Chronicle* commented: "No new Senator has ever made in so short a time such rapid strides to a commanding position in that body as Roscoe Conkling." And *Harper's Weekly* called him "young, fearless, devoted, able . . . The country no less than the state will find him a man equal to the hour."

It was clear to everyone that Roscoe Conkling's future lay in Washington. He would no longer be able to practice law in Utica as he had done, no longer be available to Jim Filkins or similar individuals. The question in many minds was whether he would complete the cases he had already begun. Jim Filkins and the Loomises were most interested in the answer.

In Roscoe Conkling's mind there was no question about what he would do. He had opened his career as a lawyer with a case against the Loomises, and now he would close it the same way. The Loomises symolized not only crime gone unpunished, but the corruption of public officials as well. Conkling talked of the need for justice, whether it be the justice of the Supreme Court or the justice of the frontier.

The case was on the docket for Circuit Court scheduled to begin June 3, 1867, in the Rome Courthouse, the courthouse in which Conkling had begun his job as District Attorney seventeen years earlier. It stood beside the ancient Indian portage connecting the Mohawk River with Wood Creek, and the ruins of Fort Stanwix were clearly visible across the green from the Courthouse steps. Fort Stanwix had been the westernmost outpost of early America, the site of treaties guaranteeing Indian land west of the Fort Stanwix Treaty Line, the promises of a young America.

On that warm June morning in 1867 people in Sangerfield and Waterville could talk of little else. Many of them journeyed to Rome to see for themselves, and they jammed the Courthouse standing side-by-side with members of the Loomis gang who had come to see justice finally carried out for Wash Loomis. The Loomis family themselves were absent, having calculated that their presence might sway the judges toward Filkins. The Honorable Henry A. Foster presided over the court, and was assisted by St. Pierre Jerred and Eli S. Bearse as Justices of the Session. The Filkins trial was one of 256 cases on the court calendar and nobody was certain when it would be called.

Roscoe Conkling was the center of attention. Connoisseurs of the courtroom realized that it might be their last opportunity to watch the legal pyrotechnics of this rapidly rising politician. Rumor was widespread that Conkling had taken a deep personal interest in the case and that he had vowed to get charges dismissed against the sandy-haired constable despite the overwhelming evidence of guilt. On that June morning there was also much speculation about Conkling's selection of his co-counsel, for it was none other than J. Thomas Spriggs. Spriggs had for eight years been the most effective Loomis lawyer—the man who had gotten charges against Grove dismissed after the incriminating evidence had been stolen from District Attorney Munger, the man who had obtained innumerable delays and dropped charges when the Loomises had been indicted, the man who had even challenged the editor of the *Roman Citizen* to a fight on the steps of that same courthouse after the editor had publicly insulted the Loomises. Yet here was J. Thomas Spriggs working with Roscoe Conkling to get charges dismissed against Jim Filkins, accused of having murdered the man who had employed Spriggs for eight years. Courtroom spectators murmured in amazement and agreed that Roscoe Conkling was indeed a very persuasive man.

Leading the prosecution was New York State Attorney General Martindale of Rochester, indicating the importance being placed on the case. Hiram T. Jenkins, still District Attorney for Oneida

County, was also a member of the prosecution team as was D.C. Pomeroy, a private lawyer from Rome retained by the Loomises. Filkins himself sat in the front of the courtroom, still free on bail on the murder indictment which had been found against him eighteen months earlier.

Various pleas, motions, and sentencings of other cases occupied most of the day; by mid-afternoon spectators wondered whether the Filkins case would be called at all. Then at four o'clock, with only one hour remaining for the day, District Attorney Jenkins called the case of the People versus James L. Filkins for the murder of Wash Loomis.

Conkling and Spriggs conferred hurriedly together regarding strategy. Then Conkling, immaculately attired in dark frock and light wasitcoat, rose and addressed the court:

> "I make the motion to set aside what is called the indictment in this case on the grounds that same was never legally found, and that the paper purporting to be an indictment was unlawfully obtained from the grand jury." He paused briefly to give emphasis to his next words: "And I propose to have Mr. Spriggs, my associate counsel for the prisoner, read the papers upon which the said motion is founded."

As Conkling resumed his seat, Spriggs arose. He was a dark, heavy-set man and the heat of the day had taken a toll. He looked uncomfortable in his new role and a few spectators snickered. "His florid countenance was bathed in perspiration and he wiped his face carefully with a white handkerchief before picking up his papers from the table at his side." He then read from papers saying that several members of the grand jury which had indicted Filkins had claimed that a key piece of evidence— the testimony of George Jones and Charles Bird—had been introduced to the grand jury as sworn affidavits without Jones and Bird themselves testifying. The affidavits asserted that they had been at the Loomises on the night of the murder and had seen Filkins with Wash about the time Wash had been murdered. It was these affidavits, said Spriggs, which had persuaded the grand jury to indict Filkins, and without them no indictment would have taken place. The affidavits had been introduced to the grand jury by Mr. C.O. Southworth, law partner of D.C. Pomeroy, and were sworn to be authentic by Mr. Southworth.

Spriggs paused to look at Pomeroy, who appeared increasingly uncomfortable. Then he went on: "The jurors did not intend to find an indictment unless the said Jones and Bird were produced and sworn before them. But District Attorney Jenkins and Mr. Southworth advised them that such affidavits were just as legal and competent evidence as if the makers of them were present and sworn." Furthermore, Spriggs went on, Jones and Bird were not produced as witnesses before the grand jury because the grand jury was told that their whereabouts were unknown. In fact they "were about in the streets of Rome, probably until after the alleged indictment was found."

By this time District Attorney Jenkins was looking uncomfortable as well. Roscoe Conkling sat quietly smiling. "Your Honor," Spriggs addressed the Judge, "I would like to read a more recent affidavit by George Jones in which this principal witness denies having made the statements submitted to the grand jury and further states that he did not see Filkins on the night of the murder."

There was an audible reaction from the courtroom. Judge Foster glanced at District Attorney Jenkins, Attorney General Martindale and Pomeroy to see whether any of them was prepared to challenge the introduction of the new affidavit. Martindale was a political appointee, as was Judge Foster himself. Hiram Jenkins had been elected by the people but had to be nominated for the position by the Republican Party. Roscoe Conkling had become one of the most powerful Republicans in New York State and was obviously going to be around for many years; this fact was as well known to the spectators as it was to the principals in the courtroom that day. Understandably, no objection was raised and Spriggs proceeded to read the new affidavit of George Jones, dated July 11, 1866, and notarized.

"I live at Rome, Oneida County, N.Y. I was at the Loomises on the night Wash Loomis was killed - also the time when the barns were burned. I did not see him beaten. It was the last of October, about the 30th. I slept in the kitchen chamber that night. Grove slept in a room adjoining mine on the same floor. There were some persons came up the stairs after him and called him down that night. There were three of them. I think I did not know any of them.

I know Pomeroy and Southworth of Rome or did at that time. I have heard that an affidavit was presented by them before the Grand Jury, purporting to have been made by me relative to the tragedy that occurred on the night of October 30th or thereabout, 1865. I never made any affidavit in regard to the matter.

I did not on the first day of November last nor at any

other time make an affidavit before C.O. Southworth of
Rome in reference to the murder of Washington Loomis.

I had some conversation (a day or two after the tragedy)
with Mr. Southworth at Rome in the office of Pomeroy and
Southworth. A person calling himself Charles Bird (alias
Charles Carr) was also present. Neither he nor I signed any
writing while we were there . . .

I did not tell Southworth that as I went into the kitchen,
Grove and Filkins were there, Filkins behind Grove and
that he struck Grove in the back of the head, nor did not tell
him anything to that effect . . . I was in Rome at the time
Mr. Filkins was indicted upon the charge of murdering
Wash Loomis. I could have attended before the Grand Jury,
was not subpoenaed to appear before them."

Spriggs sat down next to Conkling as the clock edged toward
five o'clock. It had been a trump card masterfully played. The
use of an affidavit rather than the witness himself before the
grand jury raised questions about the technical legality of the
indictment. The new affidavit cast doubt in the veracity of the
evidence upon which the indictment had been based. The integrity of Loomis' lawyer, Pomeroy, and his partner, Southworth,
had been raised, as indeed had the integrity of District Attorney
Jenkins. And finally the credibility of Jones as a potential prosecution witness had been destroyed.

District Attorney Jenkins rose. "I insist that the question of
illegality of the indictment cannot now be raised. I ask the Court
to give me until tomorrow morning to prepare affidavits to
answer the questions raised by the defense." Judge Foster then
adjourned court until the following day.

Under the headline "The Loomis Murder" the *Utica Morning
Herald* the following morning carried a full account of the previous day's testimony. The paper reported that "Jones denied
ever making the affidavit that was read before the grand jury,
and further stated that he did not see Filkins at the murder
scene." Spectators lining up for seats read the account and
discussed the character of George Jones, his police record, and
his association with the Loomis gang. A few people suggested
that Filkins might not stand trial, or be found not guilty if he did
stand trial. Yet this seemed highly improbable since everyone
west of the Hudson River knew that Jim Filkins had in fact
murdered Wash Loomis.

Court convened promptly at nine o'clock that Tuesday morning. It promised to be warmer than the previous day, yet interest

in the case, as measured by spectators trying to get into the court-room, had increased. Attorney-General Martindale opened the argument on behalf of the prosecution:

"My preliminary objections to the motion of setting aside or quashing the indictment against the prisoner, are as follows:

1. The prisoner having plead to the indictment, no motion to quash or set it aside can now be entertained.

2. The point of opposition being a defect in the proof produced before the Grand Jury, and not a defect in the record itself or in the manner of its presentment, the motion can not be entertained at all.

3. The pretended affidavits of George Jones and others are not entitled in any proceeding or action, and are extra judicial and not competent to be received.

4. All the statements in several of the papers and affidavits presented to the court, so far as they reveal the decision or opinions of any or all of the members of the Grand Jury in relation to any questions which arose before them in respect to the indictment in this action or the weight of the evidence adduced before them, are unlawful and can not be allowed in the preceding motion."

Martindale paused to see what effect his technical argument was having. Judge Foster had found the previous afternoon's testimony both interesting and disturbing, and he did not wish to rule against the motion to quash the indictment on purely technical grounds.

"I will hear all the facts of the case, and hear the whole question argued before I decide on the preliminary objections," he said.

It was the turn for the defense. Mr. Spriggs produced additional affidavits by the grand jurors who had indicted Filkins saying that they would not have voted for indictment without the evidence contained in the affidavits of Jones and Bird. In response District Attorney Jenkins produced the minutes of the testimony before the grand jury and claimed that there had been abundant testimony to support an indictment of Filkins even without the affidavits of Jones and Bird. Jenkins emphasized that George Jones had indeed made the original affidavit and had acknowledged doing so several times. Satisfied, the District Attorney took his seat. Unless the defense was able to produce George Jones in person and have him recant his orginal affidavit under oath, it was difficult to imagine how the Court could be persuaded to quash the indictment.

Roscoe Conkling rose slowly, glancing contemptuously at District Attorney Jenkins as he did so. He had few notes visible, but the thick sheath beneath his desk suggested he had prepared his case carefully. He had even put together an abstract of his arguments for the newspapers, including references to pertinent case laws, and the following day his remarks were covered in great detail.

Conkling acknowledged that "an enormous crime seems to have been committed and it concerns the public that it should be thoroughly and impartially investigated, not to satisfy the vengeance of anyone, nor to bring disgrace and accusation, if not conviction, upon any particular individual. The object is to vindicate law and order. Public history invests this view of the case with some special importance." He also assured the court that the motion to dismiss the indictment "was not made hastily and not without due consideration and reflection." He acknowledged that "a motion to quash an indictment in the ordinary sense is not looked upon with favor" because the reasons are usually purely technical. Skillfully he reminded the court that he was not asking that Filkins be found not guilty—only that he not be tried under the present indictment. Since there was no statute of limitations in bringing a new indictment, Conkling went on, "every grand jury while he lives has jurisdiction of the case." Furthermore he claimed that "it is a matter of indifference to the prisoner whether he be tried on this indictment, or another one which could be found if this were set aside."

Having laid the groundwork, Conkling went on to develop a three-part argument for dismissing the indictment. The first part, which he developed extensively, was that "the indictment was improperly and illegally found." "On the night of Monday, October 30, 1865," he began, "George W. Loomis . . . received injuries which in a few hours caused his death . . . On Wednesday, November 1, a coroner's jury assembled at the house to investigate the death. The kindred and survivors of the deceased were represented during the inquest by counsel brought from Rome. The Loomis family gave evidence, so did the women who occupied beds with Loomis men, so also did certain other men known to have been in the house when the wounds were given. But some of the lodgers were not produced or accounted for. No person appeared at the inquest on behalf of the present defendant, and as far as there was any party to the proceedings, it was the Loomis family and their counsel." According to Conkling "the case was thus left shrouded in mystery upon the partial one-sided showing of the family themselves."

Conkling then went on to discuss the murder warrant against Filkins initiated by Bill Loomis and the subsequent preliminary examination before Judge Cleveland: "One witness only, of all those lodging in the house, was found to be examined, and one other witness to collateral matter, and then the counsel who said he appeared 'at the request of the Loomis family' attempted to out-wit and circumvent the justice, and rested. Finding that the magistrate knew his duty, and meant to do it, the counsellor left the court in darkness by withdrawing. Attachments were then sent out, and every effort made during the residue of the week to command the presence of the witnesses, but by trick and fraud and defiance the witnesses were spirited away or concealed, and so the law was baffled and the proceedings defeated."

This brought events up to the crucial grand jury, and Conkling claimed the case had been "smuggled into the secrecy of the grand jury room" because "the counsel of the Loomises [was] associated with the District Attorney."

> "Haste was of the essence in the proceedings, and the matter was introduced to the grand jury at the opening session, on Monday, November 13th. All the witnesses and all the testimony which it was deemed judicious to bring forward were produced and the jury listened for two days and heard the conclusion of the whole matter. If an indictment could be legally found, everything by which it could be supported, everything upon which action could legally be based, was now before the jurors. All this, however, was insufficient. The statements of the witnesses were inconclusive or incredible, or else the witnesses themselves appeared unworthy of belief. The probable guilt of the accused was not made out, and the attempt to indict would have failed for want of proof.
>
> Had this been all, there would be nothing to point to any particular item of missing proof, nor to any particular missing witnesses. But it was made more definite. The jurors commented on the absence of Jones and Bird, as they were then called, two men admitted to have been in the house in which the alleged homicide was committed, at the time of its commission, who had not appeared either before the coroner or the magistrate, and whose absence was observed immediately after it was known that a deed of violence had been done.

Their non-appearance was suspicious because they must be able to make important disclosures. The jury was informed that these men were at a distance, no one knew where, and the requirements that they should be produced was evaded. Two or three days elapsed, and during this time these witnesses were actually in the bailiwick, at Rome, only fifteen miles off, and the Loomises and their counsel knew it. The District Attorney was kept in ignorance of it, if he was kept in ignorance at all, by fraud if not by falsehood. Jones at least says he was advised and prompted not to appear because his testimony would not be of a desirable character.

Had the matter stopped here, and ended with a supression of evidence, with the concealment of the whereabouts of essential witnesses who were sought for by the grand jury, with discouraging witnesses from appearing and testifying, there would be broad ground for impeaching the result produced, wherever it could be called in question, whatever the result might have been.

But the doings of the grand jury room in those particulars which are in no event to be disclosed, the state of mind and judgment of the jury became known outside. The counsel for the Loomises became aware that as the case stood it was a failure, and that in order to obtain an indictment, more evidence must be produced, or additional measures taken. If Jones and Bird, or either of them, were in possession of any fact which could bear against Filkins, why was not their being in Rome revealed? Why, even under the pressure of defeat before the grand jury for want of the very testimony Jones and Bird might furnish if Filkins was guilty, was the whereabouts of Jones and Bird kept secret? It can only have been because their examination would not have supported the case against Filkins.

Instead of revealing to the jury that in a few minutes these witnesses could be before them, if they had knowledge and dared to testify, resort was had to introducing into the jury room matter which was obviously illegal, and really immoral and fraudulent, even if the paper produced was a genuine affidavit, and even if its statements were true.

An attorney, the partner of the counsel for the Loomis family from the commencement, went to the grand jury room with a paper purporting to be the sworn affidavit of Jones and Bird. If this paper, illegal as it was, was to be foisted into the grand jury room by those who knew in fact as well as in law that a fraud was being committed upon the court, why not send it in and let it speak for itself? The attorney had affixed to it as notary public his signature and certificate that it had been sworn to before him. What could he add to it? What mission had he in the jury room?

It seems he was sworn as a witness, and testified that doubtless the legal evidence of these men would be the same 'substantially' as the spurious substitute presented. Thus in the role of witness or counsel he read the affidavits to the jury along with his own statements and comments, and informed them that it was right for them to receive the paper as evidence. Thus persuaded, and ignorant of the truth in fact and in law, the jury received as evidence the direct, emphatic statement contained in the paper. These statements were absolute of the guilt of Filkins and, being credited, left no question. Accordingly the jury at once found an indictment in the illegal evidence producing the result which all the legal evidence in the case had failed to accomplish.

These so-called affidavits are on their face false in the most vital particulars when read by those who know the undisputed facts of the case, or even the structure of the Loomis house, or the situation of the premises. They are yet more false in latent particulars, if the sworn statement of Jones now before the court is to be relied upon. Had the witnesses themselves been examined by the grand jury, suspicion would have been turned not upon Filkins, but in another direction. The conclusion is forced upon us that the instrumentalities of public justice have been seized upon and perverted not only to bring one man to trial by forbidden means, but also to suppress the truth in other respects and to screen the guilty and the favored.

The law has, it is believed, a remedy for this. Although it may not be of concern to the defendant to be tried upon a valid indictment rather then upon this, it is fit and wholesome that such things be done decently and in order.''

Having reviewed the sequence of events as he saw them, Conkling then proceeded to summarize the legal reasons for dismissing the indictment. For each point he buttressed his argument with extensive case law; according to one historian it was a "brilliant" citation of European and American precedents. Giving no indication of tiring, Conkling moved into the second part of his argument—an attack on the Loomis gang:

"The court cannot close its eyes to the fact, but must take judicial notice that for a series of years numerous crimes have been committed in this county and vicinity, some of them very grave crimes, some even atrocious crimes, which, with abundant evidence of their authors, have been left forever unpunished and forever veiled in mystery, and this not in consequence of any of the ordinary failures of justice. In one case a public building containing indictments has been burned to the ground, and this at a time when the statute of limitations was just ready to step in between those accused and a second indictment.

In another instance the District Attorney of this county having on his person some twelve counterfeit bills and indictments pending against the same parties, was seized in the street after midnight by two men, thrown upon the ground, and deprived of the proof which alone the indictments could be sustained. In still another case the office of the District Attorney of this county was broken open at night when indictments against the same parties were there, and a great quantity of papers carried away. Many indictments mysteriously re-appeared, other papers came back mingled with forest leaves, but the indictments against those whose conduct is in issue here never came back.

Not only have these violent modes of diverting the course of justice become matters of public history, but so also have modes like those at which this motion is levelled. Bending and manipulating the forms, the proceedings, the instrumentalities of the law, were publicly reckoned even before this came arose among the secrets and appliances of a band of offenders who pillage, rob and burn within and without the county of Oneida. Common fame has long published that certain criminals not only escape conviction, not only protect their confederates, not only bring to punishment their betrayers, not only wreck barbarous vengeance upon those who dare to pursue them, or even to testify against them, not only break through all the meshes of the law, but that bail and bail bonds, bench warrants and search warrants, indictments and the civil process of the court, do their office or stand still at the beck and nod, not of innocence, but of guilt."

It was as if the motion to dismiss the indictment against James Filkins was no longer the issue before the court. Rather the Loomises themselves were being put on trial by Roscoe Conkling. Nobody rose to object, not even the Loomis' attorney. Conkling went on:

"This subject has become a matter of record in the legislative proceedings of the State. Here is the report of the

Legislature, made by the Prison Association in January, 1866. From Page 145 onward will be found a narrative of instances in principle and character like the doings now before the court, and the actors there are the actors here. The report shows how they organize victory by laying crimes at the doors of the innocent, by manufacturing and destroying evidence, by instituting false prosecutions, by stifling and evading investigations, by polluting the fountains and defiling the ministrations of justice. This is the statement the Legislature of New York has published, and similar presentations have appeared in the public press of the whole country."

Here Conkling paused and produced several copies of his next document. Not only was the "public press of the whole country" writing about the Loomises and their evasion of justice, but Conkling noted:

"The foreign press also has given the subject to the world. Here is the London *Quarterly Review*, for January, 1867, a publication of much ability and influence, and as old as the century. It is not fond of republican government; it does not believe in democratic institutions; it has little faith in the security of life and property in an organism like ours, operating by universal suffrage; it is not friendly to America. It has an article giving reasons for its skepticism in the wisdom of our government. The article is entitled 'Crime in The State of New York.' It narrates events already referred to, and upon the doings of this family and their accomplices, and the impotency of the laws to resist or punish them, or to protect honest men from their accusations. It grounds an appeal to the British people to say whether they would change places with the people of Central New York!"

In fact the article in the influential English weekly had circulated widely in Oneida County for it overtly ridiculed the county and the state of New York. As "one of the richest, most ancient, and longest settled districts of the Union," the report said, "we are entitled to look for the highest social and administrative perfection to which the institutions of the United States can possibly attain." Instead what is found is the Loomis gang and "a state in which the boasted liberty resolves itself to a considerable extent into freedom for thieves and thralldom for honest men." The exploits of the Loomises, quoted directly from the New York Prison Association report, were detailed and the failure of justice attributed both to "official inertness and corruption" and the fact that "many of those who should prevent or punish their depredations are corrupt or intimidated." At this point Roscoe Conkling paused, looked slowly and directly at District Attorney Jenkins, then resumed reading.

The underlying reason for the Loomis gang's success, the article continued, was "the vicious system of election in America . . . by which an equal amount of political power is given to the ignorant, idle, poverty-stricken and worthless as to the well-informed, industrious, saving and estimable man . . . Instead of the wisest and most virtuous governing the most ignorant and least moral, they are governed by them and we see the consequences." The answer was to do away with democracy, to "retransfer to those . . . who as a class have received the best education . . . that political power which has been unwisely surrendered."

Roscoe Conkling had indeed elevated the proceedings. It was not the legality of the indictment which was at issue, not the issue of Filkins' guilt or innocence. It was not even the guilt or innocence of the Loomises which was being discussed. Rather the question before the court had taken on the grandeur of democracy itself. Here were the English, ridiculing democracy and calling it a failure because the Loomises had not been brought to justice. The reputation of Oneida County, of the State of New York, of the United States itself was the issue before the court. Do you want the world to think, Roscoe Conkling was asking, that Oneida County is inhabited by a band of savages?

Apparently nearing the end of his discourse, Conkling paused briefly. He had, he said, one brief additional point, the third part of his argument in favor of the motion to dismiss the indictment. Since the indictment had been obtained illegally, as he had previously shown, then to let the indictment stand would be to undermine the grand jury as a legal institution:

> "The grand jury in its best estate is an anomaly in free government," Conkling said. "It has been denounced as a monstrosity and an excrescence upon democratic institutions. Against these criticisms, however, it can be defended despite its star chamber and despotic prerogatives. It may be mistaken, it may be passionate, it must be one-sided and arbitrary, it may unwittingly blast an innocent name, or act upon specious appearances but still it may be vindicated and maintained in a wise and civilized economy, so long as it is jealously guarded from improper approach. Keep it

reasonably and practically pure, defend it against imposition and intrusion, and its ruggedness and sturdiness carry wholesome terror in their hands. But leave it open to surreptitious influences, and it becomes at once one of the most odious and unendurable of all the instruments of wrong. Let indictments be brought about by chicanery, let illegal and fraudulent statements be resorted to successfully, after legal evidence has proved inadequate, and when these things are discovered and proved to the court, let it go out that there is no remedy, no punishment, not even a loss of the illegal advantage which has been gained.

If the defendant ought to be put to trial for killing Loomis, let a grand jury say so in a legal manner, upon legal evidence. There is abundance of time and opportunity for that; but if it were otherwise, still the motion should prevail. What is the fate of the defendant, what would be his punishment, be he ever so guilty, compared with the wholesome influence of the decision now asked from the court? What example could be more reformatory and remedial, than the seal of disapprobation set upon such encroachments and infractions of law as are spread before the court."

Conkling closed by reminding the court once more that its very honor and reputation rested on the outcome of this case:

"Oneida County has suffered imputation for lax practices of her political, judicial and ministerial tribunals. Here is a glaring instance of lax and dangerous administration. The court can put its hand upon it and the occasion is of more value to the public than the life or death of any culprit whose name is borne on the roll of accusation."

Solemnly Conkling stepped down and resumed his seat. Those in the courtroom who had come to see his final performance had not been disappointed. What had at one time seemed like an impossible task—to get an indictment dismissed against a man who everyone knew was guilty of murder—had been turned into a referendum on democracy. Indeed if Conkling was correct then patriotism alone demanded that the indictment be dismissed. It was as if the whole world was watching the courtroom in Rome that June morning to see whether or not America had become civilized.

Attorney General Martindale rose to rebut Conkling. In a speech lasting one and one-half hours he complained that the prosecution had had insufficient time to prepare responses to the questions raised by the defense. He then proceeded to review the evidence on which the grand jury had brought the indictment and defended the use of the affidavits obtained from Jones and Bird. At several points he stressed the overwhelming evidence against Filkins and the fact that an indictment would have been found against him even without the affidavits of Jones and Bird. He made no mention of the reputation of Oneida County, or what Englishmen thought of Americans, but rather kept strictly to points of law. In summation Martindale argued four points:

> "1. That after a defendant has entered a plea to an indictment it is then too late to make a motion to quash it or set it aside;
> 2. That grand jurors legally cannot comment in a public manner regarding any opinions entertained or expressed by them on matters coming before them in the grand jury room, and that affidavits by them on such subjects are forbidden by law; therefore the affidavits from grand jurors introduced by the defense cannot be considered properly or legally before the court on this motion;
> 3. That even if the affidavits of Jones and Bird were improperly given to the grand jury as evidence, that error was not grounds for setting aside the indictment; and
> 4. That once an indictment has been found and there is some evidence to support it, the indictment is conclusive and no inquiry can be made or investigation gone into to ascertain upon what evidence the indictment was found or what the proceedings were before the grand jury."

Closing, Martindale warned of dire consequences if the indictment against Filkins was set aside: "Our entire system of criminal jurisprudence would be in danger if investigations are allowed into grand jury proceedings. Quashing the indictment would establish a bad precedent that would open the door to innumerable motions of any kind. It would allow culprits to escape by such proceedings without ever having a trial in a court of justice."

The arguments of Conkling and Martindale had taken the entire morning. Both sides rested, and Judge Foster adjourned court so that the justices could consider the case. As the courthouse emptied for lunch, word of Conkling's virtuoso performance spread quickly on the streets of Rome. Friends of the Loomises, several persons noted, did not look pleased with the progress of proceedings against Filkins.

The deliberations of Justices Foster, Jerred and Bearse occupied almost two hours. When the court was called back to session in mid-afternoon it was the in heat of the day, but everyone returned readily to their seats. Judge Foster opened his remarks by regretting "that in a case of this magnitude and importance more time could not be afforded for deliberation." He added, however, that "the Court is ready to give a decision now and to take the responsibility for its correctness."

He then took approximately thirty minutes to review the points of law raised by the case, quoting frequently from case law which had been cited by Roscoe Conkling. The decision, he said, then, is as follows:

> "1. That it is not too late to make a motion of this kind, after the prisoner has plead to the indictment; that such motions can be made at any time before the jury is empannelled to try the case.
>
> 2. That investigations are proper, and can be gone into as to certain matters which took place before grand jurors on the finding of an indictment; for instance, as to whether illegal evidence was given upon which the bill of indictment was found; as to whether the requisite number of grand jurors concurred in finding the bill, etc.
>
> 3. That the affidavits of grand jurors can be read on motions like this, showing that illegal evidence was received, and as to such other matters before them as they are not prohibited from disclosing.
>
> 4. That is was incompetent and illegal to read the affidavits of Jones and Bird before the grand jury on the finding of this indictment, or to give any weight whatever to that kind of species of testimony, and for that error this indictment should be set aside. The indictment is accordingly set aside."

The announcement of the decision was received with loud applause by the audience which was quickly suppressed by the Court.

The *Utica Morning Herald* on the following day headlined: "The Indictment Set Aside - Loud Applause in the Courtroom" and gave a long and detailed account of the proceedings. Most persons accepted it as the obituary for the Loomis gang. Wash Loomis had been murdered, Plumb hanged within an inch of his life, and the family home had been burned. By Thursday, June 6, there was no mention at all of the Loomises in the paper.

# CHAPTER XII

# Epilogue

The Rome Courthouse in which Jim Filkins' murder indictment was set aside is still used. Two wings and a cupola have been added over the years but otherwise it appears much as it did in June of 1867. Across the green, Fort Stanwix has been rebuilt as a tourist attraction, displaying mementos of the Treaty of 1768 which guaranteed Indians the land west of the treaty line, and the Treaty of 1784 in which the Oneidas were "secured in the possession of the lands on which they are settled." In 1984, Rome held a bicentennial celebration of the latter treaty and a few Oneida Indians were persuaded to participate.

District Attorney Hiram T. Jenkins became ill shortly after the trial and died on July 29, 1868, "after an illness of nearly a year's duration, his disease being of the nature of paralysis." Some said it was syphilis. In his thirty-five years he had distinguished himself by being thrice elected District Attorney of Oneida County and by his friendship with the Loomises. At his funeral he was eulogized by Professor Edward North of Hamilton College: "He was direct and straighforward and in everything incapable of practicing deceit or performing a mean action. His very nature was sincere and truthful, and his whole conduct in his profession was marked by the same integrity and high sense of honesty that characterized all his dealings in private life." The *Hamilton Literary Monthly* added that Jenkins' "talents, industry and character had gained for him an elevated position in the esteem of his fellow citizens."

J. Thomas Spriggs, the lawyer who had defended the Loomises for eight years but then switched sides to help Roscoe Conkling in the Filkins' trial, went on to have a distinguished career. In 1868, he was elected mayor of Utica. He subsequently ran for Congress and was defeated twice before finally winning Roscoe Conkling's former seat in 1882 and 1884.

By the time Spriggs had been elected to Congress, Roscoe Conkling had completed fourteen years in the Senate as one of the most influential men in Washington. In 1868, when the Democrats nominated Horatio Seymour, Conkling's brother-in-law, for President, Conkling "stumped the state vigorously against Seymour" and helped elect Ulysses S. Grant. Grant rewarded Conkling by making him part of his inner circle and, according to a biographer, "during the greater part of two Grant administrations [Conkling] was the most powerful politician in the country." Twice he was offered and refused appointments to the Supreme Court, once to be Chief Justice when he was still just forty-three years old.

In 1876 Conkling was a candidate to become Republican nominee for President, receiving ninety-three votes on the first round before losing to Rutherford B. Hayes. Over the years he continued to fight for the rights of Negroes and to drive a hard bargain with Southern whites in the Reconstruction Era. When Blanch K. Bruce, Negro Senator from Mississippi, took his seat in 1875, "the trembling Bruce was resolutely ignored by his new colleagues until Roscoe Conkling . . . strode over to him and warmly grasped his hand."

Although Conkling's accomplishments provided sustenance for supporters in Central New York, his detractors dined well on the viands of his vulnerability. It was not only his hauteur and acerbic tongue which made him enemies—young Clarence Darrow called Conkling "a cold, selfish man who had no right to live except to prey on his fellowmen," and another critic said "there is not the slightest evidence that his soul has ever risen above pap and patronage." But it was also his personal life—specifically his affection for women—which provided gossip traded on the streets of Utica and surrounding villages.

While his wife, Julia Seymour Conkling, and daughter stayed at home in Utica, Conkling carried on an affair in Washington with Kate Sprague, daughter of the Chief Justice of the Supreme Court and wife of an alcoholic senator from Rhode Island. Kate was "the reigning beauty of the capital," and as early as 1870 was sending flowers for Conkling's Senate desk. They were seen together in public over many years, and it seemed that it would go on forever until late one August night in 1879. On that occasion Senator Sprague returned unexpectedly to his home in Rhode Island; "a servant warned her mistress of the return just in time for the senior senator from New York to escape her bedroom through a window, with underwear hastily donned and his trousers over his shoulder."

Still in ignorance Senator Sprague retired, and the following morning went to town where a friend informed him that Conkling was at his house. Sprague returned, seized his shotgun, and found Conkling and Kate Sprague "enjoying their breakfast, the senator sitting on a lounge coolly reading a newspaper." Senator Sprague ordered Conkling out and threatened to "blow his brains out." With an aplomb which had been his trademark through a lifetime of fights in courtrooms and Congress, Conkling walked over to Kate and said: "Mrs. Sprague, your husband is very much excited, and I think it better for all of us if I should withdraw. If my departure puts you in any danger, so say, and I will stay, whatever the consequences." Conkling then left for town, closely pursued by Senator Sprague who confronted him again on the streets before a large crowd of people. Conkling finally left town, but by that time the incident was being telegraphed to newspaper offices throughout the country. The *New York Tribune* later referred to Conkling as a "patriot of the flesh-pots."

In 1881 Roscoe Conkling resigned from the Senate in a bitter fight with President James A. Garfield. A few months later Charles Guiteau assassinated Garfield in the Washington train station; when it became known the Guiteau was a Conkling supporter public wrath spilled over to the Senator from New York. The chief prosecution psychiatrist at Guiteau's trial was Dr. John P. Gray, who had taken care of Gerrit Smith in 1859 and was still the Superintendent of the Lunatic Asylum at Utica. Gray argued successfully that Guiteau's mental state did not excuse his criminal act. Two months later, while Guiteau sat in prison awaiting his assignation with the hangman, Dr. Gray himself was shot to death by an insane man in Utica.

Conkling's political careed ended with his resignation and he retired to private life in New York City. In March, 1888, he developed an abscess of his ear which spread to his brain. Heroic medical measures, including putting a hole in his skull using a mallet and chisel, failed to help and Conkling died April 18, 1888. He was buried in Forest Lawn Cemetery in Utica a short distance from the sacred stone of the Oneida Indians which marked the entrance to the cemetery. His grave site, shared by his wife, sits on a hillside overlooking Oneida Street and is marked only by a granite marker with their names and dates of entering and exiting life. One must ask cemetery personnel to find the location of the grave.

On the other side of the same hill, outside the cemetery boundary, sits a fifteen foot boulder embedded with a bronze plaque: "Roscoe Conkling Park: Given to the city of Utica for the use and benefit of all the people." The site looks northward over Utica to the Adirondack Mountains and has been, appropriately, a favorite parking place for lovers. Next to Conkling's plaque are numerous pairs of initials painted and carved on the boulder, perpetual testimony to promises and trysts.

Route 12 running south from Utica to Waterville and Sangerfield traverses well-tended farmland. Three miles before reaching Waterville an historical marker sits in a field to the right. It proclaims the "Property Line: Western boundary of civilization fixed by the Fort Stanwix Treaty, November 5, 1768." Beyond this line, it is implied, there was no civilization.

Waterville and Sangerfield are little changed from the days when the Loomises and Jim Filkins rode their streets. The railroad came to Waterville in November, 1867, but stimulated the economy only briefly. Bissell's general store is clearly discernible despite having been incorporated into McLaughlin's Department Store; the upstairs loft where Filkins and the Sangerfield Vigilantes Committee planned raids on the Loomises is still used for storage.

Hermon Clarke continued working in Bissell's store for several years and married Alice Cleveland, daughter of the Waterville physician who had taken the bullets from Filkins' arm and performed the autopsy on Wash Loomis. Clarke later went into the hop business and was elected Oneida County Clerk. He enjoyed reminiscing about the war and helped organize a veterans organization which in 1905 and 1907 held reunions with the Confederate troops against whom they had fought. The 1907 reunion was held in Roscoe Conkling Park in Utica with everyone singing "Dixie" together at the end.

Going south from Sangerfield one has to look carefully for the old country road which skirts the northern fringe of Nine Mile

Swamp, then runs along its western border to Hubbardsville. The foundations for the Loomis homestead sit in a field, clearly discernible on a summer day amidst goldenrod and Holstein cows. In front of the ruins a road runs downhill to the swamp, crossing it to meet Route 12, following the path across the swamp ridden so many times by the Loomises and their adversaries. A roadsign indicates that it is called Loomis Road, but there are no other markers of their infamy.

The local farmers know, of course, and with only a little encouragement will tell you Loomis tales which have been embellished with the years. Some of the farmers are Loomis descendants, and a few octogenarians living nearby claim to remember grandfathers describing their participation in the final raid, the hangings and the big fire. The present owners of the Loomis land are amused by questions, and graciously assent to visitors exploring the fields "but please don't knock down the fences."

Behind the ruins of the homestead the woods and maple stand are little changed. The path leading uphill through the woods shows the terracing and drainage ditches dug by the Loomises, and near the pinnacle there are remnants of the first homesite. The plateau on which the 1852 meeting of the Loomis gang was held is part of a pasture and still an excellent vantage point to see up and down the valley. If one looks closely one can almost see Jim Filkins riding south from Sangerfield with his deputies.

Nine Mile Swamp is not as wide as it was then; farmers have reclaimed its marshy edges for pastureland. From the plateau, however, it still presents a forbidding demeanor, its dark edges held in by swaths of wildflowers in the summer and by fields of snow in winter. Up close, marsh marigolds and white Indian pipe appear to welcome the visitor, but a few feet into its recesses one is forced to turn back by dank water, mud, and rotting logs. Most farmers who live on its edges still have not penetrated its interior and the hiding places of the Loomises remain undisturbed.

For the Loomises the dropping of murder charges against Jim Filkins was the final and ultimate insult. An attempt by Rhoda Loomis to rally her family was to no avail; Wash was dead and Grove, who might have assumed command, was deeply alienated from the rest of the family. It was his mother's greed, he maintained, which had led to Wash's death and the gang's downfall. Rhoda was most concerned about having enough money, and proceeded to sue law enforcement officials in Madison and

Oneida counties for twenty-two thousand dollars for the loss of their home and barns in the final raid. For counsel she retained Francis Kernan, Roscoe Conkling's original legal mentor and the man who had defeated him in 1862 for Congress. Kernan would later serve in the United States Senate from 1875 to 1881 alongside Conkling, the teacher and his student comprising New York State's two senators. Kernan, after much legal maneuvering, finally obtained a judgment for Rhoda of one thousand dollars. There was not much sympathy in the courts for the Loomis' troubles, he informed her.

Calista, Lucia, and Wash Loomis had already died, and the next of the Loomises to go was Charlotte in January of 1870. She and her husband, Asa E. Collins, had returned to Central New York from New York City and raised two children, Grove and Grace. Young Grove Collins proved worthy of his uncle's namesake, going into business for himself as a "green goods man" at a young age. He rented post office boxes at several locations, then advertised in newspapers and magazines offering easy money; "I want a few shrewd people in each locality to make thousands of dollars." To those who responded he entered into correspondence enclosing a green silk thread as a mark of identification, eventually inducing the person to send him some money as a sign of good faith. Changing his name and post office box frequently he bilked people from all over the United States, and when finally arrested had notebooks filled with thirty thousand names and addresses. He made thousands of dollars but lost it all playing the New York stock market. He was arrested numerous times for mail fraud and served time in New York's Elmira and Auburn state prisons, the Toronto Penitentiary, and a prison in Ottawa from which he escaped. He died in 1905, living in a rundown farmhouse in Tinker Hollow adjacent to the old Loomis land.

Grove Loomis settled into a small house at the edge of Nine Mile Swamp, accompanied by his mistress Nellie Smith. He had little contact with other family members for the remaining twelve years of his life, preferring instead to live quietly in the shadows of the family land now owned by others. He never lost his love for horses, and was said to steal them occasionally but was never indicted. When visitors came around, as they did infrequently, he would talk about the glories of Flora Temple or his Blackhawk stallion.

Only once in his remaining years was Grove Loomis in trouble and that was, predictably, because of a young woman. In 1874, when Grove was forty-nine, he enticed a sixteen-year-old girl named Cora Magwood to come and live in the shack with Nellie and himself under a promise of domestic work and high wages. Constable Filkins received an anonymous letter apprising him of the situation and advising him that "she has cried and taken on in the worst manner to get away but all to no avail—they will not let her go . . . You knew that all they want of her is to ruin her, and I think something ought to be done immediately to save her."

Filkins wasted little time, enlisting the support of the girl's widowed mother and then proceeding to Grove's house accompanied by two of the girl's male relatives. Since Filkins had beaten, stomped, and set Grove on fire nine years earlier, his visit was not likely to be welcomed. As recounted in a local newspaper:

> "They approached the premises quietly, and entered without warning. And right there Mr. Filkins showed what spirit of man he was. Considering the relations which exist between Filkins and the Loomises, it was an act of no little hazard for him to walk into Grove Loomis' house in the night without warning. His chance of getting the top of his head blown off was probably never better. His very boldness seems to have prevented hostile demonstrations. In the room were seated Grove Loomis, the noted Nellie Smith, three of Loomis' men, and the girl Cora, for whom they had come. Filkins told the girl she could pack up what things belonged to her without fear of being molested and come with him. While the girl was gathering together her clothing, Grove Loomis began a very free expression of his opinion of Filkins, and finally became so pointed in his remarks that Filkins invited him to 'mug up.' Indeed a row seemed rapidly approaching when Nellie Smith got Grove into the background, and took upon herself the task of entertaining the visitors. During the conversation which followed, it came out that the Loomises, through their perfectly organized system of spies, had learned that Filkins would soon be after them, and they had arranged to spirit the girl off the next day."

In March, 1878, Grove became seriously ill. Recognizing that he was dying he sent for the local minister to confess his sins and asked that the eighteenth verse of Revelations I be read at his funeral: "Fear not, I am the first and the last and the living one; I died, and behold I am alive for evermore, and I have the keys of

Death and Hades." On March 11 Grove Loomis died. At his
funeral the minister read the verse and then added: "I have no
doubt but what Mr. Loomis is in heaven with the angels. There
are many evil people who have been floated to Heaven at the
eleventh hour of forgiveness. I've heard some men say, "If I've
got to go and live with that crowd I might as well be in hell.'"

Rhoda Loomis, Cornelia and Denio were all noticeably absent
from Grove's funeral. They were furious that he had willed his
house, horses, cows and all personal possessions to Nellie Smith,
his mistress of many years, and they immediately set out to break
the will. Grove had appointed as executor of the estate his close
friend William Hathaway, Justice of the Peace in Deansboro,
and Hathaway was determined to see that the terms of the will
were carried out.

Immediately after Grove's funeral Rhoda Loomis threatened
to have Nellie killed if she did not turn over all of Grove's assets;
although Rhoda was eighty-six years old at the time, nobody who
had known her over the years doubted for a moment that she was
capable of carrying out her threat. Hathaway immediately moved
Nellie out of Grove's house and hired Charles Nash to remain
there and guard the premises. On May 1, 1878, Plumb Loomis
accompanied by Gary Penner and two other gang members came
to the house "armed to the teeth and commenced acts of lawlessness." Hathaway and Nash were both there and ordered the
Loomis group off the property. As described by the *Waterville
Times* the next move was made by Penner who, "more bold than
the rest, approached the house and endeavored to remove some
property belonging to the estate, which Nash gave him strict
orders not to touch. Penner then turned upon Nash, with an axe
in his hand, and allowed he would kill him at the first opportunity. Nash was armed with a revolver, which he drew and again
cautioned Penner, who again repeated his threat, whereupon
Nash shot him twice, one ball only taking effect. This looked like
business, a kind of business, too, which the Loomis family never
fancied, and put an end to their depredations for that day. They
left with the wounded man, Hathaway accompanying them
home." Penner was not seriously wounded, and attempts by
Plumb to press charges for the shooting were in vain. The house
and possessions remained with Nellie Smith.

Denio Loomis, the youngest of the children and just thirty
years old at the time of the final raid, continued to be closely tied
to his mother and to live with her and Cornelia at Hastings Center

until his death. His ongoing transgressions of the law were widely assumed to be Rhoda's ideas, for he had always done what she told him. In an attempt to maintain Loomis traditions he stole horses; when he was arrested in 1869 the *Utica Morning Herald* asked: "When will those Loomises cease to force themselves upon public attention? Denio, one of the worst of the family if such a comparison be possible, was held to bail to appear before the Onondaga County Court to answer for some crime . . . If one of [the Loomises] be lawfully punished it will be cause for common congratulation."

Denio jumped bail, as he did again in 1872 after being charged with grand larceny and released on a two thousand dollar bond. On the latter occasion he publicly threatened Edward Lynch who had brought the charges. Lynch refused to withdraw his complaint, and the following week his hotel and barn burned to the ground. The *Syracuse Post Standard* opined that "the work was that of a member of the Loomis gang named Denio."

In February, 1873, Denio again went to trial on charges of horse theft, this time given bail of three thousand three hundred dollars. Judge Morgan, presiding, was said by the *Onondaga Journal* to be "not the man to aid rascals in eluding justice." While the case was given to the jury, Denio went to a friend's house nearby to wait. The jury arrived at a verdict of guilty, but before the court could be resumed one of the jurors sent a message to Denio who promptly disappeared on the fastest horse in town. Several days later Judge Morgan moved to forfeit the bail, and Denio sent a telegram from Canada saying that he would appear on condition that he be granted a new trial. "How he can be entitled to another trial it is difficult to see," noted the newspaper. "If we remember correctly, the jury at his late trial found him guilty . . . Why shouldn't judgment be pronounced against the rascal and he be sent to State prison?"

When Denio finally returned he was jailed, but eventually was granted a new trial at which he was acquitted. He continued to remain out of jail for his thieving but the cost of doing so grew increasingly great. As a Syracuse newspaper saw it: "[Denio] had paid well for his liberty, and the county was well satisfied to have its depleted treasury replenished with so substantial an amount."

Denio continued stealing, and in late 1876 was indicted for taking "a horse and buggy belonging to A. Barstow of Richfield Springs . . . After much doubling over the ground the property was captured at Oneida." Before he could be brought to trial, however, he suffered a "paralytic stroke," although only forty years old, which left him disabled for almost a year. He recovered somewhat, but in late 1879 was affected by another stroke and died January 7, 1880. His body was brought to Sangerfield for burial in the family plot. The *Waterville Times* intoned: "Denio Loomis, who has been more dead than alive for several months past, shuffled off his mortal coil recently and was planted at the [Sangerfield] Centre Tuesday of this week. What shall the harvest be?"

Rhoda and Cornelia Loomis had settled at Hastings Center with Denio, and continued to live there after his death. Despite having lost their house and land in Sangerfield, Rhoda was determined to regain the financial splendor to which she had become accustomed. The biggest threat to this goal, as it always had been for Rhoda, was having to cut the family pie into too many pieces.

One person about whom Rhoda Loomis worried was Grove Loomis Jr., the son of Wash and Hannah who had been given by Wash to the Gortons after Hannah had been murdered. He would turn fourteen on February 10, 1875, and would then be legally entitled to inherit Wash's share of the family estate. On February 6, Cornelia Loomis procured papers appointing her as the boy's legal guardian. Three days later Cornelia, Denio and Plumb broke into the Gorton's house and demanded that the terrified boy be turned over to them. When the couple refused young Grove was forcibly carried from the house and taken away in a sleigh.

News of the abduction spread quickly. A large group of men went immediately to Grove Loomis' house and, not finding the boy, threatened to kill him if he did not return the boy at once. Grove, thoroughly frightened, went to a Deputy Sheriff and asked for protection. Rumors abounded that the boy had been taken to Higginsville, Hastings Center, or more distant points. As reported by the *Waterville Times*: "Some of our people think he has been taken to Canada, where one of this depraved Loomis family resides; others think he has been taken to Vermont, where some members of this family have a sinful rendezvous; and others still, who comprise the greater number, think he has been taken to the sea coast, and has been already, or soon will be sent out of country, and to some distant place, from which he will never be able to return."

It took Jim Filkins several days to learn that young Grove was being held at Hastings Center and was shortly to be taken to

Canada. Filkins immediately telegraphed Officer Lynch at Hastings Center; Lynch had lost an arm but could be trusted to help because he shared Filkins' dislike of the Loomises. On the night of February 22, Lynch and several others surrounded the Loomis house and demanded that they give up the boy. On realizing that Lynch was among the men Plumb armed himself with two guns and a knife. Rushing for the door he yelled: "That one-armed son of a bitch—he'll never leave here alive!" Waiting outside the door was Lynch, revolver aimed straight ahead at eye level. As Plumb emerged Lynch cocked the trigger and said nothing. Plumb backed slowly into the house and slammed the door. A seige ensued for several hours during which the Loomises hid young Grove's clothing so that he could not be taken away. Finally realizing that they had been defeated the Loomises gave in and released him. Filkins arrived the following day to escort him back to the Gortons and ensure that papers were initiated making the Gortons permanent guardians. When asked why the Loomises had said they had kidnapped him young Grove replied: "Aunt Cornelia and Grandmother Loomis thought I did not have good enough clothes to wear as befitted a Loomis so they took me away from [the Gortons]." Grove Loomis Jr. remained with the Gortons, lived an honest life, and died in 1937.

Denio Loomis had already suffered his initial stroke when Grove died in 1878, providing further incentive for Rhoda and her remaining children to try and break Grove's will. The number of Loomis children was becoming alarmingly few, and without them Rhoda had no hope of regaining the riches she had once enjoyed. When Denio finally died in 1879 it was said that Rhoda, age eighty-eight, gave up hope and mellowed. She continued in her aristocratic ways until the end and was described by neighbors at Hastings Center as wearing "fine silks and satins," a lace cap on her head, and as being an expert in making expensive cheeses. The children nearby called her "Grandma Loomis" and one recalled: "I felt sure that people must be mistaken about her being one of the Loomis gang as she was so nice." She died quietly on October 6, 1887, aged ninety-four, having outlived eight of the twelve children she had borne. Cornelia bought the most expensive casket available for her mother, dressed her in her best silk dress, and laid her to rest next to her husband, Wash, Grove, and Denio in the Sangerfield cemetery.

Cornelia also remained active for several years following the final raid but she was no longer the queen of the outlaws. On

June 19, 1867, just two weeks after Filkins' trial, she suffered a humiliating setback which was reported in the newspapers and led to wide ridicule. She had gone to Utica to take a train to Syracuse and thence to Hastings Center. While seating herself in the train car "three men brushed past her and diappeared. Soon after she discovered that her pocket book was missing. It contained $50 in money and some valuable papers." The *Waterville Times* concluded the account of the theft by noting that "the young men have not been found, nor the money heard from."

After her mother's death Cornelia moved to a smaller house nearby. Accompanying her was Charles Loomis, Wheeler's son who had been at the Loomis home the night of the final raid. She spent her final years in solitude with little contact with neighbors or friends, and on November 24, 1893, she had a stroke. Three days later she died at the age of seventy-two, and was buried at the cemetery in Sangerfield.

Bill Loomis withdrew from the family almost completely after Wash's death; he could not understand, he said, why the many men in the house had not come to Wash's aid. He became a respectable farmer in Higginsville, raising his children and cattle, and many of his younger neighbors had no knowledge of the thief boats or his infamous past. Bill was said to be fond of beer, but became severly arthritic as he aged. Local residents remembered him driving his horse and wagon up to the Higginsville Hotel and the bartender delivering beer to the wagon because it was too difficult for Bill to dismount. He died July 3, 1896, at the age of seventy-six, and was buried by his wife in the cemetery at Higginsville. In death as in life, Bill Loomis was the only son who was able to completely break away from the Loomis family.

Higginsville today consists of a few houses and a garage, a slight pause and sideways glance for drivers along state route 46. North of the village at the site of Bill Loomis' farm remnants of the Sidecut Canal are still discernible, filling with water in springtime but no longer able to accommodate Bill Alvord's "thief boats." To the west Hastings Center has ceased to exist on any signs, but oldtimers point to a cluster of twelve houses north of Central Square and tell you that is it. Once on the main road north from Syracuse, it was bypassed by U.S. Route 11, which in turn was bypassed by Interstate 81. Twice spurned, the village has become a collection of trailers trying to metamorphose into houses within cocoons of scrub pine.

With Bill Loomis' death only Plumb and Wheeler remained. Plumb moved back to the old family land, buying a few acres surrounding the original homestead on the hill. There he lived for many years, trying to recreate the glories of the Loomis gang but now only a faint echo. He was arrested in 1872 on charges of larceny, and implicated in petit thefts of a sewing machine, a trunk, some wood, and some chickens. Up until the time he died he was continuously involved in litigation and court suits of one kind or another, often acting as his own lawyer.

Plumb had led a charmed life, having escaped being shot and being hanged. In 1874 his horse shied in Waterville, throwing Plumb and the carriage into the ditch upside down. He escaped serious injury, as he did again four years later when he was gored by a bull. As the memories of the Loomis' criminal activities receded, Plumb became a local character of sorts and was regarded with amusement. In his sixties he was still seen at burlesque shows in Utica, and he frequented the bars of Waterville. On one occasion he confronted Jim Filkins at the American Hotel. "Jim," he said, "come and have a drink. You murdered my brother, God damn you, but come and have a drink anyway." Plumb also liked to talk about his hanging and show the scars on his neck from the rope. Over beer in the American Hotel Patrick Doyle boasted to Plumb that he had helped hold the rope that hanged him. Plumb Loomis replied that "while he might have deserved hanging he never got low enough to deserve hanging at the hands of a goddamn Irishman."

Following Nellie Smith's death Plumb moved from the hill to Grove's house at the edge of the swamp, and it was there that he died August 26, 1903, after a brief illness. He was buried with his family in the Sangerfield cemetery, and a piece of the maple tree limb from which he had been hanged was put on display at the local tavern. The branch was later acquired by the Madison County Historical Society, and in 1984 was loaned to the New York State Historical Association for use in the Farmers' Museum in Cooperstown. It was put on display in an exhibit called "Happy Times: New York Village Amusements."

Wheeler Loomis was the last of the outlaw gang, but because of the rape charge against him he rarely returned from Canada. He remained actively involved with his family's horse thieving network until the final raid, then settled into respectable farming outside Alexandria, Ontario. His son, Charles, went to live with Cornelia and Rhoda, and a daughter returned to Central New

York and settled there. On March 20, 1911, Wheeler Loomis died of cancer in Ontario. His body was brought to Sangerfield and buried in the family plot.

Today Wheeler's grave is the only one of the original family which can be found. It sits in the middle of the Sangerfield cemetery, just off Route 20, across the street from the Sangerfield Inn and Post Office. The grave is marked "Theodore W. Loomis, 1831-1911. Erected by son William." The only other Loomis grave which is marked is that of Charles W. Loomis, Wheeler's son, who lived until 1926. Somewhere beneath the adjacent sod lie George Loomis, Rhoda, Wash, Grove, Denio, Cornelia, and Plumb but the stones marking their burial have been removed or overgrown. The records of the cemetery are minimal, consisting of a single map which a cemetery official confidentially told me had been copied off an original drawn on a paper bag. A large area of the cemetery is simply marked on the map, "Old Public Burying Ground." Today broken pieces of tombstones can be found in bushes, and markers flush with the ground are being inexorably reclaimed by grass and weeds. One of the local citizens whom I consulted suggested that the Loomises had never been buried there at all. Another said he thought they had but "maybe they was moved." "After all," he said with a faint twinkle in his eye, "there's lots of folks near the swamp who swear they seen Wash Loomis' ghost from time to time."

Many descendants of the Loomises continue to live in Central New York, today often proudly claiming their heritage. One of the best known individuals thought to have been a descendant was poet Ezra Pound whose grandmother, Sarah Angevine Loomis, came from Oneida County. Pound himself believed he was related to the Loomis gang for during his undergraduate years at Hamilton College he changed his middle name from Ezra Loomis Pound to Ezra Weston Pound so as to disassociate himself from his tainted pedigree. Later Pound was indicted on nineteen counts of treason for working with the Fascists in Italy during the Second World War.

As the Loomises themselves died off, so too did the other gang members. Laverne Beebe was one of the first, being killed by Apache Indians in 1869 while "in the employ of the Government as an Indian scout." Frank Jones was arrested for stealing a horse and buggy and Salem Loucks for larceny and jailbreaking; each time such names came to public attention they were linked "to the former Loomis gang," like ever fainter echos reverberating between the surrounding hills. In 1871, John Maxwell murdered William Bennett for having been "improperly intimate in his family," and the newspaper account implied that justice had been served because both men "were supposed to be members of the notorious Loomis gang." Big Bill Rockwell moved west to Ohio. Bill Alvord died in Auburn State Prison in 1874, having spent almost half of his sixty-six years behind bars.

Interest in the Loomises flared once more briefly in 1879. Nobody had ever been charged with the 1866 murder of Phoebe Crandall but her husband, Dennison, had never given up hope of finding those responsible. Even though the intruders had worn masks, Dennison Crandall was certain he could recognize them by their eyes. Over the years he had driven to jail on many occasions, summoned by the sheriff, to look at the inmates being held. In 1878, Isaiah Belfield was arrested on charges of forgery. When Dennison Crandall saw Belfield he said yes, *that* was one of the men who had killed his wife twelve years earlier. "Those eyes—I have seen them in my dreams a hundred times."

Belfield was brought to trial in Morrisville on May 8, 1879. The case generated considerable interest, with the *New York Sun* and *New York Herald* sending reporters. Amos Cummings for the former wrote a long narrative of the Loomis gang alongside the Belfield case proceedings. The prosecution based its case on Dennison Crandall's identification and also on testimony which Nellie Smith, Grove Loomis' mistress, was prepared to give. Nellie was angry with the Loomises for attempting to break Grove's will, and told the sheriff that she had overheard Isaiah giving details of the Crandall murder to Cornelia Loomis. As far as recognizing Belfield in court, Nellie assured the sheriff that she would recognize him if she saw him "in a pudding dish."

The judge, however, refused to allow Nellie Smith to testify since she had not been in the room when the alleged conversation took place. Furthermore the defense raised questions about Dennison Crandall's eyesight and memory since he was then almost seventy-eight years old. Jim Filkins and other law officers testified about Belfield's character and criminal record but the evidence to link him with the murder was not enough. The jury found him not guilty, although he was sentenced to a prison term on the separate forgery charges. Neither Joe Crandall nor Shadrack Curtis was ever charged for Phoebe Crandall's murder, and when Dennison Crandall died shortly thereafter it was still listed as unsolved.

Jim Filkins' appearance at the Crandall trial raised once again the questions about Wash Loomis' murder, and the *New York Sun* reporter asked Filkins about it. The aging lawman denied any involvement, but told the reporter he had heard that two gang members had killed Wash in a fight. In recounting the story in the *New York Sun* the reporter added: "I asked Ephraim Conger and William V. Durfee if they had ever heard this story. Ephraim winked at Durfee, and replied that he thought it very plausible." There were never any additional indictments for Wash's death, and the persons who accompanied Filkins were not positively ascertained although the names of young Hank Bissell, Cort Terry and Civil War veteran John Garvey were mentioned most often.

Shortly after the Crandall trial Filkins retired from his official duties. "Family troubles" had broken up his home, as he had resolutely refused to allow his fourteen-year-old daughter to marry. Filkins, then fifty-five, moved to Utica and worked as a night watchman for several years. In 1892, he became sick and returned to Waterville. There on January 4, 1893, at age sixty-eight he died.

Jim Filkins was buried in the cemetery at North Brookfield, directly across Nine Mile Swamp from the old Loomis home. The cemetery lies four and one-half miles south of Sangerfield alongside Route 12. Filkins' grave sits on a hillside beneath a large pine tree, the closest grave in the cemetery to the Loomises, and the Loomis pinnacle is clearly visible. It is as if he still is watching them in death, as he did in life. Robins, orioles, and meadowlarks are the only sounds which break the stillness on a summer day.

The rolling hills to the west, beyond the Loomis pinnacle, are much as they were in 1866 when the men rode to the Loomises for the final raid. West of the village of Madison the 1837 Bouckville Hotel and 1850 Landmark Tavern, alongside a gully which was once the Chenango Canal, are still open for business. Turning right in Morrisville on County Route 101 leads directly to Peterboro five miles to the north. There the village green is flanked by twenty houses, a volunteer fire department and a post office. In the middle of the green is a stone statue of a soldier, a memorial to Union forces in the Civil War. Engraved on it: "Cheers for the living, tears for the dead."

At one end of the village green is a large lot enclosed by an iron fence. The iron gate still swings clumsily to admit visitors to what was once the Smith estate. In the middle of the lot is a clump of trees and bushes beneath which can be seen the foundation and charred timbers of the Mansion House which burned to the ground in 1936. On one side of the lot is a small red brick building marked "Peter Smith's land office." Otherwise there is no historic marker of any kind to indicate who once lived there or visited there. When I was in Peterboro in 1985 a young man approached me as I wandered around the grounds of the estate. He wanted to be helpful. "Who was this fellow who lived in the big house?" I asked. "Oh, Smith, Gerrit Smith," he replied. "What did he do?" I persisted. "Well, I know the old people used to talk about him a lot," he said. "I'm not sure but I think he was a war hero or something."

Gerrit Smith's involvement with the Civil War was completed by the release of Jefferson Davis from prison. In 1866, Smith wrote to President Johnson that Davis' "very long confinement in prison without a trial" was "an insult to the South, a very deep injustice to himself, and a no less deep dishonor to the government and the country." In May of 1867, Smith went personally to Richmond to argue for Davis' release, and in a public speech called for the North and South to live together in mutual trust and love. Finally, on November 8, 1867, Jefferson Davis was released on a bail bond signed by Gerrit Smith, Cornelius Vanderbilt and Horace Greeley.

For the rest of his life Gerrit Smith denied having supported John Brown's raid on Harpers Ferry. Brown's visits to Peterboro were very hazy in his mind, and he claimed that Brown had a "great horror of bloodshed." In the months immediately preceeding Brown's raid Gerrit Smith said he had had no communication with him whatsoever. When confronted with overwhelming facts to the contrary, Gerrit Smith took refuge in his history of insanity, as in this 1872 letter: "When the Harpers Ferry affair occurred, I was sick, and my brain somewhat diseased. That affair excited and shocked me, and a few weeks after I was taken to a lunatic asylum. From that day to this, I have had but a hazy view of dear John Brown's great work . . . My brain has continued to the present time to be sensitive on this John Brown matter, and every now and then I get little or no sleep in consequence of it."

Gerrit Smith remained true to the causes for which he had fought, however. He became a loyal Republican because he believed that party had "saved the nation." He staunchly supported the Presidential candidacy of Ulysses S. Grant with both money and speeches, and when Grant had been re-elected to a second term in 1872 Smith wrote to him:

> "I rejoice in your re-election for your own sake - for the sake of its ample vindication of your assailed wisdom and assailed integrity - but I rejoice in it more for our country's sake. What our country most needs is not prosperity in business, the speedy payment of her great debt and the increase of her wealth. Far more than this and than all things else she needs the cordial recognition and full protection of the equal rights of all her children - the black and red as well as the white. In the light of what you have already done to this end, I believe that ere the close of your next Presidential term, this recognition will be gained and this protection enjoyed. Then and not till then shall we be a favored nation."

Smith's reference to American Indians was unusual for him; he apparently was recognizing in his final years that they, like the Negroes, had been treated badly.

Smith remained vigorously involved in social causes until the last week of his life. He continued to champion temperance reform, making frequent speeches and donating money. At age seventy-six he adopted the cause of Cuban revolutionaries who were fighting Spain for independence in a Ten Years' War; Smith arranged public meetings in Peterboro and Canastota, and donated several thousand dollars to the revolutionaries' support. He also encouraged his daughter, Elizabeth Smith Miller, and niece in their efforts to achieve womens' rights. In 1869, Elizabeth Cady Stanton and Susan B. Anthony created the National Woman Suffrage Association, which would eventually secure the right for women to vote.

Gerrit Smith's grandson, Gerrit Smith Miller, contributed to the nation in a different sphere. In 1862, while a student in a private boarding school in Boston, young Gerrit founded and captained "the first organized football club in the United States." He was later recognized as one of the founding fathers of American football, which has become our most violent American pastime. The original football team organized by Gerrit Smith Miller was named the "Oneidas" in honor of those whose land his grandfather and great-grandfather had bought and sold; the team was distinguished by scarlet neckclothes which all members wore and by never having lost a football game.

Gerrit Smith went to New York City for the Christmas holidays of 1874. On December 26 he suffered a stroke, and died a few days later. When his body arrived at the railroad station in Canastota a large crowd was on hand despite a temperature outside of thirty degrees below zero. At the Mansion House "flowers adorned the rooms, and the Cuban cross stood on the table"; children from an orphanage he had founded stood around his coffin and sang his favorite hymn. Among the pall-bearers carrying him to the Peterboro cemetery a half-mile to the east were two Negroes.

Today Gerrit Smith's grave can be found in the middle of the cemetery beneath maple trees. It is marked by a rectangular block of granite with his name marked on the top, and lies near that of his father, Peter Smith. There is no historical marker nor any indication of who Gerrit Smith was. If one climbs to the summit of the adjacent hills on a clear day the Adirondack Mountains are visible. There at North Elba, on land given to Brown by Gerrit Smith and now just two miles outside the village of Lake Placid, John Brown's body lies "a-mould'ring in his grave" next to two of his sons who were killed in the raid on Harpers Ferry. Brown's simple farmhouse and barn have been restored as they were in 1859 when he died. The fields beyond and the looming peaks of the Adirondacks have not changed at all since John Brown left, unless you turn to the east and notice two ski jumps built for the 1980 Winter Olympics a few hundred yards from the grave.

Returning to Sangerfield and driving east, it is thirty-seven miles along the rolling hills of Route 20 to the village of Cherry Valley. The main road bypasses the town today, so it is necessary to turn off. On the road descending into town there is a small farmhouse on the right, and nestled into a corner of the yard is a stone marker with a cross on top. This, the sign says, was one site of the massacre. The sign recreates the scene of November 11, 1778:

> "His wife Elizabeth, at the door holding an infant, was shot down in cold blood by Walter Butler's Tories and Indians on that day. Nearby at the left stood the apple tree into which was thrown her arm brutally severed from her body."

Following the Civil War none of the American Indian groups fared well. President Grant named Ely Parker to be Commissioner of Indian Affairs, but in less than three years he was forced to resign by political pressure from a coalition of corrupt merchants, the "Indian Ring," who had been profiting from government contracts for supplies to the Indians. Parker tried to eradicate the corruption but failed, and he retired to private life in New York City.

In the West the Indians were relentlessly pushed off their land. Between 1872 and 1874 United States military troops slaughtered twelve million buffalo, virtually eradicating the Indians' main source of subsistence. It took somewhat longer to eliminate the Indians themselves who were given a choice of reservations or death; since many of the reservations were malarial the outcome was often the same. As soon as Indians got settled on one reservation government officials would move them to another, causing one chief to suggest: "I think you had better put the Indians on wheels and you can run them about whenever you wish." General Philip Sheridan advised his troops that "the only good Indians I ever saw were dead," and Colonel George Custer obliged by massacring one hundred and three Cheyenne men, women and children. When Custer and two hundred and fifty troops were killed in 1876 after foolishly attacking four thousand armed Sioux, national sentiment for exterminating the Indians intensified. By 1885 Sitting Bull, proud leader of the Sioux, had been reduced to being a traveling exhibit in Buffalo Bill's Wild West Show.

A remnant of Oneida Indians remained in Central New York and over the years has increased to nine hundred individuals. Their headquarters is a thirty-two acre reservation, the remains of over six million acres which they once owned and which were guaranteed to them by several federal treaties. The reservation sits beside State Route 46 just south of the village of Oneida and is marked by a fading, peeling sign proclaiming the "Territory of Oneida Indian Nations."

The Oneidas continue to have problems. They are divided into two factions, and when one of them opened a bingo hall on the reservation in 1985 violence flared between them. "Fighting broke out in front of the hall. Clubs and baseball bats were used and shots were fired, though no one was seriously injured." An official in the Bureau of Indian Affairs confidentially told me that the Oneidas are difficult to deal with. "They are divided among themselves," he said. "And more than most tribes they do not want anything to do with the government."

The Oneidas have tried to obtain justice for the land which was stolen from them. In 1970, they filed a lawsuit to reclaim the

100,000 acres illegally purchased by New York State in 1795 following passage of the federal Indian Non-Intercourse Act; in 1985 a partial decision in their favor was handed down by the United States Supreme Court. In 1978, the Oneidas filed additional suits claiming that the New York State purchases of 1785 and 1788 of more than five million acres of Indian land were also illegal; in 1988 a Federal appeals panel rejected these claims. In 1986, while awaiting settlement of the 1970 lawsuit, the Oneidas used earnings from their Bingo hall to buy back 47 acres of land from a local farmer, thereby more than doubling their reservation to 79 acres.

The Oneidas never forgot their sacred stone. According to a 1902 report "many times during the first twenty-five or thirty years after the sacred stone was deposited upon Forest Hill it was visited by members of its tribe; and even now at occasional intervals the cemetery employees see the figure of an Indian passing along the graveled paths to pause beside this sole remaining monument of a broken race." In 1974, the Oneidas reclaimed the stone from the cemetery entrance and with "appropriate religious ceremonies" moved it back to their reservation. When I first saw the sacred stone on the reservation it sat in front of a burned-out trailer, pieces of charred lumber and cinder blocks around it. Nearby an old car was being cannibalized for parts. When the Bingo hall was opened in 1985 the stone was moved to a more appropriate setting in an adjacent field.

It is seven miles from the Oneida Reservation to Peterboro and Gerrit Smith's grave. The road winds over a high ridge with fertile farmland stretching for as far as the eye can see. Six million acres of it were once guaranteed to the Oneidas for their assistance in achieving American independence. Groves of butternut trees still stand on the ridge, and beneath them are scarlet leaves of Indian paintbrush, reminders of a dead past.

# Postscript

From the village of Cherry Valley and the depths of Nine Mile Swamp, the waters run south to form the headwaters of the Susquehanna River. These waters, from the earliest days of America, have carried violence in their eddies. It was violence originally imported on the genes of those who selected themselves to come to the new land, nurtured by a bloody war of independence, and then encouraged by dehumanization of groups whose cheap land or cheap labor was desired. The springtime of America's history passed, but violence remained on the land as alluvial ebullitions. It is quiescent now, but periodically bubbles to the surface in a multitude of forms. In retrospect, it would be surprising if it did not.

Eighty miles south of the Loomis farm is the village of Appalachin, sitting on the bank of the Susquehanna River. There on November 14, 1957, another meeting took place. The morning fog was still lifting from the river when Sergeant Edgar D. Crosswell of the New York State Police reported to his superiors that limousines accumulating at the home of Joseph M. Barbara indicated that he was hosting more than a meeting of his soft drink distributors.

Barbara's large stone house stood on a knoll at the end of a long private driveway. It would be difficult not to notice limousines parading into the tiny village of one thousand people for they had to pass directly by the State Police Substation at the edge of town. One year earlier there had been a similar meeting but the state police had decided not to notice. Their nearsightedness had been considerably assisted, it was said, by envelopes

231

stuffed with large bills which had, even by the day of the meeting, been transformed into outboard motors, skimobiles, and downpayments on new cars. But that was a year earlier, before the friendly understanding between Joe Barbara and the police had run aground on shoals of greed.

Sergeant Crosswell was soon joined by another trooper and two agents of the United States Treasury Department's Alcohol and Tobacco Tax Unit. Barbara had been previously convicted of bootlegging liquor, had been charged with two murders, and was suspected of being an important member of the Cosa Nostra—the Mafia. It was with more than a little trepidation, therefore, that the law enforcement officials drove up Joe Barbara's driveway.

The chaos which ensued was described by news media all over the world the following day. Well-dressed men fled into fields and woods in all directions, abandoning both their host and common sense. They had committed no crime in gathering for a barbecue, but once they left Barbara's estate the police could stop them and ask for identification. Sixty-three men were stopped and identified including Vito Genovese, Carlo Gambino, Joe Profaci, and virtually every important crime boss east of the Mississippi River.

Forty others remained calmly in Joe Barbara's large living room and got on with business. Albert Anastasia had been assassinated in New York and the dons wanted to prevent gang warfare. A successor would have to be agreed upon in such a manner that both conservative and liberal factions of the family could save face. Then there was the matter of narcotics; Mafia tradition prohibited dealing drugs but younger members in New York and Chicago increasingly were adopting them as sideline businesses. Most importantly, however, the meeting was to be recreational. As later described by Joseph Bonanno, such meetings were "great social occasions for men of my world to mingle, to renew friendships and exchange views . . . [they] were both pageants of power and ceremonies that reminded us of our common way of life."

It is unlikely that the dons attending Joseph Barbara's meeting in 1957 had ever heard of the Loomises. They were, however, direct spiritual descendents of George, Rhoda, Wash, Grove and the rest of the gang which had institutionalized violence one hundred years earlier. The Mafia is merely one of many modern incarnations of an important American tradition.

# Notes

Approximately three-quarters of the information on the Loomis gang is taken from newspapers of the period and one-quarter from George W. Walter's *The Loomis Gang* (Prospect, N.Y.: Prospect Books, 1953). A slightly revised edition of *The Loomis Gang* was published in 1968 (Sylvan Beach, N.Y.: North Country Books) but reference pages in the notes below refer to the original 1953 edition. Unfortunately George Walter did not detail the origins of his information and so it is difficult to ascertain the authenticity of his stories; the people he interviewed who claimed first-hand information are now dead. I have used those stories which seemed reasonably likely in view of what else is known about the Loomis family. The original drafts and notes used by George Walter are held by the Madison County Historical Society in Oneida, New York. Two fictionalized accounts of the Loomis gang have also been published: J. Brick, *Rogues' Kingdom* (New York: Doubleday and Company, 1965) and H. M. Daniels, *Nine Mile Swamp: A Story of the Loomis Gang* (Philadelphia: Penn Publishing Company, 1941).

## PREFACE

"What is impressive": R. Hofstadter, "Reflections on Violence in the United States" in R. Hofstadter and M. Wallace, eds., *American Violence: A Documentary History* (New York: Alfred A. Knopf, 1970), p. 7.

## EPIGRAPHS

R. M. Brown, *Strain of Violence: Historical Studies of American Violence and Vigilantism* (New York: Oxford, 1975), pp. 35-36.

J. Conrad, *Heart of Darkness* (New York: New American Library, 1950), p. 69. Originally published in 1910.

Chapter I: PROLOGUE

"Robert Henderson's head": *New Jersey Gazette* quoted in D. Goodnough, *The Cherry Valley Massacre* (New York: Franklin Watts, 1968).

"Shocking sight": J. W. Jakes, *Mohawk: The Life of Joseph Brant* (New York: Macmillan, 1969), p. 109.

George Washington Loomis' birthdate and the genealogical information on the family is found in E. S. Loomis, *Descendants of Joseph Loomis in America* (Fresno: Book Publishers Inc., 1981). It was originally published in 1909 but original place or publisher is not listed. George Washington Loomis is descendant no. 2248.

George Washington's 1783 trip is described in W. S. Baker, *Itinerary of General Washington From June 15, 1775 to December 23, 1783* (Philadelphia: J. B. Lippincott, 1892).

George Washington's land dealings are described in H. L. Ritter, *Washington As A Business Man* (New York: Sears Publishing Co., 1931). See also J. Corbin, *The Unknown Washington* (New York: Charles Scribner's Sons, 1930), p. 80-81; and J. T. Flexner, *Washington: The Indispensable Man* (New York: New American Library, 1984), p. 369.

"During the later years": E. W. Spaulding, *His Excellency George Clinton* (New York: Macmillan Co., 1938), p. 231. The joint real estate ventures between Clinton and Washington are described in this book.

"They say that the General": C. Hislop, *The Mohawk* (New York, Rinehart and Co., 1948), p. 214.

Oneida sacred stone: See W. W. Canfield, *The Legends of the Iroquois* (Port Washington, N.Y.: Ira J. Friedman, 1902), pp. 187-93.

Book by Lewis Henry Morgan: *League of the HO-DE-NO-SAU-NEE Iroquois* (Rochester: Sage and Brothers, 1851).

"Feast on a Bostonian": A. M. Gibson, *The American Indian: Prehistory to the Present* (Lexington: D. C. Heath and Co., 1980), p. 252.

Oneida Indian participation in the war is described in Goodnough, op. cit., pp. 59-61; and J. Campisi, "Oneida," in *Handbook of North American Indians*, vol. 15 (Washington: Smithsonian, 1978), p. 483.

Philip Schuyler and his reaction to the Oneida Indians' living conditions in the early 1780s is in B. Graymont, *The Iroquois in the American Revolution* (Syracuse: Syracuse University Press, 1972), pp. 242-44.

The Congressional resolution of 1783 on the Oneida and Tuscarora Indians is in L. M. Hammond, *History of Madison County* (Syracuse: Truair, Smith and Co., 1872), p. 99.

Treaty of Fort Stanwix, 1784: See Graymont, op. cit., pp. 281-82 and Spaulding, op. cit., pp. 151-53.

"You are a subdued people": Graymont, op. cit., p. 281.

"Revolution means to murder and create": L. Hartz, *The Liberal Tradition in America* (New York: Harcourt, Brace and World, 1955), pp. 64-65.

Some of the pressure to obtain Oneida Indian land apparently emanated from the belief that canals could be built through Central New York to connect the eastern seaboard with the expanding midwest. George Clinton, Philip Schuyler and George Washington were all intrigued by this idea. In 1761 Schuyler as a young man had visited England and been profoundly impressed with canals being built to reduce the cost of transporting coal and agricultural products. Returning to the colonies he began exploring the possibility of connecting Lake Champlain to the Hudson River, and had shown his plans to Benjamin Franklin and others as early as 1776. Washington, meanwhile, was exploring possibilities of making the Potomac River navigable by means of canals, and had presented a plan to the Virginia legislature for a stock company to be formed. By 1779, Clinton had also become involved in canal projects, sending a man up the Mohawk River to measure the depths of the water at different places. Both Schuyler and Clinton eventually became convinced that the Mohawk River could be connected to Lake Ontario (via Wood Creek, Oneida Lake, and the Oswego River) by a canal dug along the portage at Fort Stanwix; it was for this reason that Washington and Clinton had tried to purchase that land in 1783. For details see B.J. Lossing, *The Life and Times of Philip Schuyler*, vol. II (New York: De Capo Press, 1973; first published in 1872), pp. 464-69; B. Tuckerman, *Life of General Philip Schuyler, 1733-1804* (New York: Dodd Mead and Company, 1903), pp. 259-64; Spaulding, op. cit., p. 156; and Flexner, op. cit., p. 196.

The 1785 land negotiations between Governor Clinton and the Oneidas are described in Graymont, op. cit., pp. 286-88. The price paid by New York State was $11,500 for the 500,000 acres; see Spaulding, op. cit., p. 151. The price of the land being sold by Clinton and Washington is in a July 1787, letter mentioned in Hislop, op. cit., p. 214.

The 1788 land negotiations, known as "Clinton's Purchase," are detailed in R.L. Higgins, *Expansion in New York* (Columbus: Ohio State University Press, 1931), p. 105; in the recent court suit brought by the Oneida Indians against New York State (Supreme Court of the United States: The County of Oneida and the State of New York v. The Oneida Indian Nation, nos. 83-1065, 83-1240, October term, 1983); and in Hammond, op. cit., pp. 164-65.

Details of the Indian Non-Intercourse Act of 1790 and the assurances of President Washington are in the suit brought by the Oneida Indians against New York State (Supreme Court, op. cit.). Details of the 1795 illegal purchase of Oneida Indian land by New York State are found in this same document.

"Before his death": Spaulding, op. cit., p. 232. The 1799 estimate of George Washington's wealth is in Flexner, op. cit., pp. 369-70.

Details of the 1792 allegations against Governor Clinton are in Spaulding, op. cit., pp. 235-36.

"Had the votes": D.M. Ellis, J.A. Frost, H.C. Syrett and H.J. Carman, *A History of New York State* (Ithaca: Carnell University Press, 1967), p. 129.

"The increasing population": Spaulding, op. cit., p. 233, quoting a 1772 letter from Francis Vanderkemp.

Information of land speculation in Central New York can be found in Ellis et al., op. cit., pp. 150-52; P. D. Evans, *The Holland Land Company* (Buffalo: Buffalo Historical Society, 1924); and D. D. Sowers, *The Financial History of New York State from 1789 to 1912* (New York; AMS Press, 1969; originally published in 1914).

For an account of the Ogdens see F.B. Hough, *History of St. Lawrence and Franklin Counties, New York* (Baltimore: Regional Publishing Company, 1970; originally published in 1853).

"To extricate him": Spaulding, op.cit., p. 234.

Information on John Jacob Astor is in Spaulding, op. cit., pp. 156-57 and 230-31.

Information on Peter Smith is found in R. V. Harlow, *Gerrit Smith, Philanthropist and Reformer* (New York: Henry Holt, 1939), pp. 2-5; and O. B. Frothingham, *Gerrit Smith* (New York: Negro University Press, 1969; originally published in 1878), pp. 5-9.

"To try to curtail": C.L. Todd and R. Sonkin, *Alexander Bryan Johnson* (Syracuse: Syracuse University Press, 1977), p. 25.

Information on Jedediah Sanger is in P. Jones, *Annals and Recollections of Oneida County* (Rome, N.Y.: A.J. Rowley, 1851), pp. 280-81; D. E. Wager, *Our Country and its People: A Descriptive Work on Oneida County, New York* (Boston: Boston History Company, 1896); W. Collins, "The Romantic History of Old New Hartford (New Hartford, N.Y.: Public Library, 1949, mimeo); and "New Hartford, N.Y. Centennial 1870-1970" (New Hartford, N.Y.: New Hartford Centennial Committee, 1970, mimeo).

"Many people being deprived": P. Jones, op. cit., pp. 18-19.

The naming of Sangerfield is mentioned in P. Jones, op. cit., pp. 410-411; and Wager, op. cit., p. 536.

"Wagons, stagecoaches": Ellis et al., op. cit., p. 181.

The social deterioration of the Oneida Indians is described in J. Belknap and J. Morse, *Report of the Oneida, Stockbridge and Brotherton Indians, 1796* (New York: Museum of the American Indians, 1955); and Campisi, op. cit.

"By this means": W.C. Macleod, *The American Indian Frontier* (London: Kegan, Paul, Trench, Tauber and Co., 1928), pp. 49-50. See also Macleod, p. vii.

The 1806 purchase of land by George Loomis is recorded in the Record of Deeds, Oneida County Court House, Book 12, p. 445.

"The Yankees have taken": Hislop, op. cit., p. 221.

Chapter II: MEETING

"The wagons and rigs": Manuscript entitled "The Loomises and the James Brothers" found in the George Walter collection, Madison County Historical Society, Oneida, N.Y. In these notes it is speculated that Jesse James might have been in attendance; since James was not born until 1847 this is clearly not true.

1865 New York State legislative report: *Twenty-first Annual Report of the Prison Association of New York*. Part I. Transmitted to the Legislature, January 22, 1866. Reprinted in many sources including H.W. Thompson, *Body, Boots and Britches: Folktales, Ballads and Speech from Country New York* (Syracuse: Syracuse University Press, 1979), pp. 81-84, originally published in 1939.

Crime in America: *Quarterly Review* 122 (1867): 89-100. This journal was published in London but is not the same as the *London Quarterly Review*.

"Read a man": Descriptions of Wash and the other Loomis children are taken, unless otherwise indicated, from A. Cummings excellent account of the Loomises in the *New York Sun* May 21, 1879, and from Walter.

Students with unruly behavior: In 1823 there had been a widely publicized incident at Hamilton College when students decided to get rid of a teacher who was universally disliked; "while the offensive teacher was quietly sleeping in his room one night they loaded, plugged and sanded a cannon and fired it in a hall near his door. The result was that it nearly ruined part of the building and tore in tatters the clothing and bed of the tutor. His escape from instant death was almost miraculous." See I.P. Bielby *Sheriffs of Oneida County* (Utica, N.Y.: P.E. Kelly, 1890), p. 8.

"We sometimes traded": Walter, op. cit., pp. 12-13. The account of Rhoda Loomis teaching other children to steal is in Cummings, op. cit.

The story of Wash Loomis' "stolen" boots is in Thompson, op. cit., p. 91.

"The next day": Walter, op. cit., pp. 74-75.

Wash Loomis' 1844 arrest is alluded to by Walter, op. cit., p. 17.

"Wash was a genius": Cummings, op. cit.

The 1845 indictments of Wash Loomis and Riley Ramsdell are found in notes taken from court records in the Walter collection, Madison County Historical Society. This is also the source of information on the 1847 indictments of Wash and Bill Loomis.

"Burglaries were": Cummings, op. cit.

"A sudden shower": B.J. Dew, "The Loomis Gang Again," *New York Folklore Quarterly* 10 (1954): 195-97.

"An almost inconceivable": Cummings, op. cit.

The dropping of charges in Madison County: See Walter, p. 21. The judge involved was not Joseph Mason, as Walter says, but rather James W. Nye who was the judge at the time. See Hammond, op. cit., pp. 148-49.

"A genial old man": Walter, op. cit., p. 13.

Rumors that Wash Loomis had been killed are alluded to in notes in the Walter collection, Madison County Historical Society. Rumors that he had been a member of the Oregon Legislature are in J.E. Clark, "The Famous Loomis Gang," *Morrisville Leader* no date, 1910.

"The wound was": Cummings, op. cit.

The descriptions of Grove Loomis are from Cummings, op. cit. and Walter, op. cit.

"Babies were named": Walter, op. cit., p. 46. See also B.J. Giambastiani (ed.) *Country Roads Revisited* (Oneida, N.Y.: Madison County Historical Society, 1984).

The account of how the Loomises changed the markings on horses is in Thompson, op. cit., p. 89.

"The animal whinnied": Thompson, op. cit., p. 89.

"Yessir, dat sure": Walter, op. cit., p. 48.

"There was a Mr. Wadsworth": Walter, op. cit., p. 50.

The economics of the Loomis horse thieving are described in Walter, op. cit., p. 47.

"White markings": Walter, op. cit., p. 51-52.

"One night the horse": Walter, op. cit., p. 51.

Hop growing in New York State is described in L.M. Hammond and in A.O. Osburn, Sangerfield History, Its People, Industries and Development, in *Transactions of the Oneida Historical Society 1889-1892* (Utica, N.Y.: L.C. Childs and Son, 1892,) pp. 147-48.

"Grew at least": H.F. Jackson and T.F. O'Donnell, *Back Home in Oneida: Hermon Clarke and His Letters* (Syracuse: Syracuse University Press, 1965), p. 14. The other quotes on hop growing are also from this book.

The account of the Abbey brawl is from Cummings, op. cit., and Walter, op. cit., pp. 18-20.

"So thick and impenetrable": Cummings, op. cit.

"Excursionists were able": J.J. Walsh, *Vignettes of Old Utica* (Utica, N.Y.: Utica Public Library, 1982).

The work of Samuel F.B. Morse in Cherry Valley is documented in material at the Museum of the Cherry Valley Historical Society, Cherry Valley, N.Y.

Martha Ann Burdick was pregnant: The marriage date of February 11, 1853 and birth of their first daughter on May 28, 1853 are listed in Loomis, op. cit. Bill Loomis is descendant no. 5004.

Bill Loomis' counterfeiting activities are detailed in Walter, op. cit., pp. 33-34, and his theft from the butcher shop is described in C. Brutcher, *Joshua: A Man of the Finger Lakes Region, A True Story Taken From Life* (Syracuse: no publisher listed, 1927), p. 67.

"I never take"; Walter, op. cit., p. 26

The story of the stolen horse in Camden is in Walter, op. cit., p. 71.

"With a whinney": The Wygart mare story in various forms is in Cummings, op. cit.; *Utica Sunday Journal* July 7, 1895; and Walter, op. cit., pp. 26-27.

The Loomis family connections in northeastern Pennsylvania included Griswold O. Loomis of Lenox, Pa., a fifth cousin, whose uncle lived in Bridgewater which is just seven miles from Sangerfield.

Hiding a gang member in Susquehanna, Pa., is mentioned in Walter, op. cit. p. 72.

The jailing of a gang member in Montrose, Pa., is described in Brutcher, op. cit., p. 68. The account of the fire is from the *History of Susquehanna County, Pennsylvania*, p. 274, kindly supplied to me by Ms. Betty Smith, Curator of the Susquehanna County Historical Society. The Brutcher account of the fire claimed that "even the jail burned down" but official records show that this was not the case.

Descriptions of Bill Rockwell and his confrontation with Wash are from Brutcher, op. cit., pp. 5-7, 70-77, 95-95.

"The horses were led": Brutcher, op. cit., p. 75.

"As many as fifty": Dew, op. cit.

Accounts of Bill Alvord are taken from the *Onondaga Standard* March 30, 1853, and from notes in the Walter collection, Madison County Historical Society.

"About sixteen": "The Loomises and the James Brothers," op. cit.

Chapter III: DISCORD

The descriptions of Rhoda Mallet are from Walter, op. cit., p. 7. Other information on her is from A. S. Mallet, *John Mallet, The Hugenot and his Descendants: 1694-1894* (Harrisburg: Harrisburg Publishing Company, 1895); Cummings, op. cit.; and *Utica Morning Herald* May 20, 1879.

"I want you to": Walter, op. cit.

Medicine in the nineteenth century is described in P. Starr, *The Social Transformation of American Medicine* (New York: Basic Books, 1982), p. 30ff.

The 1815 purchase of more land by George Loomis is recorded on a deed filed in the Oneida County Courthouse, book 27, p. 396, filed Sept. 27, 1815.

The accounts of women in frontier New York are from M. P. Ryan, *Cradle of the Middle Class: The Family in Oneida County, New York, 1780-1865* (Cambridge: Cambridge University Press, 1981), pp. 21-22, 32-33, and 74. The story of the bed-warming pan is from Walter, op. cit., p. 9.

"We soon learned": Walter, op. cit., p. 13.

"Did not want them to associate": *Utica Morning Herald* May 20, 1879.

"Of all the sources": A. M. Schlesinger, *The Age of Jackson* (Boston: Little, Brown and Company, 1945), p. 376.

"State very frankly": Ryan, op. cit., p. 170. Other details on the education of the Loomis daughters are from the *Utica Morning Herald* May 20, 1879.

The descriptions of the Loomis homestead are in Cummings, op. cit., and Walter, op. cit., p. 10.

"Homestead literally overflowed": These are the recollections of Thomas L. Hall in Walter, op. cit., p. 16.

Daily farm chores in central New York are described in O. Hamele, *And They Thanked God* (no publisher listed, 1944), pp. 10-18.

The entertainment and shows in Utica are described in Walsh, *Vignettes* . . . , op. cit., p. 88ff.

"Walked into a Waterville": Walter, op. cit., pp. 24-25. Another account of shoplifting by the Loomis girls is in Thompson, op. cit., p. 86.

"Before my mother was married": Walter, op. cit., pp. 23-24. The incident is also referred to by Cummings, op. cit., and by Dew, op. cit.

Corruption in early New York State banking practices is described in D.S. Alexander, *A Political History of the State of New York* (Port Washington, N.Y.: Ira J. Friedman, 1969; originally published in 1909), pp. 190-96.

"Never before": Brown, *Strain* . . . , op. cit., p. 99.

Charges of counterfeiting against George Loomis and his bribery of a member of the grand jury are mentioned in the *Utica Morning Herald* June 19, 1866, and also Cummings, op. cit.

References to court papers regarding George Loomis' money lending activities and the role of Othniel Williams are in the Walter collection, Madison County Historical Society.

George Loomis' counterfeiting during the 1830s is referred to in Bielby, op. cit. p. 9.

The 1838 indictment of Willard Loomis is referred to in notes in the Walter collection, Madison County Historical Society. The Loomis genealogy of E.S. Loomis, op. cit., lists Willard Loomis as having died on December 3, 1835, but the Oneida County court records show him to still be alive in 1838.

The 1829 reference to an Oneida County sheriff's concern about Loomis thefts is mentioned in Bielby, op. cit., pp. 8-9. The 1836 search of the Loomises is alluded to by Cummings, op. cit.

The 1837 indictment of George Loomis for arson is in notes of court records in the Walters collection, Madison County Historical Society.

"The old members": Bielby, op. cit., p. 9.

"For want of moral honesty": Bielby, op. cit., pp. 11-12.

"His shrewd and ingenious": Bielby, op. cit., p. 13.

"It was known": Cummings, op. cit.

Descriptions of Plumb and Denio Loomis are taken from Walter, op. cit., p. 15. Denio is also described in Thompson, op. cit., p. 86. See also Dew.

The story of Cornelia buying the oxen has many versions. See, for example, Cummings, op. cit.; Walter, op. cit., pp. 34-35; and Thompson, op. cit., p. 87. The description of Cornelia as an outlaw is by her niece and is in Walter, op. cit., p. 16.

Jane Alvord's running away from the Loomises is described in Walter, op. cit., pp. 115-16, and in C. Carmer, *Listen for a Lonesome Drum* (New York: David McKay Company, 1936), p. 274.

Chapter IV: OPPOSITION

"Was a natural": Jackson and O'Donnell, op. cit., p. 19.

George Eastman was born in Waterville, July 12, 1854. His father was a shop-keeper. Dan Rice's circus was advertised in the *Waterville Times* August 10, 1855. P.T. Barnum's lecture in Waterville took place in January, 1855, and was printed in the *Waterville Times* January 20, 1855. In 1865 Barnum published a book called *The Humbugs of the World* and in 1871 he launched his circus, later merged with one run by James Bailey.

The history of the San Francisco Vigilance Committee is described in R.M. Brown, op. cit., pp. 135-37. The editorials in support of vigilantism are found in H.H. Bancroft, *Works*, vol. 37 (San Francisco: The History Company, 1887), pp. 552-58. The reference to President Andrew Jackson is in R.M. Brown, op. cit., p. 162.

Roscoe Conkling's background and appointment are from D.M. Jordan, *Roscoe Conkling of New York: Voice in the Senate* (Ithaca: Cornell University Press, 1971), pp. 3-10. The descriptions of Conkling's appearance are from D.B. Chidsey, *The Gentleman from New York: A Life of Roscoe Conkling* (New Haven: Yale University Press, 1935), pp. 1 and 9. His illegitimate offspring are mentioned in Chidsey, ibid., p. 116.

"Would throw open": Jordan, op. cit., p. 12.

"Method, order": A.R. Conkling, *The Life and Letters of Roscoe Conkling* (New York: Charles L. Webster and Company, 1889), p. 20.

"He could quote": Chidsey, op. cit., p. 10.

Descriptions of Conkling's courtroom style are quoted from Chidsey, ibid., pp. 1 and 39.

"To be confined": Walter, op. cit., p. 25. Roscoe Conkling's record of convictions is mentioned by Jordan, op. cit., p. 9.

Conkling's defeat in November, 1850, is in Jordan, op. cit., p. 10. The Loomis' control of 500 votes in Oneida County is mentioned in the *Utica Morning Herald* May 20, 1879.

Conkling's political activities in the 1850s are summarized in Jordan, op. cit., pp. 12-16.

"The day is too": Conkling, op. cit., p. 379.

The descriptions of Jim Filkins are from Cummings, op. cit.; *Utica Daily Press* January 5, 1893; Walter, op. cit., pp. 53-54; J.B. Hoban, "That Loomis Legend," a manuscript dated May 16, 1929, in the Colgate University Library, Hamilton, New York; and J.B. Hoban, Roscoe Conkling and the Loomis gang, *New York History* pp. 433-449 (Oct.) 1941. Much of the information on Filkins in the Walter book must be treated with skepticism for one of the author's main informants had a strong personal dislike of Filkins as was duly noted by Walters. For example one story (p. 53) alleged that Filkins was sent to prison by the Loomises in an episode in which Plumb stole a cow in 1841; Plumb would have been only seven years old at the time.

"Horses, harnesses": *Madison Observer* no date, quoted in Walter, op. cit., pp. 78-79.

"Lashed out in true": Dew, op. cit.

"Knocked off the knob": Walter, op. cit., p. 72.

The burglary of the pistol factory is in Walter, op. cit., p. 76. The shooting of the farmer is in Walter, op. cit., p. 73. The shooting of a burglar in Oriskany Falls is in the *Waterville Times* March 3, 1855. The murder of the farmer near Morrisville and subsequent trial are in notes in the Gerrit Smith collection, Olin Library Rare Books Room, Cornell University.

The "thief boats" are mentioned in Walter, op. cit., p. 90.

"I wish my dogs": Walter, op. cit. p. 11.

"You'll need about": Thompson, op. cit., pp. 92-93.

"Told Grove about it": Walter notes, Madison County Historical Society.

"Who was employed": Dew, op. cit.

The story of Grove Loomis' recovery of his friend's horse and buggy is from Hoban, "That Loomis Legend," op. cit.

"Perry Risley": Walter, op. cit., p. 95.

"Realizing that they might": Walter, op. cit., pp. 95-96.

"I promptly hitched up": Walter, op. cit., pp. 94-95.

"I always kept": Thompson, op. cit., pp. 93.

Methods of keeping Loomis associates in line are mentioned in Thompson, op. cit., pp. 90-91.

"At the trial": Walter, op. cit., p. 79.

The murder of the Negro gang member is mentioned in Cummings, op. cit., and Walter, op. cit., p. 93.

Chapter V: MILIEU

"The next day word": Hoban, "That Loomis Legend," op. cit.

"She was repeatedly": *Twenty-first Annual Report . . .*, op. cit.

"Sometimes in one": Bielby, op. cit., p. 11.

"Large family of interesting": G.C. Van Deusen, *Thurlow Weed: Wizard of the Lobby* (Boston: Little, Brown and Company, 1947), p. 105.

Thurlow Weed's having worked briefly for the *Sangerfield Intelligencer* is mentioned in the *Waterville Times* April 28, 1855. His indictment in Cooperstown in 1815 is in Van Deusen, op. cit., pp. 11-13.

"My Lord Thurlow": Ibid., p. 109.

"That to the victor": Ellis et al., op. cit., p. 145.

Accounts of Whig corruption in Albany are described in Van Deusen, op. cit. pp. 104-109.

"At least one man's": Ibid., p. 108.

"Bribery by the Whigs": Ibid., p. 107.

"Outrageously corrupt": Ellis et al., op. cit., p. 238.

"Do I know him": Jordan, op. cit., p. 33.

"Manipulation was an instinct": Chidsey, op. cit., p. 15.

"Reeking everywhere": Charles Dickens' *American Notes* quoted in F. Browning and J. Gerassi, *The American Way of Crime* (New York: G. P. Putnam's Sons, 19), p. 136. The information on the New York gangs is from this book pp. 137-51.

William Tweed's appearance and activities are quoted from A. B. Callow, *The Tweed Ring* (New York: Oxford University Press, 1966), pp. 10-15 and 23; S. A. Pleasants, *Fernando Wood of New York* (New York: Columbia University Press, 1948), pp. 39-45; and E. K. Spann, *The New Metropolis: New York City, 1840-1857* (New York: Columbia University Press, 1981), pp. 299-301.

"Would reach from City Hall": Spann, op. cit., p. 251.

"Became so incensed": Ibid., p. 252.

"As New York's": Browning, op. cit., p. 151.

"Series of bankruptcies": Spann, op. cit., pp. 10-11. The other New York City accounts of fraud are from the same source.

"Lottery, gambling": Ibid., p. 437. This case occurred in 1843.

"Was discovered to have": Spann, op. cit., p. 306.

"The gross betrayal": Ibid., p. 308.

"Extraordinary increases": Ibid., p. 305.

"A blubberous": Spann, pp. 150-51.

The account of Daniel Drew is in Ellis et al., op. cit., p. 273.

"Hardly trust": Spann, op. cit., p. 10.

"Hundreds escape punishment": Ibid., p. 319. Another reader of the accounts of crime in New York in the 1850s was almost certainly Karl Marx, the German philosopher who was writing *Das Kapital* in England. From 1852 to 1862 Marx was a regular writer for Horace Greeley's *New York Tribune*, contributing over five hundred dispatches in all. See B. Davis, *The Civil War: Strange and Fascinating Facts* (New York: Fairfax Press, 1982), p. 74.

"That environment, not innate": R. Horsman, *Race and Manifest Destiny* (Cambridge: Harvard University Press, 1981), p. 98.

"The animals": Ibid., p. 113.

For a history of phrenology see S. J. Gould, *The Mismeasure of Man* (New York: W. W. Norton, 1981), p. 57.

"Eyes never rested": S. L. Chorover, *From Genesis to Genocide* (Cambridge: MIT Press, 1979), p. 146.

"Our manifest destiny": This phrase was first used by John L. O'Sullivan on December 27, 1845; see Schleisinger, *Age* . . . , op. cit., p. 427.

The 1818 "hangings" are recounted in Bielby, op. cit., p. 7, and in Wager, op. cit., pp. 182-83.

"The intensity of feeling": J.E. Smith (ed.), *Our Country and Its People: A Description and Biographical Record of Madison County, New York* (Boston: The Boston History Company, 1899), pp. 488-89. See also Hammond, op. cit., pp. 157-58; and B. Peel, The Hanging of Morrisville's Mad Dad, *Syracuse Herald American* November 13, 1983, p. 23.

The 1832 cholera epidemic is described in Walsh, *Vignettes* . . . , op. cit., pp. 110-112.

"Nearly in a state": J. Fowler, *Journal of a Tour Through the State of New York in the Year 1830* (New York: Augustus M. Kelley, 1970), p. 84. Originally published in 1831.

"Provided for the removal": Campisi, op. cit.

"The huge boulder": Canfield, op. cit., p. 191.

The activities of Gerrit Smith are described in Frothingham, op. cit., and Harlow, op. cit. Smith's home as part of the underground railroad is described in E.C. Stanton, *Eighty Years and More: Reminiscences 1815-1897* (New York: Shocken Books 1971; first published in 1898), pp. 51 and 62-64. The friendship between Smith and Alfred Conkling is mentioned in this book, p. 52.

Conkling's 1852 defense of the abolitionists is cited in Harlow, op. cit., p. 300.

"Do you want": Conkling, op. cit., p. 406.

"Two carriage-loads": Stanton, op. cit., pp. 62-63.

Gerrit Smith's land giveaway is described in Harlow, op. cit., pp. 242-47; Frothingham, op. cit., p. 235.

Details of John Brown's early life are found in J. Redpath, *The Public Life of Capt. John Brown* (Freeport, N.Y.: Books for Libraries Press, 1970; first published in 1860); and B. Stavis, *The Sword and the Word* (New York: A.S. Barnes and Company, 1970).

"To establish five": P.S. Foner, *Frederick Douglass* (New York: Citadel Press, 1969), p. 138.

The initial meeting of Smith and John Brown is described in Redpath, p. 59. See also Frothingham, op. cit., p. 235, and Harlow, op. cit., p. 246. Some sources claim that Brown bought the land from Smith but this seems highly unlikely given Brown's deep indebtedness at the time.

"Resembles the ape": Charles Caldwell quoted in Horsman, op. cit., p. 119.

"The Negro south": This is from the *Utica Morning Herald*, no date, quoted by Walter, op. cit., p. 81.

"A man so noble": J.R. McKivigan and M.L. McKivigan, "He stands like Jupiter": The autobiography of Gerrit Smith, *New York History*, April, 1984, 189-200. Originally written in 1856 but not previously published.

"A fool's tongue": C.C. Cole, *The Social Ideas of the Northern Evangelists, 1826-1860* (New York Octagon Books, 1977), p. 124.

"It struck me": Stanton, op. cit., p. 79.

"Heigh! ho!": The introduction of bloomers is described in Stanton, op. cit., pp. 200-203, and in E. Griffith, *In Her Own Right: The Life of Elizabeth Cady Stanton* (New York: Oxford, 1984), pp. 70-73.

"Woman's dress is": C.N. Robertson (ed.), *Oneida Community: An Autobiography 1851-1876* (Syracuse: Syracuse University Press, 1970), p. 294. The sexual beliefs of the community are described on pp. 265-69. See also E. Wilson, *Upstate: Records and Recollections of Northern New York* (New York: Farrar, Straus and Giroux, 1971), pp. 22-25.

"An unmanly sight": Robertson, op. cit., p. 18.

"Woman has done": *Waterville Times* March 10, 1855.

Gerrit Smith's brief career in Congress is described in McKivigan and McKivigan, op. cit.; Foner, op. cit., p. 165; and Frothingham, op. cit., p. 226.

"Made a very fiery": Redpath, op. cit., p. 81. John Brown's plan to liberate slaves in Louisiana is mentioned in Redpath, op. cit., p. 63.

"I have only a short": Stavis, op. cit., p. 53.

"Not earnestness": Ibid., p. 51.

"Our sacred work": O.G. Villard, *John Brown 1800-1859* (New York: Alfred A. Knopf, 1943), p. 287.

"I am ready": Frothingham, op. cit., pp. 232-33.

Brown's 1856 visit east is mentioned in Stavis, op. cit., p. 58. That he visited Rochester is confirmed in Foner, op. cit., p. 405. There is no mention of Brown specifically stopping in Peterboro on this trip but it seems likely that he did since Gerrit Smith was his principal source of financial support and Peterboro is directly en route from Rochester to Boston.

"A volcano": Stavis, op. cit., p. 59.

"A few men": Redpath, op. cit., p. 206.

"Give a slave": Ibid. See also p. 193.

"We must not shrink": Harlow, op. cit., p. 394.

"Spent the next several": Stavis, op. cit., p. 60.

"If God be for us": Villard, op. cit., p. 321.

"As the sun": Ibid., p. 322. See also Frothingham, op. cit., p. 237; Harlow, op. cit. pp. 396-98; and Stanton, op. cit., p. 54.

"Are ready to go" and "I expect to effect": Villard, op. cit., p. 322. See also Stavis, op. cit., p. 9.

Chapter VI: RAIDS

"Indictments against": Bielby, op. cit., p. 16.

DeWitt Dennison's arrest and release are mentioned in Walter, op. cit., p. 73.

"An excited crowd": Walter, op. cit., p. 30. Other references to Grove's arrest are found in Cummings, op. cit.; the *Waterville Times* March 27, 1858; and J.J. Walsh, "Trials and Tribulations in Oneida County," unpublished manuscript.

"What are you doing?": Thompson, op. cit., p. 90.

"Fetters and chain": *Waterville Times* April 10, 1858. See also Walter, op. cit., p. 31.

Information on J. Thomas Spriggs is from H.J. Cookinham, *Recollections of the Oneida Bar* (Utica: Thomas F. Griffiths, 1905), pp. 132-33.

The robbing of the District Attorney is described in the Walsh manuscript, op. cit., and in Walter, op. cit., pp. 32-33. The *New York Tribune* account is in April 10, 1858.

"So many sheep": Cummings, op. cit.

"He was arrested": Walter, op. cit., pp. 40-42. The attempt of the Loomises to arrest Clark is from the *Waterville Times* June 26, 1858.

"Outran him": Cummings, op. cit. See also Walter, op. cit., pp. 54-55.

"Grove's hounds": Walter, op. cit., pp. 64-65.

"As Peebles and Thompson": *Utica Morning Herald*, date uncertain, quoted by Walter, op. cit., p. 65.

"The Utica papers": *Waterville Times* July 24, 1858.

"Should a bolt": *Roman Citizen*, date uncertain, quoted by Walter, op. cit., p. 58.

The raid by Filkins, Humphrey and Hall is described by Cummings, op. cit., and Walter, op. cit., pp. 60-62.

The account of Salem Loucks' escape is in Cummings, op. cit.

"Who is it?" Walter, op. cit., pp. 42-44, and also alluded to in the *Waterville Times* July 3, 1858.

"After waiting": Walter, op. cit., p. 44, quoting the *Utica Morning Herald*, date not given.

Attempts to arrest Grove and his response are detailed in Walter, op. cit., pp. 59-60.

"I laughed": *Waterville Times* August 21, 1858.

"The time is coming": *Waterville Times* November 20, 1858.

"The Loomises amused": *Waterville Times* October 16, 1858.

"Grove Loomis is": *Waterville Times* November 20, 1858.

"The community is really": *Waterville Times* January 22, 1859.

"Mr. Ray has been called": *Waterville Times* January 29, 1859.

Filkins' raid of November 13, 1858, is described in Walter, op. cit., p. 66.

Filkins' raid of November 20, 1858, and its aftermath are described in Cummings, op. cit.; and Walter, op. cit., pp. 67-68.

"A tenant of": *Waterville Times* November 29, 1858.

"Wash must be tried": Walter, op. cit., p. 68.

"Say Wash": Walter, op. cit., pp. 68-69. The *Waterville Times* claimed the story was true but another newspaper in Hamilton denied that it happened. Whether the story is true or apocryphal is therefore uncertain.

"Free as the soaring": *Waterville Times* April 30, 1859.

John Brown's offer of $2.50 for the capture of President Buchanan is mentioned in A. M. Schleisinger, *The Almanac of American History* (Greenwich, Ct.: Bison Books, 1983), p. 275.

"Do you hear": Harlow, op. cit., p. 403.

Accounts of the April 1859 public lecture by John Brown in Peterboro are taken from Harlow, op. cit., pp. 403-04; Villard, op. cit., p. 395; and Frothingham, op. cit., p. 237.

Preparations for the raid on Harpers Ferry are detailed in Redpath, op. cit., p. 240ff. See also Frothingham, op. cit., p. 242.

"Intelligent black men": *New York Tribune* August 27, 1859.

"A monster in human": Harlow, op. cit., pp. 406-07.

"The sage of Peterboro": *New York Herald* September 5, 1859.

"Didn't want to have": Redpath, op. cit., p. 255.

"Had I interfered": Stavis, op. cit., pp. 159-60.

The outpouring of public support for John Brown following his trial is detailed in Stavis, op. cit., pp. 167-68, and in Redpath, op. cit., frontsheet.

Material on Gerrit Smith's mental state is taken from his psychiatric case records at Utica State Hospital. There is no suggestion in these records that Smith was faking his symptoms. In modern terminology Smith would have been diagnosed as having a brief reactive psychosis with manic features. Smith had a family history of mental illness with a brother affected with what was probably schizophrenia and a father who was said to be very eccentric in his later years; see Harlow, op. cit.

"The crimes of this": Stavis, op. cit., p. 169.

"Even now as": Davis, op. cit., p. 85.

Stonewall Jackson's attendance at Brown's hanging is cited in Davis, op. cit., p. 84. John Wilkes Booth's attendance is mentioned in Stavis, op. cit., pp. 171-72.

"One of the blackest": Chidsey, op. cit., p. 10.

"The largest majority": Jordan, op. cit., p. 19.

"Large number of friends": Jordan, op. cit., p. 20.

"Planted himself": Jordon, op. cit., pp. 21-22.

"By contributions of money": Harlow, op. cit., p. 413. See also Foner, op. cit., p. 182.

"But a hazy view": Harlow, op. cit., pp. 415-18 for the account of Smith's distancing himself from John Brown.

"Slavery in all": Stavis, op. cit., p. 168.

"I feel confident": Harlow, op. cit., p. 428.

"For six long months": Jordan, op. cit., p. 25.

Hermon Clarke's background is recounted in Jackson and O'Donnell, op. cit., pp. 19-20.

"There is even now": Brown, *Strain* . . . , op. cit., p. 3, quoting an 1837 Lincoln speech.

"The town was": F.G. Beardsley, *A Mighty Winner of Souls, Charles G. Finney* (New York: American Tract Society, 1937), p. 13.

Reference to George Loomis' participation in the war is in Walter, op. cit., p. 7. The activities of New York State militia units are chronicled in Wager, op. cit., pp. 168-73; Ellis et al., op. cit., pp. 140-42; and A.M. Schleisinger, *The Almanac*, op. cit., pp. 194-195.

The August 1859 burglary of a store is mentioned in the *Waterville Times* August 27, 1859.

"The Loomises bear": *Utica Morning Herald* March 10, 1860.

Lincoln's train stop in Utica in February, 1861, is mentioned in Jackson and O'Donnell, op. cit., p. 20.

"Atmosphere with noxious vapors": Jordan, op. cit., p. 30.

"Petrified with fear": Ibid., p. 31.

Fernando Wood's proposal is in Ellis et al., op. cit., p. 242.

Chapter VII: WAR

"Undigested immigrants": B. Caton, *The Civil War* (New York: American Heritage Press, 1960), p. 20.

Mobilization of troops in Oneida and Madison counties is described in Wager, op. cit., p. 196, and Smith, op. cit., p. 194.

"I have never spoken": Harlow, op. cit., pp. 428-29.

"Not one word": Harlow, op. cit., p. 431.

Ely S. Parker's background and attempts to enlist are found in D. Brown, *Bury My Heart at Wounded Knee* (New York: Holt, Rinehart and Winston, 1971), pp. 174-75; and in W.H Armstrong, *Warrior in Two Camps: Ely S. Parker, Union General and Seneca Chief* (Syracuse: Syracuse University Press, 1978).

Grant's 1854 resignation from the Army is mentioned in Davis, op. cit., p. 178.

The role of the Indians in the Confederate Army is detailed in Gibson, op. cit.

"Common sense teaches": Harlow, op. cit., p. 437.

"Because of a bad heart": Walter, op. cit., p. 81.

The attempts of the Loomises to kidnap and jail Filkins are described in Cummings, op. cit., Walter, op. cit., pp. 82-86; *Waterville Times* May 10, 1861; and *Utica Daily Press* January 5, 1893.

"One of Utica's": Bielby, op. cit., p. 15.

The theft of documents from the office of the District Attorney is described in Cummings, op. cit.; and Walter, op. cit., p. 91.

"I believe every": Jordan, op. cit., p. 37.

"Gaudy clothing": Caton, op. cit., pp. 41-42 and pp. 47-48, is the source of information on the first Battle of Bull Run.

Ball's Bluff and Conkling's response to it are detailed in Conkling, op. cit., pp. 138-47.

"Invincible in peace": Jordan, op. cit., p. 35.

"I am a workingman": Conkling, op. cit., p. 407.

Details of the Budge murder case are in Chidsey, op. cit., pp. 29-31, and Jordan, op. cit., p. 51.

Conkling's 1861 defense of Filkins is mentioned in Walter, op. cit., p. 86.

The murder of Hannah Wright is detailed in Cummings, op. cit.; Walter, op. cit., pp. 116-118; and the *Utica Morning Herald* November 30, 1861. Wash Loomis' placement of his son with the Gortons is mentioned in Walter, op. cit., pp. 212-13, quoting an undated *Waterville Times* article.

"He could enumerate": Cummings, op. cit.

The burning of the Beebe barn is in Cummings, op. cit.; Walter, op. cit., pp. 76-78; and the *Utica Morning Herald* November 2, 1861.

"I'm going to teach": Walter, op. cit., pp. 63-64.

"Was this spring chosen": *Waterville Times* April 25, 1862.

"A most rigid examination": Cummings, op. cit. See also Walter, op. cit., pp. 100-102.

"Plumb and Denio": Walter, op. cit., pp. 102-103.

"Tell me, Mr. Loomis": Cummings, op. cit. This episode is also described in Walter, op. cit., pp. 99-100 although Walter asserts that it involved Denio rather than Plumb Loomis.

Henry M. Stanley (real name, John Rowland) being at Shiloh is mentioned in Davis, op. cit., p. 72. The descriptions of the Monitor and Merrimac are from Caton, op. cit., pp. 77 and 79.

"Always saw a larger": Jordan, op. cit., pp. 38-39.

"Sending reinforcements": Schleisinger, *Almanac . . .*, op. cit., p. 118.

"John Brown's Body" was composed anonymously and can be found in P.E.

Ernest (ed.), *The Family Album of Favorite Poems* (New York: Grosset and Dunlop, 1959), p. 448. The story of Julia Ward Howe's writing of "The Battle Hymn of the Republic" is in Davis, op. cit., p. 73.

Rallies and mobilization in Central New York in 1862 are detailed in Wager, op. cit., pp. 196-97; Smith, op. cit., pp. 195-96; Durant, op. cit., p. 644; and Jackson and Donnelly, op. cit., pp. 21-22.

"There is a multitude": Jordan, op. cit., p. 41.

The origin of the term "Copperhead" is mentioned in Caton, op. cit., p. 229.

"In 1862 that force": Browning and Gerassi, op. cit., p. 190.

"The river is beautiful": All of Hermon Clarke's letters are quoted from Jackson and Donnelly, op. cit. A few of them were in fact written by other member's of Clarke's company but for simplification I am using them as if they had been written by Clarke himself.

"Never before": Caton, op. cit., p. 85.

"There is no doubt": Caton, op. cit., p. 106.

Horatio Seymour's beliefs and Conkling's responses are found in Chidsey, op. cit. pp. 41-42.

"Take care of wounded": Davis, op. cit., p. 26. Mary Todd Lincoln's four brothers are mentioned in Davis, op. cit., p. 24; two of them were eventually killed in battle.

"Personal in the lowest": Jordan, op. cit., p. 48.

"Yesterday afternoon": Jackson and Donnelly, op. cit., p. 56.

Chapter VIII: RAPE

Mention of Bissell's letter to Hermon Clarke is in Jackson and Donnelly, op. cit., p. 45. This letter is not reproduced, but Bissell would certainly have brought Clarke up to date on the latest Loomis happenings as Clarke's family would also have done.

The Loomis' horse stealing is described in Brutcher, op. cit., pp. 78-79. Stealing the same horse twice is mentioned in the *Waterville Times* February 11, 1864.

"He discovered Beebe": Notes in the Walter collection, Madison County Historical Society.

"When the loud knocking": *Waterville Times* February 20, 1863.

"Harboring, concealing": *Waterville Times* October 29, 1863.

The Charles Hopson case is detailed in Chidsey, op. cit., p. 42, and Conkling, op. cit., p. 196.

"Sir, a thing": Jordan, op. cit., p. 52.

"Friend Jenkins": Walter, op. cit., p. 105.

Arson attributed to the Loomises is described in Walter, op. cit., pp. 106-08;

and in N.R. Cowen, "Loomis Family History," a manuscript of the Waterville Historical Society.

"50 men 25 feet high": Caton, op. cit., p. 132.

"I have been to Washington": Jackson and Donnelly, op. cit., p. 65.

New York draft riots: The details are from Browning and Gerassi, op. cit., p. 195; Davis, op. cit., pp. 114-15; and Ellis et al., op. cit., p. 337. The Richmond bread riot is described in Davis, op. cit., p. 117.

"The women and children": Jackson and Donnelly, op. cit., p. 83.

The remark by the Prussian general is found in Caton, op. cit., p. 151.

Gerrit Smith's war efforts are detailed in Harlow, op. cit., pp. 433-37. Frederick Douglass' speech is mentioned in Foner, op. cit., p. 199.

The losses of the Madison County regiment at Gettysburg are given in Smith, op. cit., p. 200.

"Dear Sir": Walter, op. cit., p. 127. Other accounts of Filkins' shooting are in Cummings, op. cit., and the *Utica Daily Press* January 5, 1893.

The arrest of Wheeler Loomis for rape is found in Cummings, op. cit.; Walter, op. cit., pp. 120-24; and the *Waterville Times* October 22, 1863. The previous rape charge against him and dropping of the charge is detailed in notes in the Walter collection, Madison County Historical Society.

"Gentlemen of the jury": The account of Frances Van Dee's charges and Filkins' trial is taken from Walter, op. cit., pp. 126-27 who got the story from a letter from Thomas L. Hall of Hamilton, New York, and from the *Waterville Times* July 23, 1863.

"Fifty [men] were": Jackson and Donnelly, op. cit., pp. 111-18.

"Men enlisted": Chidsey, op. cit., pp. 47-48. The enlistment bonuses in Oneida and Madison counties are mentioned in Wager, op. cit., p. 197, and Smith, op. cit., p. 205. The story of the abduction of the soldier in Syracuse is in Browning and Gerassi, op. cit., p. 196.

Corruption during the Civil War among officials is in Browning and Gerassi, op. cit., pp. 190-193.

The prices of goods during the war are listed in Ellis et al., op. cit., p. 340.

"The fighting was": Jackson and Donnelly, op. cit., pp. 131-32.

"Our lines are": Jackson and Donnelly, op. cit., pp. 142-43. Such fraternization on the lines was apparently not uncommon during the Civil War; see, for example, Davis, op. cit., p. 49.

"The Niggers charged": Jackson and Donnelly, op. cit., p. 142.

"The radicals serenaded": Jackson and Donnelly, op. cit., p. 44.

The death rate of Indians fighting for the Union is in Davis, op. cit., p. 219. Indians fighting for the Confederacy are described in Gibson, op. cit., pp. 367-72.

"I saw the body": Brown, *Bury* . . ., op. cit., pp. 85-90.

Hermon Clarke's 1864 letters are in Jackson and Donnelly, op. cit., pp. 139-78.

"An impossibility": Chidsey, op. cit., p. 47.

"Had been for private": Jordan, op. cit., p. 54.

"No one could be": Ibid.

Laverne Beebe's arrest and release in Canada are in notes in the Walter file, Madison County Historical Society.

"We have heard": Cummings, op. cit. See also Walter, op. cit., p. 135, and Thompson, op. cit., p. 96.

The burning of evidence in Conger's barn is described in Walter, op. cit., pp. 109-10. The burning of the Madison County Courthouse is found in Cummings, op. cit.; and Walter, op. cit., pp. 110-13. The cost of replacing the Courthouse is mentioned in Smith, op. cit., p. 206.

"While we lay": Jackson and Donnelly, op. cit., p. 185.

Wilmer McLean's role in the war is described in Davis, op. cit., pp. 19-23. The role of Ely S. Parker in the surrender ceremonies is found in Armstrong, op. cit., pp. 108-11, and in H. W. Felton, *Ely S. Parker: Spokesman for the Senecas* (New York: Dodd, Mead and company, 1973), p. 89.

Chapter IX: SCALPING

"A great and spontaneous": Jordan, op. cit., p. 58.

"It was interesting": Jackson and Donnelly, op. cit., pp. 191-95.

"You white men": Armstrong, op. cit., p. 113.

Denio Loomis' horse theft is in the *Onondaga Journal* June 24, 1867; he was indicted and brought to trial but obtained a hung jury.

"The intruders": *Syracuse Journal* May 12, 1865.

"Well, Sheriff Crocker": Cummings, op. cit.; see also Walter, op. cit., p. 132.

"Three years ago": Conkling, op. cit., pp. 245-46. See also Jackson and Donnelly, op. cit., pp. 203-04.

"The Rebellion": Chidsey, op. cit., pp. 48-49. See also Conkling, op. cit., pp. 213-17.

"The South": From "No Treason in the Civil War," a pamphlet printed by the New York American News Company, 1865, and found in the Gerrit Smith file in the Syracuse University Library.

Gerrit Smith's suit against the *Chicago Tribune* and the newspaper's response is in Harlow, op. cit., pp. 450-54.

Details of the 1865 Loomis crime wave are found in Walter op. cit., p. 133, and in notes in the Walter collection, Madison County Historical Society.

The formation of the Sangerfield Vigilantes Committee is mentioned in Walter, op. cit., pp. 136-37.

"We are not quick": R.D. McGrath, *Gunfighters, Highwaymen and Vigilantes: Violence on the Frontier* (Berkeley: University of California Press, 1984), p. 243; it was taken from a Nevada newspaper in 1881.

The transcript of the coroner's inquest on the death of Wash Loomis was printed in the *Utica Daily Observer* November 3-6, 1865.

The funeral of Wash Loomis is in the *Waterville Times* November 9, 1865. Grove Loomis making his own funeral arrangements is in Walter, op. cit., p. 218.

The accounts of Filkins' preliminary hearing and grand jury indictment are taken from the *Utica Morning Herald* November 13, and 14, 1865; Cummings, op. cit.; Hoban, op. cit.; Walter, op. cit., p. 151ff; and notes in the Walter collection, Madison County Historical Society.

"The [Loomis] case will": *Utica Morning Herald* November 14, 1865.

"Mr. Filkins, we understand": *Onondaga Journal* November 20 and 21, 1865.

"The pestilence": Conkling, op. cit., pp. 386-87.

The account of the bail hearing is in Walter, op. cit., pp. 158-61, and taken from the *Utica Morning Herald* November 21, 1865.

Chapter X: LYNCHING

"Had not the roads": *Waterville Times* November 30, 1865.

"Previously been allied": Thompson, op. cit., p. 96.

The bounty on Filkins' head is in the *Utica Daily Press* January 5, 1893. The confrontation between Filkins and the Loomis gang members in the Park Hotel is described in the *Waterville Times* November 30, 1865.

"On that same night": Brutcher, op. cit., pp. 132-34.

"I'm damned if": Davis, op. cit., p. 226.

"The men of the North": Schleisinger, *Almanac . . .*, op. cit., p. 295.

"About early candle light": The account of the Crandall murder is from Walter, op. cit., pp. 163-68; and the *Utica Morning Herald* December 12, 1865.

"Ran like a deer": *Utica Observer* March 17, 1866, and Walter, op. cit., pp. 169-71, are the sources of information on this raid and the subsequent arrests.

"We are good, honest": *Waterville Times* March 8, 1866.

"There stood the fair": Walter, op. cit., pp. 124-25.

"There is a family": *Twenty-first Annual Report,* op. cit.

Plotting his assassination: See Schleisinger, *Almanac . . . ,* op cit., p. 304, and Jordan, op. cit., p. 71.

"Cannot by oath": Conkling, op. cit., p. 382.

"Three hundred thousand": Ibid., pp. 382-84.

The criticism of Conkling is in Chidsey, op. cit., p. 40, and Jordan, op. cit. p. 80.

"For a mighty nation": Brown, *Bury* . . . , op. cit., pp. 152-53.

"The treaty of 1788": *Utica Morning Herald* February 5, 1866.

The poisoning of Loomis maple trees is described in Walter, op. cit., pp. 171-72.

The return of the prisoners from Iowa is detailed in notes in the Walter collection, Madison County Historical Society; Walter, op. cit., p. 172; *Utica Morning Herald* June 22, 1866; and *Madison Observer* June 20, 1866.

"Left Waterville for": This account is from an official deposition made by Filkins and was fully reported in the *Utica Morning Herald* June 11, 1866; *Waterville Times* June 14, 1866; and the *Madison Observer* June 20, 1866.

"Coppery skin": Walter, op. cit., p. 164.

"Shook her head sadly": Notes in the Walter collection, Madison County Historical Society.

"And in the course": *Madison Observer* June 20, 1866.

"None of the Loomis": *Utica Morning Herald* June 12, 1866.

"Discussing the affair": *Utica Morning Herald* June 11, 1866.

"No apologies were needed": *Utica Morning Herald* June 28, 1866.

"The fact that civilized men": S. Jacoby, *Wild Justice* (New York: Harper and Row, 1983), p. 12.

The account of the June 16 raid and hangings is a composite from the following sources: Cummings, op. cit.; *Utica Morning Herald* June 18 and 19, 1866, and May 20, 1879; *Utica Sunday Journal* July 7, 1895; *Onondaga Journal* June 19, 1866; Walter, op. cit., pp. 179-87; Camer, op. cit., pp. 277-78; Brutcher, op. cit., pp. 68-69; and W.S. Leete, "Rounding up the Loomis Gang," a manuscript in the Madison County Historical Society.

Chapter XI: TRIAL

Excerpts from Mrs. Mason's diary are in notes in the Walter collection, Madison County Historical Society.

"We reached the Loomis place": *Utica Morning Herald* June 19, 1866.

"Mrs. L. did not": Ibid.

"Men, forgetful of what": *Utica Morning Herald* June 18, 1866.

"The act committed": *Waterville Times* quoted in Carmer, op. cit., p. 278.

"On his deceitful errand": Jordan, op. cit., pp. 82-83.

"Despite the retribution": *Waterville Times* October 25, 1866.

Plumb Loomis' sentence is in the *Waterville Times* December 20, 1866. The announcement of sale of Loomis land is in the *Waterville Times* November 22, 1866.

"The desperado lying": *Waterville Times* September 20, 1866.

"The fastening which held": *Waterville Times* November 1, 1866.

"He was calling himself": *Utica Morning Herald* April 23, 1867.

"To see if Judge Harris": Jordan, op. cit., p. 85.

"An odd genius": Ibid., pp. 32-33.

"Grotesque and harmless": Ibid., p. 86.

"Great sums of money": Conkling, op. cit., pp. 286-87.

The newspaper praise of Roscoe Conkling is in Conkling, op. cit., p. 291, and Chidsey, op. cit., p. 115.

The account of the trial of Jim Filkins is a composite from the following sources: *Utica Morning Herald* June 4-6, 1867; *Rome Sentinel* June 11, 1867; Walter, op. cit., pp. 189-96; notes in the Walter collection, Madison County Historical Society; Hoban, "Roscoe . . . , " op. cit.; Conkling, op. cit., pp. 293-94; and J.J. Walsh, "Trials and Tribulations in Oneida County," unpublished manuscript.

"One of the richest": The *Quarterly Review* article had been published in London in vol. 122, pp. 89-100, 1867. Shortly after it appeared a reference to it also appeared in *The London Review* (vol. 14, p. 188, January 26, 1867) ridiculing the article's conclusions: "This Conservative habit of regarding every calamity [the Loomises] as a judgment for [their political viewpoint] is about as reasonable as the notion of some Irish Protestants that the potato blight is the immediate result of Popery."

## Chapter XII: EPILOGUE

"He was direct": Notes in alumni files at Hamilton College, Clinton, New York, and from the *Hamilton Literary Monthly* 3(1868):66-67 and 4(1869):124.

Spriggs political career is reviewed in Cookinham, op. cit., pp. 132-33.

"Stumped the state": Chidsey, op. cit., p. 136.

"During the greater part": Chidsey, op. cit., p. 4.

"The trembling Bruce": Jordan, op. cit., p. 432.

"A cold, selfish": Ibid.

"There is not the slightest": Ibid., p. 433.

"A servant warned": Details of Conkling's affair with Kate Sprague are in Chidsey, op. cit., pp. 117-18, and Jordan, op. cit., pp. 204-05 and 310-11.

"A patriot of": Jordan, op. cit., p. 433.

Hermon Clarke's later life and the Civil War reunions are recounted in Jackson and O'Donnell, op. cit., pp. 205-09.

"Green goods man": Hoban, "That Loomis . . . ," op. cit. See also Cowen, op. cit.

"She has cried": *Onondaga Journal* date uncertain, 1874, obtained from Onondaga Historical Association. It appears to have been based on an account of the event in the *Waterville Times*.

"They approached the premises": Ibid.

"I have no doubt": Walter, op. cit., p. 218.

"Armed to the teeth": *Waterville Times* May 2, 1878.

"When will those Loomises": *Utica Morning Herald* March 12, 1869.

"How he can be": *Syracuse Post Standard* February 24, 1873.

"A horse and buggy": *Onondaga Journal* November 10, 1876.

"Denio Loomis, who has been": *Waterville Times* January 15, 1880.

"Some of our people": *Waterville Times* February 25, 1875; see also March 4, 1875, and Walter, op. cit., pp. 212-17.

"Fine silks and satins": Walter, op. cit., p. 230.

"The young men have not": *Waterville Times* June 27, 1867.

Bill Loomis' last years are described in Walter, op. cit., pp. 233-34.

Details of Plumb Loomis' final years are from Walter, op. cit., pp. 226-28 and 235-37, and from the *Waterville Times* November 21, 1872.

Ezra Pound: See E.F. Torrey, *The Roots of Treason: Ezra Pound and the Secret of St. Elizabeths* (New York: McGraw-Hill, 1984), pp. 18-20. Whether Pound was truly related to the Loomis Gang has never been established with certainty. One source says that his grandmother was the daughter of "N.S. Loomis, a lawyer in Oneida County" and if this is true, Pound is probably not related. See J.B. Hoban, "Ezra Pound and the Loomises: A Genealogical Note," *Philobiblon* (a publication of the Colgate University Library, June 1961).

"In the employ of": *Waterville Times* August 26, 1869.

The trial of Isaiah Belfield is described in Cummings, op. cit.; Cowan, op. cit.; and Walter, op. cit., pp. 221-23.

"Very long confinement": Frothingham, op. cit., p. 318.

"When the Harpers Ferry": Ibid, p. 246-47. See also Harlow, op. cit., pp. 452-54.

"I rejoice in your": Frothingham, op. cit., p 340.

Gerrit Smith Miller's life and involvement in the founding of American football is found in the Gerrit Smith file, Madison County Historical Society.

Gerrit Smith's death is described in Frothingham, op. cit. pp. 354-58.

Ely Parker's postwar career is detailed in Brown, *Bury My . . .* , op. cit., pp. 176-77 and 184-86.

"I think you had better": Ibid, p. 285.

"The only good Indians": Ibid, p. 166. Over the years popular usage has changed this quote to: "The only good Indian is a dead Indian."

"Fighting broke out": C. D. May, "Divided Oneida Tribe Seeks End to Feud," *New York Times* December 29, 1986.

"They are divided": Interview with official in U.S. Bureau of Indian Affairs, 1984.

The U.S. Supreme Court decision regarding Oneida Indian land claims can be found in "Supreme Court Upholds Claim by Oneida Indians," *New York Times* May 5, 1985. The 1988 court action is described in "Court Refuses Oneidas' Claim for Treaty Land," *New York Times* November 2, 1988. The purchase of land by the tribe is in "Oneida Indians Buy N.Y. Land Involved in Tribal Claim Case," *Washington Post* September 10, 1986.

"Many times": Canfield, op. cit., p. 192.

"Appropriate religious ceremonies": *County Courier News* May 29, 1974, in the files of the Forest Hills Cemetery office.

## POSTSCRIPT

"Great social occasions": J. Bonanno, *A Man of Honor* (New York: Simon and Shuster, 1983), p. 204. Information on the meeting in Apalachin is from this book and also from N. Gage (ed.), *Mafia, USA* (Chicago: Playboy Press, 1972), pp. 120-123.

# INDEX

188, 191, 192, 210
Washington, George, 3-5, 7-8, 10, 25
Washington Mills, 21
Waterville, 11, 13, 17-19, 23. 39, 40, 42,
  45, 48, 52, 53, 55-56, 71, 73, 81, 90,
  102, 106, 108, 113, 115-118, 121, 124,
  125, 127, 128, 133, 136, 137, 141, 143,
  149, 152, 153, 158, 159, 161, 168, 169,
  179-181, 185, 186, 193, 212, 221
Wayne County, PA, 190
Weed, Thurlow, 65-66, 72
Welch, Decatur, 187

Welles, Gideon, 138
White Antelope, 141
Whitesboro, 44
Whitestown, 37
Whitman, Walt, 97
Whittier, John Greenleaf, 97
Windsor, CT, 1-2
Wirz, Henry, 168
Wisconsin, 132
Wright, Hannah, 113
  *(see Loomis, Hannah Wright)*
Younger brothers, 132